THE SWORD AND THE SHOVEL

The Battle for the Biblical Family

— Revised Edition —

GEORGE C. SCIPIONE

Institute for Biblical Counseling & Discipleship
La Mesa, California

Revised Edition

ISBN: 0-9720407-0-6
Library of Congress Control Number: 2002104129

Cover illustration by Dinca Lyons.

Printed in the U.S.A. by
Morris Publishing
3212 East Highway 30
Kearney, NE 68847
1-800-650-7888

To E.T.

May His grace equip you to preach Christ and Him crucified, risen and crowned.

George C. Scipione

Do not be afraid of them; remember the Lord who is great and awesome, and fight for your brothers, your sons, your daughters, your wives and your houses.

Nehemiah 4:14

To George and Rita,

godly parents who started the process of making me what God intends me to be, and whose fifty-two years of marriage are a testimony of God's faithfulness.

To Eileen,

a godly wife who is the best "complement" I've ever received and who has continued what my parents started.

To Paul, Ruth, Nicole, Arielle and Deborah,

great children who belong to God and who will finish off whatever my parents and wife have missed!

I thank my God in all my remembrance of you, always offering prayer with joy in my every prayer for you all, in view of your participation in the gospel from the first day until now. For I am confident of this very thing, that He who began a good work in you will perfect it until the day of Christ Jesus.

Philippians 1:3-6

THE SWORD AND THE SHOVEL

4 ~ WHERE'S THE BATTLE?

5 ~ WHAT'S THE STRATEGY?

6 ~ CAN MY FAMILY HELP?

APPENDICES

ACKNOWLEDGMENTS

Few people accomplish anything on their own; I'm no exception. Many people helped in this project but of special note are the following: Howard and Roberta Ahmanson and Dr. Marvin Olasky, who encouraged me to write this book; Michael and Linda Pasarilla and Garnet Young, who typed the original draft; Rosemary Buerger who typed and retyped the many subsequent drafts; John and Sandra Cully of Evangelical Bible Book Store, who gave me free books to help the project (not to mention the family budget!); Anna Whitten of Westminster Theological Seminary in California's library, who cheerfully tracked down needed titles on the inter-library loan system; Dr. Andy Peterson, my co-worker at the Institute for Biblical Counseling and Discipleship and Westminster Theological Seminary, who constantly challenged me and suggested many "must" titles; Jay Adams, who reworked the manuscript; Rebecca Jones, who refined it even more; Bonnie Graham, my Administrative Assistant, without whom the revised edition would not have come about; and my wife, Eileen, who consistently encouraged me. Finally, I wish to thank the many relatives and friends who prayed faithfully to our triune God, to Whom the glory be given. Any good that comes of this work is His doing; the mistakes, gaps and flaws are mine.

INTRODUCTION

A tidal wave of books on marriage and child-rearing inundates Christian bookstores, sweeping the patron out the door. So why another book on the family?

If you wade through the flotsam and jetsam, you find little that is distinctively biblical. Instead, you find psychological and sociological ideas attractively packaged and sprinkled with a few proof texts. These books will *not* help you think clearly or develop a Christian worldview. Even books that attempt to be biblical are not systematic. No systematic theology of the family exists. As a result, many Christian families do not function much differently from those in homes that surround them. My goal is to set out the biblical view of the family in a systematic way.

Why insist on being biblical? Why not just observe families and ascertain needs? Why not turn to research, science or to marriage, family and child therapists? What is so special about the Bible? Yes, it is God's Word. Sure, it is helpful for salvation. But why study the Bible in order to study the family?

The Bible exhibits four essential characteristics. First, it is *necessary*. People need clear verbal instruction from God. Even before their fall into sin, Adam and Eve needed instruction.[1] Now that humanity is in rebellion against God, His Word is even more necessary. The first chapter of Romans describes the result of thinking and living apart from biblical revelation. Second, the Bible is *authoritative*. As the Word of the Living God, it is infallible and inerrant.[2] The Word judges us, not vice versa.[3] Third, the Bible is *sufficient*.[4] It can equip us to do all God requires. The Word gives discernment that can be obtained nowhere else.[5] Fourth, the Bible is *understandable*.[6] It is not some mysterious Gnostic document. The Holy Spirit makes it clear to all obedient believers.[7]

What do these essential qualities equip us to do? Why are we in this world? The Bible answers: God put us here to glorify and enjoy Him forever.[8] Jesus gives His people eternal life, which He defines as knowing the only true God, and Jesus Christ whom He sent.[9] As we come to know the Father through the Son, the Holy Spirit produces His moral character in our lives.[10] As they reflect this same glory, Christian families not only enjoy fellowship with God, they show God's love and glory to a world yearning for true fellowship and joy. Perhaps nowhere can such qualities be seen more clearly than in a Christian family that pleases God.

To think biblically about the family, we must realize two things: first, the gospel of Jesus Christ, found in the Bible, is not shameful; it is the power of God unto salvation.[11] We are not to be ashamed of it intellectually. The biblical world-and-life view is not only cogent and complete, it is *the only true view*. The apostle Paul compellingly proves that men have rejected God's truth.[12] To the extent that man rejects the Bible, his thinking, whether informal, formal, or scientific, will be distorted and false.

Such distortion occurs overtly in non-Christian religions. It comes out more subtly in academic and scientific endeavors. The field of psychology, especially counseling psychology,[13] provides one of the clearest examples of intellectual apostasy. Now that Marriage, Family and Child Therapy is a separate field of study and the Family Systems approach to therapy is well-established as a way of looking at families, we can expect more and more deviations from a biblical view of the family. False views become popular *because* the biblical view of the family has been abandoned. If your presuppositions about God, the world, yourself, sin and redemption are not biblical, then your view of the family will be false.[14]

Second, although the Bible does not tell us everything about the family, we must mine its depths before we can make observations or build theories. Thus, the method I used to develop this book took the following steps:

Step One: I read the Bible through, listing all passages dealing with the family—directly or indirectly. The list, found in Appendix 1, is extensive, if not exhaustive.

Step Two: I exegeted the passages.

Step Three: I categorized the texts.

Step Four: I looked at popular Christian books and studied theological works on the family. (See Sections 1 and 2.)

Step Five: I researched academic work on the history of the family in Western civilizations since biblical times. (See Section 3.)

Finally, I tried to develop biblical solutions based upon my knowledge of the Word and my pastoral experience. (See Sections 4, 5 and 6.).

I live in San Diego. Southern California is trendy and transitory, a land of fun and funky bumper stickers. But fun does not eradicate cults, Satan worship, and the raging spiritual warfare.[5] A host of pagan forces, armed for battle against the family, stands in the California sun, but all over America, we are fighting for our families, for our churches, and for our culture. The evil one wants to destroy godly families, biblical churches, and the remaining vestiges of Christian influence in Western culture. Nothing short of God-ordained revival—especially in families—can prevent a neo-dark age,[16] soaked in pagan idolatry.[17] I pray that we may live to see the third Great Awakening in America. To reform America, our families must first be reformed—thousands of Christian homes that will hold out light to a dark age. If you are not committed to the God of the Bible, nor saved by the life, death and resurrection of Jesus His Son, nor guided by God the Holy Spirit, I pray you will be,[18] so that your family can contribute to the bright flame.

San Diego, 2002

Notes:

Introduction

1. Adam had to care for the garden and name the animals, an act of classification. This is very "scientific." However, God instructed him and his wife, Eve, about the task He gave them to be fruitful, to multiply, to fill the earth and rule over it. God fellowshiped with and instructed them daily *before* the fall. Man was to exercise scientific, cultural activities *within God's verbal revelation*.

2. 2 Pet 1:16-21.

3. Heb 4:12, 13.

4. 2 Tim 3:15-17. The Westminster Confession of Faith says: The whole counsel of God concerning all things necessary for His own glory, man's salvation, faith and life, is either expressly set down in Scripture, or by good and necessary consequence may be deduced from Scripture.

5. Ps 119:97-100; Heb 5:11-14.

6. Deut 30:11-14; Rom 10:6-15.

7. See C. Van Til's "Nature and Scripture," *The Infallible Word: A Symposium by members of Westminster Theological Seminary* (Phillipsburg: Presbyterian and Reformed, 1978), 263-283.

8. Westminster Shorter Catechism answer to question #1. Cf 1 Cor 10:31; Rom 11:36; Ps 73:25-28.

9. John 17:3.

10. 2 Cor 3:17, 18.

11. Rom 1:16.

12. Rom 1-3.

13. See D. Powlison's excellent article, "Which Presuppositions? Secular Psychology and the Categories of Biblical Thought," *Journal of Psychology and Theology*, 1984, vol 12, no 4, 270-278, which is the best written scholarly article on how your presuppositions affect your scientific research and conclusions. "Eeny, Meeny, Miny, Mo: Is Biblical Counseling It or No?" *Journal of Pastoral Practice*, G. C. Scipione, 1989, vol IX, no 4, 44-57, is written in a more popular style, but deals with similar issues.

14. H. Schlossberg and M. Olasky, *Turning Point: A Christian Worldview Declaration* (Westchester: Crossway, 1987) grasp the connection between Christian belief and the practical consequences that result from it.

15. Eph 6:10-20; Rev 12:1-9; 19:11-16.

16. C. Colson, *Against the Night: Living in the New Dark Ages* (Ann Arbor: Servant, 1989). Colson, one of the better known analysts of our culture, shows the danger we face.

17. H. Schlossberg, *Idols for Destruction: Christian Faith and Its Confrontation with American Society* (Nashville: Thomas Nelson, 1983), is

perhaps the best biblical analysis of modern Western civilization and is must reading for any serious Christian.

18. John Blanchard's *Right with God* (Carlisle: The Banner of Truth Trust, 1971) is an excellent place to start if you are not a follower of Jesus Christ. This book was written for those who want to be right with God but realize they are not. May God bless you as you read.

Section 1

~

WHY BOTHER?

~

CHAPTER 1

The Family: God's Basic Building Block

When you go to a movie, don't you hate to miss the first five minutes? It's so hard to figure out the story if you do. Beginnings are important. Yet in our age of quick fixes and process thinking, we've so idolized change and flux that we've forgotten the first five minutes of our human story. But God knew that we would need to know what happened in the first five minutes, in order to understand the rest. Biblical revelation begins with God's narrative of the beginning, Genesis. To think clearly about our world and our own life, we must "think God's thoughts after Him." God considered the beginnings of our human race to be extremely significant.

The apostle Paul often settled disputes between Christianity and pagan philosophies within the churches. In disputes over proper roles of sexuality or gender, he appealed to the beginning, to God's creation order.[1] In this, Paul agreed with Jesus Christ, who often went back to the original order and intent of God the Father in creation.[2] This original order is viewed *as the way things should be*. Pre-Fall perfection was made by God's heart and hand.[3] So the question really is, if you had a world to make, would you start it the way God did?

How did God begin? The Bible is clear: God created the world. God Himself was center stage. The creation of the world and its subsequent history revolved around the eternal God, who created out of nothing by the Word of His power. He spoke and it came into being.[4] All He created was good, in fact, the best.[5] Since God's ways are perfect and above human criticism,[6] to find out how God designed the world is to discover the best.[7] Nothing about Adam's life was independent from God or His Word.[8] We, too, must begin and end with God Himself if we want to understand the story, if we want to think and live correctly.

God made man to reflect Him and gave man authority and dominion over the rest of creation. This control mirrors God the Creator.[9] Man's life and work, his vocation, is personal service to God under God's control and for His glory.[10]

The first man, Adam, served as a prophet, priest and king under God. He was to use creation in a covenantal, sacramental way. We don't use "covenant" much anymore, but it means a legal agreement. In this case, God sets up the legal relationship with man, who is to serve God with all his heart. God's part of the agreement is to rule, love and care for man.[11] All creation was at man's disposal to aid him in his service to and worship of God. This may well have been the symbolic sacramentalism behind the tree of life.

God placed man in a family relationship to accomplish the task He gave him.[12] How did God begin our story? He created the world out of nothing, placed it under man's dominion, and placed man in a family. God created a *family*. He did not start with a church, a government, a business, or a voluntary organization. He started with a family—a husband and wife who were to rule over the creation and procreate godly offspring.[13] These godly children were to start new families and spread out to fill the earth. We shall see that all other societal organizations were present within the family in germinal form and developed out of the family to become separate entities with their own jurisdictional authority.[14]

Under certain circumstances the family can function as a business, church, or government. However, such structures cannot replace the family. It is God's basic building block, with which He builds nations, governments, churches, business enterprises, charitable institutions, etc. The centrality of the family lies in its unique nature and function. Nothing can replace it. In His infinite wisdom, God created the family; it is not a man-made institution.[15] Anyone who ignores, bypasses, or tries to reconstruct it rejects God's plan, and those who try to replace it will fail. To fight the family is to do battle against God Himself, and rebellion against God always leads to death[16]— for cultures as well as individuals.[17] Whole cultures perish when they ignore or tamper with God's design for life.

God's *purpose* for the family involves great covenantal responsibility. Man's kingly rule was to extend over all the creation through the legitimate multiplication of royal families. In a creaturely way, man reflected God's creative and providential care over creation. He was to enjoy the fruits of his labors in sacramental, sabbatical joy, just as God took the sabbath to rest and to enjoy His creation. The Fall did not free families from their covenantal obligations to their Creator King. After the Fall, fruitful multiplication and work were cursed with pain and death,[18] yet the obligation remained: in spite of sin, God still held out the mandate to serve Him by fruitful work and procreation. Of course, He also provided the means by which sinful man could attempt an otherwise impossible venture. After the Fall, the task had to be undertaken through the power of Christ, who conquered death. This promise was given even to Adam and Eve, so that they might not lose hope.

God emphasized the continuity in His purpose when, after the Flood, he renewed the covenant with man. God promised a creation that would sustain life and allow for the pursuit of the cultural mandate:

While the earth remains
Seed time and harvest,
And cold and heat,
And summer and winter,
And day and night
Shall not cease.[19]

God blessed Noah and his sons: "Be fruitful and multiply, and fill the earth."[20] The covenant was reissued, and God protected the life He saved by ordaining governmental punishment of murder.[21] Again, He repeated the mandate to be fruitful and multiply,[22] and gave the covenant sign of the rainbow.[23] The family, its labors—productivity and procreativity—are still the centerpiece of God's providential care over creation. This second start repeats what He said to Adam. Even the Flood, which involved judgment and salvation, did not eradicate the family or its role in history.[24]

God's word *defines* the family, as well as declaring its purpose. The family is a man and a woman in lifelong covenantal companionship serving God by taking dominion over creation. Under His guidance, and in fellowship with Him, they seek to be fruitful, to fill the earth, to subdue it, and to rule over it to God's glory.

Procreation is a God-ordained part of family life, and childlessness is a curse (though it does not negate a marriage or make a couple a non-family).[25] The creation account in Genesis and other passages shows the marriage-family bond to be a covenant of companionship.[26] We will examine this later. It is sufficient to note here that the family is a male-female unit serving God. As covenantally-yoked, complementary[27] companions who are no longer alone, they serve God by exercising dominion. Individually and jointly they reflect God's character. This is the family.

If we fail to understand it as God's basic building block, the family will not be central in our thinking. Other structures will replace it. Our priorities will be wrong, thus distorting our whole life, including our relationship with God Himself. The family is a reflection of the very reality and nature of God.

Notes:

Chapter 1

1. Rom 1:26, 27; 1 Cor 11:8, 9; 2 Cor 11:3; 1 Tim 2:13, 14. Paul believed that creation took place in time-and-space history and that knowledge of it is significant and normative for us after the Fall.

2. Matt 19:3-12. Jesus argues that Moses' legislation was permitted due to sin and non-repentance and argues (v 8) that at the beginning it was different, due to God's design in creation (v 4).

3. Isa 40:12-17. Note Isaiah's irony and sarcasm!

4. Gen 1:3, 6, 9, 14, 20, 24, 26; Ps 33:6; 2 Cor 4:6.

5. Gen 1:31.

6. Rom 11:33-36.

7. F. Schaeffer, *Genesis in Space and Time* (Downers Grove: InterVarsity, 1972). Schaeffer points out that *if* these are *not* space-time historical accounts, we lose everything: creation, Christ, salvation and a reliable, inerrant, infallible revelation of God and His will.

8. J. Adams, *A Theology of Christian Counseling: More than Redemption* (Grand Rapids: Zondervan, 1979), chapters 3 and 4, shows how God's Word is the very environment in which man lives. See also J. Calvin, *The Institutes of the Christian Religion*, in the Library of Christian Classics, vol XX, trans. F. L. Battles (Phila: Westminster Press), Book 1 Chapter 1.

9. Gen 1:26. The first Hebrew term is *selem*, which can mean (1) a shade or shadow, or (2) an image or likeness. The second Hebrew term is *demut*, which can mean (1) a likeness or image, (2) a model, or pattern, or (3) an appearance, form or shape. Man is the shadow or reflection of God who is the real substantial one.

10. Ps 8.

11. This is a simple explanation of a complex notion. For a full understanding of the covenant, you can read O. Palmer Robertson's *Christ of the Covenants* (Phillipsburg: Presbyterian and Reformed, 1981).

12. Gen 1:26-31; 2:18-25.

13. Gen 1:28; Ruth 4:12; 1 Sam 2:20; Mal 2:15.

14. See Chapters 5 and 6.

15. J. Adams, *Christian Living in the Home* (Phillipsburg: Presbyterian and Reformed, 1972), 43-45.

16. Gen 3; Rom 1-3.

17. Rom 1. Paul traces the degeneracy of the Gentile cultures, which do not have special revelation from God. Common family problems, such as disobedience to parents (v 30), and lack of love (v 31) precipitate the decline into depravity. Homosexuality is so unnatural that it destroys the family.

18. Gen 3:16-19. To forget God's mandate is not only a case of mental

or cultural amnesia, but "folly" in the biblical sense of the word as seen in the wisdom literature. This folly is a moral, covenantal term meaning “wicked rebellion against God” (v 17).

19. Gen 8:22.

20. Gen 9:1.

21. Gen 9:2-6.

22. Gen 9:7.

23. Gen 9:8-17.

24. 1 Pet 3:18-22.

25. Biblical examples abound: Abraham and Sarah, Elkanah and Hannah, as well as Zechariah and Elizabeth. All were godly.

26. J. Adams, *Marriage, Divorce, and Remarriage* (Phillipsburg: Presbyterian and Reformed, 1980), 11-12. The key passages are Prov 2:17 and Mal 2:14.

27. Gen 2:18. The first Hebrew word is *'ezer* and means “help” or “helper.” It comes from a verb that means (1) to surround, enclose, or (2) to help, succor, aid. The woman aids or helps the man. The second Hebrew word is *neged,* which means (1) before, in the presence of, or (2) in front of, over against. It means "as over against him." This woman is his opposite or corresponding unit.

CHAPTER 2

The Family: God's Reflection

Andy and Beth are in their early forties, have been married twenty years, and have three children, ages seven, ten and fifteen. For Andy, who has studied with New Age teachers, evil and sin do not exist. He feels no guilt about his recreational use of drugs, his occasional drunkenness, his unwholesome speech, his lust for other women, or his sullen self-centered withdrawal from Beth and the children. Andy thinks himself sinless.

Beth attends a liberal church that teaches semi-traditional morality but nothing of personal commitment to Jesus Christ. Beth sees herself as a victim of Andy's selfishness. A people-pleaser, she has reached out to leaders of several congregations, always holding Andy accountable. She is angry and afraid, desperate to control or change Andy. Hostility and arguments mar their communication. At Beth's insistence they had tried secular counseling, which had produced despair, hopelessness and an extended separation. Now they sit in my office.

Both claim they want to salvage their marriage and family. Andy says, "I've done nothing wrong; all she does is bitch and complain. If she'd get off my back, everything would be fine." Beth moans, "The first eighteen years were fine. The last two he's been into this new age stuff. He's changed. I don't like it. He's withdrawn since he's gotten into it. Show him how wrong he is."[1]

What is going on? Many things. However, many passages in the Bible (e.g. Ps 115:8, 135:18 and Isa 44:6-23) warn us that people become like the gods they serve. Beth and Andy as individuals, and their family as a unit, reflect the gods they serve. Andy withdraws and does his own thing because his god is an impersonal, immoral force. Little personal love exists.

Beth's God is personal and caring but amoral and powerless to cleanse and change people. Therefore, Beth must try to fill the gap as a semi-benevolent dictator, who controls a world careening out of control. Neither has the strength to change permanently. People are only as good as the gods they serve (Matt 6:19-25). Beth and Andy and families like theirs shrivel up and die because they feast on the food of futility, offered by the false gods they serve.

Your Family Reflects the Reality of God

*Family members reflect the **reality** of God.*

Every part of creation reflects the reality of God (Rom 1:18-32).[2] Every sub-atomic particle has the signature of the triune living God written on it, but man alone is stamped with God's special, personal image and likeness.[3] You and your family members are individual reflections of God's personal reality. Your sin clouds and distorts this reflection like a circus mirror. To see the real you, you need to look at God's mirror, the Scriptures. In them you find that you don't need to pretend that the image is wonderful. You cannot change the image, but you can change the person standing in front of the mirror, by coming to Christ to be regenerated and sanctified. The closer you come to Him, the more the image of God in you will shine clear.[4] Sin does not totally obliterate the ability to reflect your God.[5] Each one in your family, for better or worse, reflects God.[6] But as important as this truth is for life, the family as a whole is our specific concern. That you are personally the image of God may not be a new thought or perspective but you may never have considered that:

*Your family unit reflects the **reality** of God.*

Your family, as a unit, reflects the reality of God in a way that individual members do not. Yes, you, as well as your spouse and children, are the image of God. But a man and woman *in a lifelong covenantal union* for the purpose of dominion under God, also reflect the reality of God. The God you serve shapes you. Others will see the reality of that God in your lifestyle. Likewise, your family and its corporate life reflect your gods.

Satan knows this. The destruction of a life in the womb obliterates one reflection of God's reality. The destruction or distortion of God-ordained family relationships obliterates another. Since the reflection of God's glory is man's main purpose,[7] Satan will stop at nothing to destroy man.[8] As Satan dulls, damages and destroys the family, God's glory is eclipsed. Satanic substitutes for biblical families are one of the major strategies in his war against God. Andy and Beth and their children, individually and corporately, reflect other gods than the true triune God. They are damaged and ultimately may be destroyed. God is dishonored by their lives.

Your Family Reflects the Nature of God[9]

Family members reflect the ***nature*** *of God.*

The first and second chapters of Genesis tell us God made man "in His image". You reflect not only the reality of God's existence but also, in some ways, His very nature. You are not divine, nor will you ever be, but you are a creaturely analogue of God's character. In these two chapters of Genesis, four individual characteristics stand out.

- *You are a* ***person.***

The God who created you is personal. As a person, you reflect His personhood.[10] Picture yourself as Adam. As you name the animals, you can't get overly enthusiastic about communicating with or marrying a giraffe. You yearn for fellowship and intercourse with another human. God gives you a partner who is your personal counterpart.

Thank you, God! People need other people. The effects on babies and small children of a lack of personal contact are well-documented.[11] Members of your family need physical affection, verbal communication, laughter, friendship, and all the other delightful forms of personal communion God has provided by creating the family.

- *You rule.*

God is sovereign over all; man is to rule the creation under God. You and your family members need responsibility and freedom to rule; these add satisfaction to life. While in Egypt, Israel became slaves without freedom and responsibility to determine their own lives, and became fearful and lazy. They ceased to be free men, then ceased to think and act like free men. After God freed them, they wandered in the wilderness, complaining like slaves and displaying animal-like instinctual lusts. Slaves to their sins, they died at God's hand (Ps 39:8-11; 49; 106). Family members need responsibility.

- *You work.*

God works six days; man must work. In the pastorate, I counseled Carl, who had recently professed faith in Christ and had joined a Bible-believing church. Carl was in his late twenties, married, and the father of three small children. A gifted musician, he wanted to earn a living performing, but his music did not provide for his family. His church leaders encouraged him to get other work, but he refused their counsel. As a result, his family lost several places to live and never had enough to eat. Carl turned back to drinking, which compounded his problems. The church helped the family and tried to work with Carl, who refused to change. According to Christ's instructions in Matthew 18:15-20, the church finally excommunicated him. He deserted his family and is now worse than an unbeliever (1 Tim 5:8). I wish I could have found the key to Carl's problem, but Carl also refused my counsel.

Carl's case shows us what a man becomes without work—an instinct-driven creature. Without work, you and your family will die.

♦ *You rest and worship.*

God works six days and rests to enjoy the labor of His creative hands. God gave us the seventh day for rest and refreshment.[12] When I was first in the pastorate, I took no time off. There was so much to do! Because I was proud and feared failure, I didn't follow God's plan. My wife suffered because of my depression and crabbiness. I began having stomach pains. My doctor said I was developing an ulcer and prescribed medicine that included tranquilizers. How convicted and ashamed I was about my sinful neglect of God's gracious plan. Once I focused on pleasing God and began to take days off, my health returned and I became a better husband.

You need sabbath rest and sacramental fellowship. Your family members need time to rest and experience the joy of worship and Christian fellowship. Seven day weeks crammed with all work and no rest turn you into a cloudy mirror, reflecting a *dull* image of God.

Many Bible teachers have noticed these individual aspects of the image of God. However, few note that:

♦ *Your family unit reflects the nature of God.*

Look at Genesis 1 and 2 again. Not only does your family corporately reflect the *reality* of God, it also reflects the very *nature* of God. Of course your family will never be divine, but it is a creaturely analogue that reflects God's character in ways that individual members cannot.[13] In these chapters, three corporate characteristics stand out.

♦ *Your family is a multiple-person unit.*

Because a family consists of more than one person, it reflects God's tripersonal unity.[14] This attribute has great significance for culture and history.[15] Though the Trinity is a mystery richer than any creaturely reflection, the family best represents it. Two aspects of family life reflect in a creaturely way this divine attribute:

The One-flesh Relationship between Husband and Wife[16]

Ed is in his late thirties and has his M.A. in electrical engineering. He meets Faith at church. She is a shy nineteen-year-old in her first year of college. They love each other, and desire a home and children. They marry and agree to postpone having children until she completes college. Ed works so Faith can get her degree. As her confidence grows, Ed encourages her to get an M.A. in performing arts. By the time she has finished, he is in his forties and longs for children. Faith, however, has set her heart on a Ph.D. and demands to continue her schooling and career. Ed insists on their original agreement. She divorces him. Individual desires kill their unity. A biblical view of "oneness" before God could have saved this marriage.

God gave Francis and Edith Schaeffer this unity. Their marriage reflected the one-fleshness God intended for couples. They were a marvelous, harmonious unit while their individual diversity was seen in their lives and writing. The Schaeffers and their community at L'Abri were God's model of how two individuals may remain separate persons, yet become almost one in their lives. You probably know other godly couples who personify this mysterious unity while flowering as individuals. Great beauty, unity and harmony in marriage can exist without the death of the individual.

Satan attacks this balanced one-fleshness in order to distort the triunity of God. We all need a deep sense of unity without the loss of individual identity. God's nature provides a model of unity and individuality. God's created structure of marriage reflects it. Both are possible. But Satan wants no testimony to the hope and beauty God holds out.

The Image of the Parent in the Child[17]

I once watched a cute five-year-old girl drink tea at an elegantly set table with her English mother. Though she inherited her jet black curls from her father, she curled her pinky finger in the air when she drank from her china teacup—just like her mother. Attitudes and behaviors are learned and mirror parental models just as physical characteristics reflect their genetic image.

Imagine Adam's amazement when he looked at Cain and Abel, and later at Seth—mini-Adams, mirroring him. I'm amazed at how easily my five children are identified as Scipiones.[18] So much similarity between parents and children exists that children often seem to be extensions of Dad and Mom; yet they remain uniquely individual. When parents abort offspring or children rebel at being like their parents, Satan again obliterates the reflection of the unity and individuality that reflects God's character.

♦ *Your family is a* ***hierarchy of equals.***

The Father, the Son and the Holy Spirit are co-equally God, but in creation, providence and redemption they work in a hierarchy to accomplish goals.[19] This is a reality against which Jesus and the Spirit do not rebel. Two aspects of family life reflect, in a creaturely way, this divine attribute:

The Headship of the Husband over the Wife

Faith divorced Ed over the issue of career vs. children. She refused to follow his leadership in an area of conflict. She refused to obey her vows before God and refused to keep her promise about children.

I met George and Harriet while making an evangelistic call in a town near my church. Both were doing drugs and lived in a duplex that they owned. Jake, who lived next door, often partied with George. Eventually, Jake and Harriet had an adulterous affair.

George refused to stop them and finally, Harriet moved in with Jake. George saw no problem with this arrangement, and felt no need to bring Harriet home or to evict Jack from the duplex.

These cases illustrate the inevitable breakdown of marriages with no authority structure.[20] Feminism and male cowardice contribute to a breakdown of authority in Western civilization. Our civilization struggles to survive. (See Appendix 2).

The Headship of Parents over Children

While I was a pastor in New Jersey at Calvary Community Church, our congregation sponsored three refugee families. The first was from Vietnam and lived with us for a year.[21] While an Oriental view of the family is not biblical, it retains a vestige of respect for elders and parents often absent in American families. My wife and I noticed how the children responded to their parents. After a year, they moved into their own home. As the years went by we saw a modern American attitude creep into the children. There was no question who was boss when they came. As the initial respect lessened, one non-biblical view of the family was replaced by another.

Can you imagine Jesus the Son arguing with the Father? "Jesus, I want you to become a man and die for our people's sins." "No, I won't go; send the Holy Spirit, send an angel, but not me." Preposterous, you say. Yet, a similar egalitarianism is supported in academic, government, and even church circles as the ideal way to raise children.[22] A biblical relationship between children and parents reflects the holy relationship within the Godhead. Just as the husband-wife relationship mirrors inter-trinitarian harmony, so parent-child interaction reflects the Father-Son relationship in the Godhead. Just as the subordination of the wife to the husband does not negate her equality as an image-bearer, so the subordination of the child to the parent does not negate his equality as an image-bearer.

- ♦ *Your family is a stable* ***producer of new people and new families.***

You cannot create something out of nothing as God can, but, in a creaturely way, you reflect the divine creativity of God. Out of His eternal, unchangeable being, by His word, come new creatures. So too out of the family come new things: out of an intimate knowledge of Eve, Adam produced children in his likeness (Gen 1:27; 5:3). A woman who lies on the delivery table after giving birth sees the new creation in which she and her husband have participated. They share the intense and joyful satisfaction of God in having brought into existence a new person. These children in turn generate new families.[23] The birth of children and new family units are reminders that God created us. Although the fellowship of the Godhead was not incomplete, God created man for fellowship; a husband and wife have in each other all they need, yet they too produce new life for fellowship. Satan hates new children as well as marriage, and tries to destroy both.

Karen and Larry, both in their late sixties, sat wearily in my office and poured out their tale of agony. They had been happily married for ten years, when Karen got pregnant. She was angry because she thought that the child would "ruin everything." Sensing how selfish her attitude was, she became depressed. When her son was born, she tried to overcome her guilt and depression by smothering mothering and spent the next thirty years in and out of mental institutions. I told her the good news about Christ's forgiveness. Karen's rejection of God's plan to receive children as blessings created real guilt, which she did not know how to cleanse. Karen needed the compassion and blood of Jesus Christ. Children are an inheritance from the Lord (Ps 127, 128), and are a reflection of His life-giving creativity. The refusal to obey God's mandate to fill the earth (Gen 1) denies God's creativity.

New life, whether physical life in the womb, or spiritual life created by the regenerating work of the Holy Spirit, gives hope. Satan knows that people cannot live without hope. He tries to wash any reflection of the God of Hope from our hearts with a flood of despair.

Your Family Is Needed

By now, you can see that ideas, especially those about God and the family, have serious consequences. You, your family and your reflection of God's character are at the heart of our culture war. Too few families are living reflections of God. To abandon or distort the individual or corporate reflections of God's nature destroys pointers to the reality and nature of God.[24] Yes, if you wanted to keep people from coming to God, you'd try to destroy the family. Satan knows this. Losing the Biblical view of the family is serious because to distort or destroy Biblical families is to eclipse a reflection of God's glory.

The stakes are high: lose the Biblical view of the family, and you lose God and His Word. Lose the living, true, triune God and His Word, and you lose everything: man, family and civilization. If your family's structure and life are twisted, your relationship with God will be twisted. Your relationships to other humans and the stability of those relationships will also suffer. In short, family and culture will grind to a halt and disintegrate before your unbelieving eyes.

Notes:

Chapter 2

1. Andy and Beth are real people. I have altered names and added details from other real cases to create composite examples. This pattern is followed throughout the book wherever cases with first names are used.

2. Job 12:7-9; Ps 19:1-6; Rom 1:18-23. Through the structure of creation God clearly, though indirectly, reveals truth about Himself and about the spiritual, unseen realm. All of Creation is real, but points to realities beyond itself. This witness to God is available to all people at all times. Because such revelation is general and seen in the created realm, theologians label it "general" or "natural."

God also directly and personally gives special, supernatural information about Himself and about the spiritual, unseen realm. John, in the prologue to his gospel (John 1:18), alerts us to this fact. Although no one has ever seen God, Jesus makes Him known. Christ's teaching and preaching indicate this, especially as reported by John (John 5:19-23). Jesus says and does exactly what the Father says and does. What God's prophets do and say by the Holy Spirit's power is part of special or supernatural revelation (2 Tim 3:16, 17; Heb 1:1, 2; 2 Pet 1:19-21). All the words of the Bible are included.

Man's unique position as the apex of general revelation parallels the unique position of Jesus Christ in special or supernatural revelation. Jesus is the final, ultimate revelation of God (Heb 1:1, 2). Similarly, man is the pinnacle of general revelation. Man, as the image of God, is greater than the rest of creation. Jesus, as God's Son, is greater than the rest of God's direct revelation. However, Jesus, the eternal Son, who became the Messianic Son, stands on the divine side of the Creator-creature distinction, whereas man is never apart from or separate from creation.

For an excellent discussion of these issues and their implications for our knowledge in general and of man specifically, see L. Berkhof, *Systematic Theology* (Grand Rapids: Wm. B. Eerdmans, 1941), 26-40.

3. Gen 1:24-31; 5:1; 9:6; 1 Cor 11:7; Jam 3:9. Man is a creature like other creations of God. However, he alone is the image or likeness of God. Gen 2:7-25 shows that man had special creative attention from God. Both Adam and Eve were special, direct creations of God: this makes man unique, different from all other creatures. Angels are not in God's image, though some of their attributes are similar to man's.

4. Rom 8:29; 1 Cor 15:49; 2 Cor 3:18; Col 3:10.

5. Jam 3:9.

6. Is it any wonder abortionists use impersonal terms such as "prenatal tissue"? If the reflection of God is not a person, then God's triune personhood can be obscured or obliterated. Rebellion against God becomes easier, Rom 1:18-32.

7. See the *Westminster Larger Catechism,* question 1.

8. For an extended treatment of this, see J. Adams, *The Biblical View of Self-Esteem, Self-Love, Self-Image* (Eugene: Harvest House, 1986), chapter 7, especially 81-83.

9. Man is not, and never will be, God. Therefore, he cannot share certain attributes of God, e.g., infinity, eternity. Theologians call these incommunicable attributes. Man shares certain other attributes of God—love, peace, justice. Theologians call these communicable attributes. See Berkhof, op. cit., 52-76 for a helpful discussion. This distinction preserves both the Creator-creature distinction (which protects against occult pantheism and monism), and man-as-the-image-of-God (which protects against naturalistic materialism). Theologically, God and man are preserved. Even some of the non-communicable traits, however, are reflected in man on the familial, though not on the individual, level. *Always*, the Creator-creature distinction needs to be maintained. See R. J. Rushdoony's *Foundations of Social Order: Studies in the Creeds and Councils of the Early Church* (Phillipsburg: Presbyterian and Reformed, 1972), chapter 6.

10. The key concept is heart. See Berkhof, op. cit., 84-85. Cf Gen 6:6; Job 9:4; 1 Sam 13:14; 2 Sam 7:21; 1 Kgs 9:3 (2 Chr 7:16). For a fuller discussion of "heart", see my unpublished Th.M. thesis, "The Pauline Concept of *Suneidesis*" (Philadelphia: Westminster Theological Seminary, 1973), 38-44. Also, see J. Adams, *A Theology of Christian Counseling* (Grand Rapids: Zondervan, 1979), 113-115. These discussions show that we have more than "just" anthropomorphic language.

11. J. Bowlby, *Maternal Care and Mental Health. Deprivation of Maternal Care: A Reassessment of Its Effects* (New York: Schocken, 1966).

12. Since the resurrection, Christians are given their rest and refreshment up front. We receive the Holy Spirit as a down-payment of good things to come (Rom 8:23, 2 Cor 1:22; 5:5; Eph 1:14), and we receive the Lord's Day as a foretaste of Sabbath rest (Heb 4). Note that we get rest *before* labor. In redemption the emphasis changes. The seventh day Sabbath becomes the first day fellowship of the Lord's Day of resurrection. This switch is shadowed in the Old Testament. Ex 20:8-10 emphasizes creation; Deut 5:12-15 emphasizes redemption from bondage in Egypt.

13. See endnote 9. Some family systems, like the classical Chinese model, fail to distinguish between the reflection and the reality. The mistaken idea that eternity resides in the family and not God, is a sinful, idolatrous mistake with far-reaching practical results.

14. Berkhof, op. cit., chapter 8, "The Holy Trinity."

15. Ps 103:19; 1 Tim 1:17; 6:15, 16.

16. Gen 1:26, 27; 2:18-24. This relationship is a great mystery (cf Eph 5:22-33). A mystery is a divinely revealed truth that could never be inferred. Paul says that marriage reflects the mystery of the incarnation of Christ and

the salvation of His people, but that does not mean it is a sacrament that imparts automatic grace. How can two unregenerate partners get saving grace from marriage? This also does not mean actual ontological unity occurs, as it does within God. What it means is that in a creaturely, finite way, marital union reflects God's character and that a *real* unity and diversity exist and are preserved.

For a comprehensive study of the important but incorrect view that marriage is a sacrament, see the third volume of the series "Marriage in the Catholic Church," by Theodore Mackin, S. J., *The Marital Sacrament* (Mahway: Paulist Press, 1989).

17. Gen 1:26-27; 5:1-3; Lk 3:23-38; 1 Cor 15:49. These passages show the genetic and character unity between generations. Yet, sufficient individuality exists so that no one is an exact clone of another; not even identical twins.

18. They, on the other hand, are appalled at the idea of growing up to look like me. God is gracious; they look more like Mom!

19. H. O. J. Brown, *Heresies: The Image of Christ in the Mirror of Heresy and Orthodoxy from the Apostles to the Present* (Grand Rapids: Baker, 1984). Chapters 7-9 outline the dangerous deviations from true trinitarianism and how they affected the church. These chapters are an important contribution to the centrality of the Trinity and specifically address the issue of subordinationism.

Theologians call the equality of being in eternity and time the *ontological trinity*, whereas the working relationship of the persons in the Godhead in eternity and in creation, providence and salvation is known as the *economic trinity*. The order in the economic trinity is a reflection of the relationship within the ontological trinity. See Berkhof, op. cit., 89.

20. I do not mean to imply that this is the *only* problem in these marriages, but it is the major cause of failures in both of these marriages. The authority structure must be God's and must be followed if a marriage is to work and last.

21. Lest you think us "martyrs" for Christ, the church had a seven-bedroom, two-kitchen parsonage surrounded by seventeen acres of land. The Nguyens lived upstairs and cooked in the basement. The manse was a two-family dwelling.

22. William Coulson was Carl Rogers' right-hand man but he has come to see the folly of this approach to children (J. DeWyze, "An Encounter with Bill Coulson," *The Reader*, vol 6, no 33, Aug. 20, 1987). Coulson is a lapsed Roman Catholic who has returned to practice his faith. He now is trying to undo the damage he did in promoting egalitarian education. For a poignant video interview, see D. James Kennedy's *The D. James Kennedy Hour* (Coral Ridge: Coral Ridge Ministries, March 29, 1992). "Rogerian Influence in Counseling and Education" has W. Coulson's testimony, as well as mini-

interviews with Dr. Andrew Peterson (my associate at CCEF-West in San Diego), and a couple who was nearly destroyed by humanistic counseling but marvelously transformed by the Holy Spirit's use of Biblical counseling. (What was not mentioned was that Dr. Peterson was God's instrument in this process!)

Feminists often claim that hierarchical thinking *causes* abuse. See R. L. Clarke, *Pastoral Care of Battered Women* (Westminster: John Knox Press, 1986), M. M. Fortune, *Keeping the Faith: Questions and Answers for the Abused Woman* (New York: Harper & Row, 1987).

23. Genesis is structured around the phrase "These are the generations of." The history of new families that result in nations is dealt with in Appendix 3.

24. For the best material on the image of God, especially the corporate image, see J. Frame, "Men and Women in the Image of God," *Recovering Biblical Manhood and Womanhood*, eds. J. Piper, W. Grudem (Wheaton: Crossway, 1991), 225-232.

CHAPTER 3

The Family: God's Servant

Inez is a lonely seventeen-year-old, pregnant from one of her occasional one-night encounters. Her fifteen-year-old brother is in Juvenile Hall. Her father used to beat the family, until he left when Inez was only eight. Her mom has a live-in boyfriend, a drunkard who hates Inez and her brother. "Get out, you slut!" he yells at Inez, as he slobbers through his brown-stained, broken teeth. On the street, the warm California sunshine embraces her, but gives no comfort. In desperation, she contacts a crisis pregnancy center that places her in a shepherding home with a Christian family. Very immature, she wets her bed, sulks, withdraws, throws temper tantrums and manipulates. The family gives her love and structure. Although she appreciates the love and occasionally tries to reciprocate, she resists the structure, refuses to change and never responds to the good news about Jesus. The family perseveres, encourages her, and tells her she will not be able to handle her child if she does not mature. Inez gives birth to a little girl.

She insists she can make it on her own, gets a job and an apartment. However, she lives for parties, drinking, drugs, and boyfriends. While she is in jail for possessing drugs and resisting an arresting officer, her shepherding family cares for her baby daughter. Inez places her daughter up for adoption through a Christian agency and begins to drift aimlessly, living out of her car. She moves from one temporary relationship to another and has another illegitimate child. In her mid-twenties, Inez is already a bitter, broken woman.

How many Inezes are there? Family units like Inez and her mother, whether in the inner city or in wealthy suburbia, do not create stability and growth.

God created the family as a hothouse in which He grows five major social units. Without these units, society cannot remain stable enough to exercise the dominion God requires in Genesis 1:28. You and your family are necessary for each of these units to exist and prosper. You and your family are *that* important to society.

1. The Individual

Inez's antithesis is Ken, a godly young man, the son of an American missionary. Ken learned of Jesus from his father and mother, through whose gracious, generous, godly, sacrificial love God planted a church in a foreign culture. Now Ken works as a businessman in a country which officially prohibits all Christian activities. Ken's friends love him, and his testimony, though quiet, is powerful.

How do Inez and Ken differ? Primarily, in their families. "But," you argue, "surely God can overcome family background." Yes, God redeems the lost and changes them. Sure, there are exceptions. Some wonderful saints grew up in rotten families but as a rule, the family shapes the individual.

Children are genetic images of their parents (Gen 4:1; 5:1-4). Procreation results in infants who are image-bearers of their parents as well as of God. But numerous Scripture passages show that children also reflect the moral patterns of their parents (1 Pet 1:18). Parental modeling starts with the basic genetic inheritance and shapes it: Inez is like her mother, Ken like his father.

Edith Schaeffer notes that the individual's abilities are trained and honed in the family:

> One family and the children of that family can do marvelous things to affect the world or devastating things to destroy it. Hitler was one man born in one family. We could use many contrasting examples to emphasize that the old-

> fashioned saying, "The hand that rocks the cradle rules the world" is not just a group of quaint, idiotic, romantic words—it just happens that they are true. The problem today is that people want to have computers rock the cradles, institutions take over from that point on, and have no human influence involved at all. What career is so important as to allow the family to become extinct? The family which has continuity for not just one lifetime, but for generations, gives solidity and security and environment that cannot be duplicated and which spreads in a wide circle.[1]

A recent study, *The Girl Scout Survey on the Beliefs and Moral Values of America's Children*, states:

> Despite the diversity of perspectives among children, one thing is clear, the family has a decisive place in their world of meaning. The family—whatever its configuration—is the institution most children trust to solve America's problems. Marriage and a good family life is their chief priority as they face the future. And closer to their everyday experience, the family is their greatest source of emotional support and moral guidance.[2]

It goes on to conclude that:

> Among other things, those genuinely interested in children cannot ignore the importance of the family. No other institution, whether the state, the church, social service organizations or the many youth organizations, it would seem, could ever be an adequate substitute for the family. Nevertheless, other local and community organizations have a decisive influence on the lives of children. Their task is to continue to complement and thereby strengthen the family.[3]

The family gives birth to, nurtures and molds individuals. As a rule, stable families produce stable individuals; conversely, ungodly, unstable families produce ungodly, unstable individuals. Nothing replaces the family. God did not create Adam and Eve—and a day care center. The kibbutz or any other substitute for the family will fail.[4] Without a godly family, the individual is impoverished.

2. The Family

Inez is like her mother; her little family unit is the image of her mother's. Peter says that we inherit a futile way of life from our forefathers, yet there is hope because the blood of Christ redeems from this slavery (1 Pet 1:18-9). However, the rule remains: the family gives birth to new families in its own image.

My own family reflects this principle. My wife and I are sinners, raising five beautiful sinners. We are Christians and have His Spirit reconstructing our lives, but both Eileen and I had what Inez never did—godly parents. As we grew up, through all our sin, rebellion and struggles, we had godly models who loved God and us, and who raised us in the "nurture and admonition of the Lord." In the midst of the challenge of raising our children, we have had several individuals and families live with us as we ministered to them. We trust God that our children and our guests have found in our parents and us models to emulate.

Gen 4-6 tells us that the Cain-Lamech line was rebellious, while Seth's line obeyed and produced Noah. God wanted Israel to know its true family identity in contrast to the surrounding nations. Seth's family resulted in a group of people committed to the Lord, and although the sons of God forgot their roots and lusted after worldly women, there was *no* covenant keeper in Cain's line. Seth's line fulfilled God's command to "fill the earth and subdue it." Cain's failed.

The original family gave birth to other families that were to reflect the original by spreading out, filling the earth, organizing and ruling it to God's glory. Stable, godly families produce other stable families; unstable, ungodly families produce other unstable families:[5] this is the rule.[6] Government programs and private efforts to develop stable families will fail if there are no godly homes to train the next generation of families.

3. The Economic-Cultural Unit

Imagine Adam enjoying the challenge of naming and classifying animals. After God gives him Eve, they learn together. Even after the fall, they learn and pass these lessons on to their children. Early in our racial history, skills develop in the context of the family, as Cain's line develops tent-making, advanced livestock-breeding, metallurgy, and the fabrication of musical instruments. Sin did not obliterate man's desire or ability to discover and develop; it only perverted this creative attribute. Seth's line produces Abraham, who develops wealth and worship. These advances continue in Isaac, then in Jacob as this family helps to advance culture. Moses observes several things: first, creativity starts in the family as individuals develop new skills (Gen 4:17, 20-22). Second, the family passes these new skills on to the next generation. Third, the family leaders, the elders, regulate commerce between families and cities. Fourth, the elders enforce the contracts made between individuals and groups (Gen 23; 34). The family was the heart of economic advancement and cultural progress.

In his book, *Cause of Progress: Culture, Authority and Change,*[7] sociologist Emmanuel Todd claims that the type of family structure dictates the economic structure and progress of a particular society. Some family types promote and others hinder cultural advancement; the family is the key to progress and functions itself as an economic unit that is hard to match.[8]

Only stable, productive families pass on knowledge and wealth. Inez and her mother are not productive. In fact, they drain society. Only productive families stabilize an economy and culture. Economic and cultural progress is hampered without godly families.

4. The Church

Exciting things happen in a growing church in northern New Jersey planted by the church I once pastored. People confess sin publicly, are converted at church suppers, and work hard at worship and witness. Lots of factors contribute to its liveliness: faithful preaching, good elders, etc., but central to the story is one godly family. Andrew and Brianna were members of a church that began to drift in its commitment to God and His Word. Although they tried gently to return it to God's Word, their efforts met with hostility and indifference. Prayerfully, they resigned, got help from others and started a new church, only to have the leaders there change the original doctrinal position and exclude Andrew and Brianna from church membership as the new church was formed. They quietly withdrew and traveled great distances to worship in a sound church. Did they give up? No! They persevered in prayer, and when some people left their original church because things got even worse, Andrew and Brianna were there to help start a third church. This faithful family who had suffered much now saw a sound church planned and planted. Because they refused to give up, God's kingdom advances.

Moses recorded the genesis of worship in the family.[9] Worship was family-based until God formed Israel as His congregation. After Sinai, worship still occurred in the home, Passover being the chief example.[10] The New Testament did not change this family orientation. Although the change from the Passover meal to Communion as the covenant meal put the church family in the foreground, the family remains the underlying foundation for corporate worship.[11]

What does family worship do for the church? Three things. First, it trains worshipers' attitudes. As hearts are trained and attention spans are stretched in family worship at home, adults and children alike become godly, effective worshipers. Secondly, it models how the church should function as the family of God. The family teaches worship in the context of love, discipline, reconciliation and service. Thirdly, the home and family worship train leaders for the church (1 Tim 3: 4-5; Tit 1:6). The family is the minor league where church leaders are seasoned as they learn loving leadership and the roles of management.

B. M. Palmer says:

> Two principles emerge into view from the general survey, which really determine the matter. The first is, that in the Family are to be found both the State and the Church in embryo, perpetuated as they both are, through its continuance, until the end of time. The second is, that in both alike, the civil and ecclesiastical status of the child is defined from that of the parent, by right of birth.[12]

The family contains the church in embryo.[13] Godly families produce stable, growing churches; unstable families produce ungodly churches that often split. You will be a blessing to your church if you make your family and its worship a top priority after your relationship with God and your spouse. Because the church is God's salt and light in the world, to preserve culture you must preserve the church; to preserve the church you need godly families. The family and church are inextricably interwoven with cultural blessing (Ps 128). Inez, her mom and their families are not families that will make a church salt and light.[14] Without godly families, worship and witness are impoverished.

5. The State

Imagine yourself seated between Bethel and Ai in Abram's tent, looking at livestock as far as you can see, listening to Abram and Lot talk. Abram says, "Lot, we are brothers, relatives. Let's not fight. Don't let our herdsmen bicker and quarrel. Look, isn't the whole land before you? Please, separate your stock from mine. If you go left, I'll go right, or if you go right, I'll go the other way." Lot nods, gets up, leaves and goes into the Jordan valley while Abram stays in Canaan. This family split leads to three nations: Israel, Moab and Ammon.

Lot goes to Sodom: he marries, is captured by Chedorlaomer, is delivered by Abram, protects God's angels, escapes God's wrath, loses his wife, hides in caves, gets drunk twice and is seduced by his daughters. Moab and Ammon, the two illegitimate sons of Lot, become enemies of Israel and continually cause them to stumble into sin.[15] An unstable family and its sin results in two wicked nations that despise God's kindness and antagonize and attack God's people for generations to come. One family can alter world history—for good or for ill.

Abram's family is a positive example. God covenants with Abram, Isaac and Jacob, whose twelve sons become God's nation that receives the Mosaic and Davidic administrations of the Abrahamic covenant. Jesus the Messiah comes and administers the final covenant and by Him all the nations and families of the earth are blessed. Without him, all of us are aliens, headed for hell (Rom 1-2; Eph 2:11-22). Through one family we are saved. The family is important to the formation, character, and development of nations in general and of God's nation in particular. One family can profoundly affect world history and eternity.

Abram acted as a civil magistrate and a military commander (Gen 14). In doing so, he followed the pattern set by the first family of Adam,[16] and the renewed family of Noah.[17] The rest of the Old Testament confirms the family as the original court of social and governmental adjudication,[18] and for a time it retained many of its governmental functions after formal governments developed.[19]

Normally, the elders of the extended family became the elders of the formal government and ruled over the major functions of society: economic[20] and political,[21] as well as religious.[22] Moses records that all the nations of his day developed out of individual families.[23] The family was the womb of nations.

B. M. Palmer states that the family is the state in embryo. Emmanuel Todd, in *The Explanation of Ideology: Family Structures and Social Systems*,[24] shows how the very structure of the family determines the kind of political structure a society will have. Todd's crucial work contains important implications for the family and its structure.

What does the family do for the State? Five things.

1. The family trains its citizens.

Palmer says:

> Thus the Family is the school in which men are trained for the duties of citizenship; for the strongest government would be shattered in a day were not the concurrent wills of which it is composed taught how to blend with mutual concessions.[25]

2. The family models good citizenship.

The family remains the controlling model for how the state and its citizens treat each other. The working relationships between authorities and subordinates are modeled in the family. Justice, mercy and love are mastered in the family.

3. The family preserves stability.

Marxist-Leninists believed that a Soviet Union without religion and capitalism would become a secular utopia. Egalitarian to the core—at least in theory—they despised the traditional hierarchical structure of the family, legislating against Christianity, capitalism and the family. This failed so miserably that in the late 1930s they had to protect the family by legislation so the Soviet Union would not fall apart.[26] Yet they continued to oppose the biblical understanding of family. By the early 1990s they began looking for Western capital to feed a starving nation and they allowed Bibles, preaching and even a few Christian schools to nourish a nation of starving souls.[27]

4. The family trains leaders for the State.

Just as the family is the minor league for church leaders, so it is for the State. In fact, the State should choose its leaders from family trained leaders who have proven their worth in the church. Only when a man can rule and manage these two smaller units is he prepared to lead society at large.[28] There can be no permanent growth or national stability without godly leaders.[29] The Massachusetts Bay Colony knew better than we.[30] The rule is: godly, stable families produce good and godly political leaders; unstable ones do not. Without godly families, the nation and its government are impoverished.

5. The family offers social welfare, volunteerism and altruism.

The family can perform deeds of necessity and mercy for needy people as no other unit can. By its presence, structure and resources, the family prevents a society from degenerating into either a self-centered, fatalistic neglect of the poor and needy, or into a sterile, statist institutionalization of love and compassion.[31]

Do you catch the vision of how much depends on your family? The stability and growth of these five major social units depend on it. The chapter title is no exaggeration. God has ordained three institutions: the family, the church and the state.[32] He started with the family—a husband and a wife—not with a pastor and a parishioner or with a king and a subject. The other two grew out of the family: the family is the one renewable resource necessary for society. Today if there was a nuclear holocaust and only your family survived, you could begin society over again. A group of elders or government officials—as such—could not.

While your family is the basic governmental unit, it is not independent of the other two. Scripture records the flow of history and indicates that the family has become interdependent on the church and state while remaining God's building block, the basic governmental unit.[33] The family needs the church's preaching, sacraments and discipline to support and help it.[34] It also needs the state's protection.[35] Yet, we've seen that the church and state cannot function without godly families. You and I and our families carry a lot of weight on our shoulders. In chapter 1, I asked, "If you were going to start a world, how would you start?" I ask you now, "If you were going to destroy the world, where would you start?"

Yes, like Satan, you would start with the family. You and I must protect our families. Every social revolutionary aims at the family, as do the ACLU and NOW. Just as God and theology are tied to the family, so society and the family are bound together and reflect each other.

Lose the family and you lose everything. You lose God and theology; the world becomes very dark. You lose authority, stability and progress; the world becomes chaotic. But ultimately and most horribly, lose the family and you lose eternal life; your world becomes hell forever. Why? Because the family not only reflects the reality and nature of God, not only is it the foundation of stability and dominion under God—it is also the foundation for redemption.

Notes:

Chapter 3

1. Edith Schaeffer, *What Is a Family?* (Old Tappen: F. H. Revell, 1975), 48.

2. R. Coles, *Girl Scouts' Survey on the Beliefs and Moral Values of America's Children* (New York: Girl Scouts of America, 1989), 102.

3. Ibid., 103.

4. See D. J. Ayers, "The Inevitability of Failure: The Assumptions and Implementations of Modern Feminism," *Recovering Biblical Manhood and Womanhood: A Response to Evangelical Feminism*, J. Piper, W. Grudem, eds. (Crossway, 1991), 319-321. His comments on the kibbutz system and its daycare are helpful. See also O. R. Johnston, *Who Needs the Family?* (Wheaton: Intervarsity, 1979), 29-30.

5. Edith Schaeffer, op. cit., reminds us that the family is a formation center for human relationships, where people learn how to get along with others so they can properly manage their own new families.

6. There are exceptions, I realize, but the rule holds. Biblical examples abound: many of the same sins existed in Eli, Samuel, David and Solomon, and their families. Again, the good news is redeeming grace. For a modern example, see J. Miller, *Come Back, Barbara*, 2nd edition (Phillipsburg: Presbyterian and Reformed, 1997).

7. E. Todd, *Cause of Progress: Culture, Authority and Change* (Oxford: Blackwell, 1987). Especially fascinating is his observation on Jewish family structure as influenced by the Old Testament.

8. Nancy Pearcy shows the importance of the family to economic endeavors and, in turn, those endeavors to the family. "The Family that Works Together," *The World and I* (March 1989); "Is Love Enough? Recreating the Economic Base of the Family," *The Family in America*, vol 4, no 1 (Jan. 1990). "Working Together: Family Spirit '91," *USA Weekend* (Nov. 22-24, 1991), 4-6, 8, 11, 13-16, 19-20, 22, 24. This is the fourth annual tribute to family spirit and highlights over 600 families who work together in businesses and other endeavors. The article also uses statistics from *Family Business*, a magazine started in 1989 (Family Business Pub. Co., 1845 Walnut St., Ste. 900, Philadelphia, PA 19103). Many ideas can be gleaned from this issue.

9. Gen 4:3-12, 26; 8:20; 12:7-8; 13:4, 18; 22:9; 26:25; 33:20; 35:1-7. See also Ex 12:1-20.

10. Ex 12:1-20; 13:1-16; Lev 23:4-8; Num 28:16-25; Deut 16:1-8.

11. For cogent arguments upholding the present validity of this duty, see "To the Christian Reader, especially Heads of Families," *Westminster Confession of Faith: The Larger and Shorter Catechisms with the Scripture*

Proofs at Large (Free Presbyterian Church of Scotland, 1970), 3-6; J. H. M. d'Aubigne, *Family Worship: Motives and Directions for Domestic Piety in the Family* (Dallas: Presbyterian Heritage, 1989), a sermon preached in Paris in 1827; J. W. Alexander, "Thoughts on Family Worship" in *The Family* (Harrisonburg: Sprinkle, 1981), a reprint of the classic 1847 work. For a historical view on the father's role in worship, see K. Ptacek, "Family Worship," *The Bulletin of Greenville Presbyterian Theological Seminary*, vol 5, no 4 (Nov/Dec 1992), 3.

12. B. M. Palmer, "The Family in its Civil and Churchly Aspects," in *The Family* op. cit., 209, a reprint of the 1876 classic.

13. Palmer's first chapter in section 2 is "The Family, the Germ of the Church, Historical Development." He develops the following headings:

> 1. At the very beginning, under a system of natural religion, Adam was constituted the head and organ of a religious commonwealth.
>
> 2. Equally so after the fall, the first man becomes, in the Family, the minister of the religion of grace.
>
> 3. Under the patriarchal economy which ensued, the traces of religious service are found still in the bosom of the family.
>
> 4. Under the institutions of Moses, when the structure of the Church was so greatly enlarged, the tie is not severed which connects it with the Family.
>
> 5. Under the New Testament economy, where the Church assumes her final form, the family is again her home.

14. Of course God could change them. Even if He did, the church comprised of such broken family units would be hard to grow. We should not despise single parent homes, but, they require a longer period of time to bring a church to maturity. I have a friend who is just now, after twenty years of ministry in an inner city context, seeing male leadership develop.

15. Num 25:1-9; 31:16; 2 Pet 2:15-16; Jud 3:12-14; 10:17-18; 1 Sam 8:1-9; 12:12-13; 2 Sam 8:12; Zeph 2:8-11.

16. Gen 4:13, 14. After God tells Cain he will be a vagrant and wanderer because of his murder, Cain complains of the severity of his punishment. He does not recognize that it is only because of God's grace that his life is not taken. He sees that the vagrant wandering is rough, that being driven from God's presence is worse, and that people—obviously his family—will try to avenge Abel's death. The family was the government or judicial system. For helpful commentaries on this passage, see H. C. Leupold, *Exposition of Genesis* (Grand Rapids: Baker, 1968), 208-211; C. F. Keil and F. Delitzsch, *Biblical Commentary on the Old Testament: The Pentateuch*, vol 1 (Grand Rapids: Wm. B. Eerdmans, n.d.), 113-115.

17. Gen 9:4-6; Num 35:6-34; Deut 19:1-21. The avenger of blood was a blood relative.

18. See especially Gen 32–34.

19. Gen 14. Abraham, as head and governor of his large household, delivers Lot from kings. As long as a family/clan structure exists in the world, where no formal government exists, it will retain some or all of these functions. My brief trips to Uganda have confirmed this observation. The interaction of tribal governments with modern nation states would be an interesting study.

20. Gen 12:10, 20; 13:8, 9; 23:1-20.

21. Gen 14:1-24; 21:22-34.

22. For the classic sociological work on these three areas, their interrelationship to each other, and to the family, see Fustel de Coulanges, *The Ancient City: A Study on the Religion, Laws and Institutions of Greece and Rome* (Garden City: Doubleday Anchor, n.d.)

23. Gen 4:17; 10:1-32, especially 32; 11:1-9, especially 8, 9. The theme and organizational structure of Genesis is "These are the generations of" (*'elleh toledot*; see 2:4; 5:1; 6:9; 10:1; 11:10; 11:27; 25:12; 36:1, 9; 37:2). These references and the surrounding passages record the history of the nations around Israel. This data is sufficient to trace the roots of most modern nations. There is no legitimate argument against the family as the womb of the nations.

24. E. Todd, *The Explanation of Ideology: Family Structures and Social Systems* (Basil: Blackwell, 1985), 6.

> There is one ubiquitous theory which may be detected in political thought all over the world from Confucius to Rousseau, from Aristotle to Freud. It is the idea that family relations—those between parents and children, between husband and wife—provide a model for political systems and serve to define the relationship between the individual and authority. It is a theory which until recently was as unusable as it was indestructible, for the embryonic state of social anthropology (which is concerned with studying and classifying family forms) has never before allowed any systematic comparison between family models and political structures.

25. Palmer, op. cit., 116.

26. C.C. Zimmerman, *Family and Civilization* (New York: Harper and Brothers, 1947), 528-9; Johnston, *Who Needs the Family?* (Wheaton: InterVarsity, 1979), 27-9.

27. Nor is Russia an isolated example. Similar attempts in ancient Greece, Rome, the Middle Ages and eighteenth-century France all failed (Zimmerman, op. cit., 161, 210, 395-6). For an excellent, brief statement of how values in general, and Christian values in particular, are transmitted by the family and

become cultural glue, see John A. Sparks, "The Unseen Governors of American Society," *Special Report* #44 (Public Policy Education Fund, 161 E. Pine St., Grove City, PA, 16127). As I write, the Soviet Union is dead. The experiment has failed. Without the proper family type, society will unravel.

28. God did not want a non-covenantal person to rule Israel and gave strict rules about whom the Israelites could choose as king (Deut 17:14-20; 1 Sam 8): the king could not be a foreigner but had to be part of the covenant community (i.e., a worshiper of Jehovah), read the law every day, follow it, not be proud and not exalt himself over his brothers. In short, godly government can only be exercised by godly men.

29. The biblical model would spare us leaders who are moral disasters, like Ted Kennedy, and allow us better men, such as Judges Bork and Thomas. The Clinton debacle only reinforces this observation.

30. Many leaders in the American experiment understood the connection between authority and family. The Massachusetts Bay Colony and much of Puritan New England agreed that a citizen needed to respond well to authority while under it before he bore it. The sequence was: first, self-control by submission to the Holy Spirit; second, submission to the rule of leaders in a godly congregation; third, godly oversight of a household in marriage; fourth, wise ownership and control of land; fifth, the right to vote. Only after showing proper submission to and proper use of authority could a man take office.

Today, the only requirements to vote and rule seem to be: to be alive and not to be a felon—maybe. Edmund S. Morgan's *Puritan Political Ideas: 1558-1794* (Indianapolis: Bobbs Merrill, 1965), gives the New England Puritan leaders' views of the relationship of the family, church, and state and their interaction in a portion of colonial America. This view necessitates two things: faithful preaching of God's Word, and God's grace in continuously creating new hearts in the citizens. This, in fact, was the problem in Israel as a nation. Judges shows what happens when revival, reformation and righteous rule are separated.

Though New England emphasized the above qualifications for voting (as opposed to economic qualifications in England), the percentage of active voters was as great or greater than that of England. See Samuel T. Logan, Jr., "New England Puritans and the State" in *Theonomy: A Reformed Critique*, W. S. Barker, W. R. Godfrey, eds., (Grand Rapids: Zondervan, 1991), 369-370, especially notes 36, 37.

31. M. Olasky, *The Tragedy of American Compassion* (Washington, D.C.: Regnery Pub., 1992).

32. P. Woolley, *Family, State and Church—God's Institutions* (Grand Rapids: Baker, 1969) shows the biblical justification of groups in general and specifically the three major ones.

33. A thorough study of the interrelationship between these three

institutions is beyond the scope of this book. However, your view does impact your view of the family and how it functions. See my "Who Owns the Children of Divorce?", *Journal of Pastoral Practice*, vol 8, no 3, 1986, 46-47.

Edmund S. Morgan, *The Puritan Family: Religion and Domestic Relations in Seventeenth-Century New England* (New York: Harper and Row, 1966), 18-19, reflects on the New England Puritan view of these three authorities:

> The Puritans indeed honored every kind of superiority among men as spark of the divine order: old men were superior to young, educated to uneducated, rich to poor, craftsmen to common laborers, highborn to lowborn, clever to stupid. These differences in age, wealth, birth, and talents, however, did not constitute the order of any particular social group. They were differences similar to the differences between inferior creatures, say between a horse and a dog, differences which merely added richness and complexity to the social order. The order which God had constituted in society presupposes his "appointment of mankind to live in Societies, first, of Family, secondly Church. Thirdly, Commonwealth." For each of these groups He had established a special order, consisting of the relationships which the members were supposed to bear to one another; and respect for this order was the first thing that He demanded in all societies, whether of family, church, or state. "Order is the Soul of Common Wealths and Societies," said one minister. "It is the forme of societies," said another, and he added, "Formes are essential without which things cannot be." "Be lovers of order," urged a third; "learn to know it that you may love it." And they all taught their congregations that "whatever is done against the order that God has constituted is done against God."

34. Even in the Old Testament, once God called Israel as a political-ecclesiastical entity (a kingdom of priests, Ex 19:6, Deut 7:6; 10:15), worship was regulated by ordained men in a central place (Deut 12:1-32). The family had certain freedoms, but worship was restricted and controlled by the Levites, not the father.

In the New Testament, the ordained leaders oversee worship. Baptism (Matt 3:1; John 3:22-4:3; Acts 2:41; 8:12, 36; 10:48; 11:16; 16:15, 33; 18:8; 19:5; 22:16, 1 Cor 1:14) is always regulated and administered by ordained men. The same is true of the Lord's Supper (Matt 26:26; Mark 14:22; Luke 22:19; Acts 2:42, 46; 20:7, 11; 1 Cor 10:16; 11:26). Only something as extreme as the anarchy of war could change this and allow the family to control worship again. Of course, peace would restore the New Testament order.

35. Rom 13:3-4. Even in the Old Testament, the family's governmental powers were limited. For example, parents could not execute their rebellious children but had to go to the civil authorities (Deut 21:18-21). The civil authorities had the power to prevent parental abuse of children, even in family inheritance issues (Deut 21:15-17).

In the New Testament, there is no indication that parents are given any more powers than they had in the Old Testament. You should assume that the same limitations accrue, unless explicitly changed. Again, only the anarchy of war could temporarily change this.

CHAPTER 4

The Family: God's Model

How do you learn about God's grace? Most often, you learn through reading the Bible or hearing it preached, but you also learn through godly people. Lewis and Ruth Grotenhuis were that example for my wife and me as I learned to pastor God's sheep. Pastor Grotenhuis founded and pastored Calvary Community Church in Harmony, New Jersey. For forty years he and Mrs. Grotenhuis set a standard of Christian service and hospitality that I have yet to see matched. Lewis is now with the Lord; Ruth continues to bless people with her joy. The Grotenhuises raised seven children. At mealtime, twenty people sometimes sat around their table. Many strangers found food, shelter and wise counsel in that home. Once they found someone in their basement who had not been there when they had gone to bed; he only stayed six months! Seminary and all the books in the world could not replace this model. From them, Eileen and I learned how to serve. The family serves as God's model of salvation.

The family is both the *means* and the *model* of redemption. God always uses the family to bring redemption to His people. At the same time, He employs it as His living model of that redemption. Consider both.

The Family as the Means of Redemption

The family is always involved in redemption as the *means* or instrument of God's salvation. It is God who saves, but He always uses the family to bring His grace to His people. After the Fall, God promises the Seed who will save (Gen 3:15). Even though family life is cursed by God because of sin, His grace triumphs. Imagine Adam and Eve's pain over Abel's death at the hand of

Cain; imagine their joy knowing Seth is a replacement. Fruitfulness now means more than dominion; it means salvation. The family is the instrument of God's covenantal grace.

Noah finds grace in God's eyes (Gen 8:20–9:17). His family, not a tribe, people or nation, is spared from the flood. He becomes like Adam; to him also God gave the mandate to be fruitful and rule. Imagine watching the animals go back into the wild, seeing the smoke arise from the altar, gazing at your wife, children and daughters-in-law and knowing you had a world to subdue. What a family worship service that was! Again, we see the family as God's instrument of covenantal grace.

Abram is called by God and responds. God covenants to make his family great and through him to bless all the families of the whole earth (Gen 12:1-3). God promises to bring both the descendant, (Gen 15:1-21), and many nations out of Abram (Gen 17:1-8). He changes his name to Abraham to reflect this promise (Gen 17:1-8) and gives a family sign—circumcision. God's covenantal promises are not just to an individual but to a family, in fact, to many families. Imagine your excitement and laughter at Isaac's conception and the honor of your family blessing the whole world. Once again, the family is God's instrument of covenantal grace.

In the fourth administration of God's covenant of grace,[1] the family is still the instrument of salvation. While Israel is a nation, four particulars evidence that the family's centrality has not changed. First, its leaders are taken from the family elders (Ex 24:1-11). Second, the national structure is built on twelve family tribes. Third, when God threatens to destroy Israel and start over, He offers Moses the opportunity to be a second Abraham (Ex 32:10; Num 14:12). God's method is to pick a particular family when He wants to reissue His gracious covenant. Imagine the temptation for Moses to accept God's offer. He could have started from scratch, instead of interceding for the people. Fourth, God forbids intermarriage, an important Satanic strategy (Deut 7:1-

6). As in the previous administrations, the family remains God's instrument of covenantal truth and grace.

Imagine you are David sitting before the Lord, talking to Him. You love Him and want to build His temple. He tells you He does not need a house, but He will make a covenant with your family so that you will always have a descendant on the throne. God is going to build *you* a living house. Yes, you'd be excited as was David. The family is center stage again.

In the final administration of the covenant, Jesus mediates the new covenant in a family context. Like Seth, Noah, Abraham and Moses, the second Adam (David's greatest son, Jesus) comes into a family. Joseph and Mary, a godly stepfather and mother of Davidic descent, are entrusted with His education. The exact influence they had on His human development is hard to estimate, but no doubt it was great. At the cross Jesus takes care to provide for His mother. The new covenant comes by way of a Davidic family.

Clearly the family is the means or instrument of God's redemption. Not one administration of God's covenant fails to involve the family. Thus, you need to look with new respect and awe at the family. From start to finish, creation to consummation, the family is the means by which God brings covenantal renewal and growth. The life and death of Christ is in the context of the family. God takes the family seriously and gives it great centrality in the plan of redemption.

The family or household is not only the transmitter of salvation; it is a recipient of Christ's redemption. Just as individuals can come to God through Christ, so can households. The New Testament phenomenon of whole families coming to Christ is very strange to twentieth century Western European Christians. The New Testament data on conversions is not extensive, but household conversions are mentioned as often as individual conversions.[2] Rarely, if ever, do modern Christians think of groups of people being the recipients of the covenant of redemption, yet, in the early days of the new covenant, the family and groups were primary targets of evangelism. Only in modern times has the individual become the exclusive target of gospel evangelism. Fragmentation of the family and growth of existential thinking have invaded the Church. Ignoring the New Testament approach has hurt evangelism and the unity of the body of Christ. In an age of infidelity, divorce, individualism, and sexual impurity, there must be a focus on the family's importance to the Church and society. Individualism is one more way the world presses the Church into its mold.

The Family as the Model of Redemption

However, the family is not just the vehicle of redemption, it is also the realistic *model* of or pattern of redemption. By this I mean that the family of husband, wife, and children models the reality of the family of God. This model or metaphor is real because the Church is not only *like* a family, it *is* the family of God. God causes dead men to be born from above by the Holy Spirit's power (John 3:3-8); they are given the right to become sons of God (John 1:12, 13). The Holy Spirit, who is the Spirit of adoption, seals men into God's family and helps them cry out, "Abba, Father" (Rom 8:12-17). Christians are referred to as the household or family of believers.[3] The parallel natures of the family and the kingdom of God are seen in Luke 11:11-22. In two different settings Jesus shows a precise parallel between an earthly father and his care of his household and the heavenly Father and His care for His kingdom: the household is a mini-kingdom; a kingdom is an expanded household. Thus the human family is to be a model of the heavenly kingdom.

The physical family also models this reality. The structure and function of the family are a reflection of the character of the Church, Christ the Savior, and the relationship between them. Evangelism largely depends upon these living metaphors, the families in the Church, and the vibrancy of their reflection of redemption. Three family relationships stand out: the husband-wife, the parent-child, and the adoptive parent-child relationships. Keep in mind the interactive, analogous relationship between God and man mentioned in chapter 2 which helps to explain why these living metaphors exist.

The husband-wife relationship

The husband-wife relationship is a covenantal union that reflects the covenantal union between God and His people. The Old Testament often uses this analogy.[4] For the prophets, Judah and Israel are the bride of Jehovah. The New Testament picks up this theme and clarifies it by portraying Jesus as the Messianic bridegroom (Rev 19:6-9; 21:2, 3; 22:17); Jesus thought of Himself in these terms (Matt 22:1-14; 25:1-13).

Ephesians 5:22-33 is the most explicit teaching on this relationship: the husband is to be like Christ and the wife like the Church. Much could be said about this, but for now note that this is no mere analogy. Paul refers to the one-flesh relationship of Genesis 2:24 and says that this union reflects the great mystery of the relationship between Christ and the Church; therefore, a profound spiritual mystery is reflected in the husband and wife relationship; their union reflects the true union between Christ and His bride, the Church. Both intercourses are mysteries.

To alter the nature of the husband-wife relationship reflects on the Savior-Church relationship, changing the perception of the nature and reality of salvation. To change the reality of God's nature or salvation is to endanger your life and the lives of everyone around you. Heresy does not change God, but it does pervert people's view of Him and thus prevents them from coming to Him. You must come to God as He is and not to your own image of Him.[5] Today's attempts to alter the husband-wife relationship attack God's plan of salvation. Could anything be more serious? Whether the attempts are deliberate or not is important, yet intentions do not soften effects. Alter the lordship of Jesus Christ and you alter salvation. Paul's warning against this in Galatians should sober anyone who tampers with the marital structure. The husband-wife relationship, and the marriage union, mirrors the mystery of the incarnate Lord of glory redeeming His sinful bride.

This relationship has profound practical effects on teaching and evangelism. A poor husband-wife relationship can turn people away from the gospel. Consider a pastor whose marriage is so poor that his marital conflicts become apparent to all. His ministry becomes ineffective not only to non-Christians but to his own church members. He does not love; she does not submit. He eventually leaves the gospel ministry and the church folds.

On the other hand, a godly relationship can be a tremendous witness. Once, an older street lady stayed with us for several months. As she was leaving, she mentioned that she had stayed in other Christian homes, but this was the first in which she had not been propositioned, and in which the husband loved his wife. Thank you, Lord. She saw a living model of Christ and the Church.

The father-son relationship

Closely related to the husband-wife relationship is the second family relationship, the father-son relationship. Interestingly, the Scriptures hold both these family relations close to each other. In Jeremiah 3:1-10, the bride of Jehovah addresses God as "My Father." This address of respect shows that both the husband-wife and father-son relationship have authority and submission built in. To change the nature of either of these relationships is to distort the nature of salvation.

The father-son relationship reflects the relationship between Jehovah and Israel.[6] In the New Testament, "Father" becomes the best way to address God. The eternal trinitarian Son becomes the Messianic Son; earns the right for us to be born from above and adopted into God's family; earns our inheritance (Rom 8:15-17); and, with the Father, gives the Holy Spirit,who makes us like our Brother when He returns (1 John 3:2).

There are also practical implications for evangelism. Poor parent-child relationships can kill evangelism. I wish I could forget an incident that happened years ago. We had neighbors who were not Christians but who allowed us to take their children to church. One day during family worship I asked our children if our young neighbors enjoyed church and would come to love God. "No!" came the fervent reply from one of our children. "You're always scolding them to be quiet or to sit still." I had not reflected the gentle hospitality of our holy God and Father. May God grant us the grace to reflect Him.

On the other hand, I know a couple whose example has affected many. The husband was a Christian school principal and an elder in a church. He and his wife have done evangelistic ministry in Uganda, Kenya, and in the USA They are now in Holland doing church planting under the leadership of their oldest son. Their family and parenting influenced many who lived with them or observed them as models of God's love and discipline. Because their godly children reflected their godliness, many of their guests wanted to come to Christ.

The adoptive parent and the adopted child

The third relationship is an adoptive parent and child. Everything said of parent-child relationships is true here. In addition, adoption includes going out of the way to incorporate a child who is a stranger by nature. Of course, this is a picture of God's grace to us. Sometimes when stepfathers or adoptive fathers sexually molest children, the children grow up with distorted views of fathers. While God's grace can overcome such sin, it makes it more difficult for such children to come to God. The very idea of "father" is distorted. On the other hand, a couple in the church I pastored adopted their son. Their consistent love, as great or greater than any natural parent, has borne fruit: their son was a short-term missionary in Japan, a glowing example of a lay evangelist who loved Christ. He is now an ordained pastor. This adoptive relationship speaks volumes for the gospel.

Since the Church is the family of God, a distorted view of the family will also pervert one's view of the Church. Today, attacks on authority in the Church grow more and more vicious. Disrupt the Church and the light of the gospel is dulled. Remember what we learned concerning God, revelation, and theology. Remember Todd's work on politics and economics. But above all, remember the Savior on the cross. Yes, above all, keep your eye on Jesus. No other blood can cover your sin; no other Lord can save you and your family; no other Lord can salvage, save, and sanctify society.

One major problem with feminism and egalitarianism is that they force you to a graceless, save-yourself-by-your-own-bootstrap theology. The flow of divine, sovereign grace pouring out from an exalted, glorified, enthroned Jesus Christ is dammed. His covenantal, kingdom mercy is lost, as all authority is damned—crucified on the cross of egalitarianism. No room is left for adoption as sons through the blood of the Son. The subtle siren sounds of the serpent softly say that we will be as gods; the only god these ideas produce is a "goddess" running naked in a Satanic coven.

Much is at stake. If you lose the family, you lose everything: God, reality, revelation, society, and redemption. Many voices call out modern renditions of old lies. Yes, the stakes are high. Lose the family, and you lose the reflection of the reality and nature of God, the foundation for stability and progress in society, and the reflection of redemption. We must humble ourselves and listen to God. The Church had better humble itself and listen to its Lord and Master. Modern Western European culture had better humble itself and listen to God or it will soon join Assyria, Babylon, Greece, and Rome on the garbage heap of nations. If God did not spare Israel, He will not spare us. May He grant us mercy to listen and to obey.

Notes:

Chapter 4

1. O. Palmer Robertson's *The Christ of the Covenants* (Phillipsburg: Presbyterian and Reformed, 1981) is the best explanation of what a covenant is and how God's covenant of redemption works in history. You must grasp this if you are to see the family's centrality. Otherwise, you will drift into an atomistic individualism that undermines the unity of Christ's redemption in history and the unity of the body of Christ. Western civilization has been fragmented for many reasons. Individualism is both a cause and a result of this and we are left with families and a society of individuals with little or no sense of community.

2. John 4:53; Acts 10:2; 11:14; 16:15, 34; 18:8; 1 Cor 1:16.

3. Gal 6:10; Eph 2:19; 1 Tim 3:15; 1 Pet 4:17.

4. Isa 50:1-3; Jer 3:1-10; Ez 23; Hos 1:2-9; 2:1-23; 3:1-5.

5. Many today believe the Alcoholics Anonymous idea that God will accept you on your terms. This idea is not biblical, and amounts to saying, "God will pretend to be someone He is not, just so I can get His help." The Lord does not change (1 Sam 15:29; Jer 4:28; Mal 3:6; Heb 7:21). One of Israel's problems was that it wanted Jehovah *on its terms*. The classic example is Jeroboam, and his changes for political expediency (1 Kgs 12:25-33). God was not at all happy (1 Kgs 13:1-6). Perhaps more graphic for faithful followers of God was the incident with godly David, Uzzah and the ark (2 Sam 6:1-11). See also M. and D. Bobgan, *12 Steps to Destruction: Codependency Recovery Heresies* (Santa Barbara: Eastgate, 1991); W. L. Playfair, *The Useful Lie* (Wheaton: Crossway, 1991).

6. Deut 1:31; 32:6,18; 2 Sam 7:14; 1 Chr 17:13; 22:10; 28:6; Ps 2:7; 68:5; 89:19-29; 103:13; Isa 9:6; 63:16; Jer 2:27; 3:19; 31:9; Mal 1:6; 2:10.

Section 2

~

DOES GOD CARE?

~

CHAPTER 5

The Family: God's Overview

As you turn to these chapters on the theology of the family, you may say, "The Bible is fine, but Systematic Theology? Are you writing these chapters to show off?"

No. I do love the Bible and have been trained in the original languages, in systematic theology, and in preaching God's law and grace. But remember what I said in the introduction: I'm praying for a third Great Awakening in the United States of America. In order for our families to become the salt and light that will spark such an awakening, God's Word and Spirit will be required. Serious biblical input is imperative.[1] You need God's, not man's counsel on the family, no matter how well-intentioned the latter might be. You need the real thing.[2]

I make no claims of being a brilliant systematic theologian. I only pray that this simple presentation will help you in several ways. You will know what God says about family life. You will be able to measure your views against God's. You will be able to evaluate so-called expert views, to discern and avoid ungodly counsel, hating evil and clinging to what is good. You will be able to adjust your views and actions, thereby becoming saltier "salt" and more brilliant "light" in your family life.

God Defines the Family

1. Household: The Basic Unit

The Bible does not use the word family,[3] but prefers the word house,[4] the equivalent of our word "household." Whether in a tent, a house, an apartment, a condo, or a palace, people live in a house. Several elements comprise the family as defined biblically. The family, in its most irreducible form, rests upon God's creation ordinance of marriage. "In Hebrew culture, society was built on the family, and the family in turn on the institution of marriage."[5]

A man leaves his father and mother and cleaves to his wife (Gen 2:24). However, the Bible views the family as more than a married couple; a household includes children (Gen 1:28). Childlessness does not negate a marriage,[6] therefore a childless couple does not cease to be a family. Nonetheless, children are an expected part of the family. A family includes dependent relatives: brothers or sisters until married; grandparents and perhaps other kinsmen.[7] A family could even include non-relatives such as hired servants, slaves, and sojourners,[8] non-relative dependents who needed short-term hospitality. Later, Levites, widows and the fatherless could be included so that the family remains the basic unit of corporate or social welfare.[9]

This basic unit of society is different from our modern nuclear family which includes only husband, wife and children (preferably not too many of those). Daily life then was different and in many ways richer than today's family experience. In addition, the Old Testament applies the term "house" in even broader ways.

Importantly, "house" is applied to a household or family: Jacob's household (Gen 35:2), a family of descendants as a corporate group, Abraham's house (Gen 18:19) and David's house (2 Sam 7:11), the Hebrew people as house of Jacob (Gen 46:27) and house of Israel (Ex 16:31), the father's house in the sense of a clan or family (Num 1:2). In the Old Testament there is a solidarity between a man and his house (Josh 2:12; 6:22; 7:1-5; 1 Sam 7:15). So Joshua informs the Israelites that he and his house will serve the Lord (Josh 24:15).[10]

Therefore, the household is not just a larger version of today's family—a couple with more children—but is comprised of different kinds of people than those in our families. Further, composition is not the only difference: there is also a cohesiveness or solidarity to the family. The family unit has a vital community, a solidarity foreign to us today.

There has long been recognized in the Old Testament a certain solidarity between a man and his house. If a man committed a serious sin, God's punishment fell on him and his house (Josh 7:1-15, etc.). Similarly, God delivered an innocent man and his house from punishment (Gen 7:1; Josh 2:12; 6:22; 1 Kgs 17:15). Joshua tells the Israelite assembly at Shechem that he and his house will serve Yahweh (Josh 24:15; cf also Acts 16 in the New Testament.)[11]

The household is viewed as a covenantal unit. Things are done as a unit and not just as individuals living in the same dwelling. God often deals with whole households.

The Scriptures are much more corporate-minded than we are today, and the Old Testament use of "household" reflects that difference. God does not deal with each believer in a merely atomistic fashion. Once Abraham believed, then his whole household was considered to be in the covenant and the males were required to receive the covenant sign, circumcision. God gave a charge of holiness not only to Abraham, but also to his whole household (Gen 18:19). He commanded various religious ceremonies to be observed by the household as a unit: the Passover (Ex 12:3f.; 2 Chron 35:6), the sin offering on the Day of Atonement (Lev 16:17), the sacrifice of the firstborn of the flocks (Deut 15:20), tithing (Deut 12:7; 14:26), and eating of the Levitical tithe (Num 18:31). God punished not only Korah, Dathan, and Abiram, but also their households (Num 16:32; Deut 11:6). Conversely, when God blessed Obed-edom for taking care of the ark, He also blessed "all his household" (2 Sam 6:11).[12]

This corporate attitude is significant, not only for the individual household, but for the larger social context. The household is not only viewed as a unified whole, but also united to a broader covenantal context.

2. Extended Family

The Bible never views the household in isolation, but as connected to larger units. The first is "the house of their fathers" (Num 1:2, 4, 20). This is an extended family, probably including sons and their families, as well as the original household (Gen 7:1; 46:26, 27). In the census in Numbers, chapter 1, God tells Moses how to muster and register his warriors: first tribe, then clan, then the father's house, then house, and finally individuals. When Achan sins and causes Israel's defeat at Ai, Joshua seeks the offender, searching from tribe to clan, clan to house, house to man (Josh. 7:14). Joshua takes the tribe of Judah, then the clan of the Zerahites, then the household of Zimri, then the man Achan, who is the son of Carmi, the son of Zimri (7:16-28). This household includes at least three generations: son, father, grandfather.

Yet a *bayit* (household, family, or house) must not be thought of as being too large. It is not to be identified with a clan *(mispaha)*, which is a subdivision of a tribe; rather, it is a subdivision of the clan (Josh 7:14).[13]

The next group is the clan.[14] This is larger than the house and the house of their fathers. In Joshua, chapter 7, the clan seems to be several related houses or "houses of their fathers."

The next group is the tribe, which is comprised of all the clans that come from one of the sons of Jacob.[15]

The final unit is the people of God,[16] or the sons of Israel. The whole people can be viewed as a congregation in worship or a nation as a political unit[17] or a total family. This structure is seen when Solomon calls all the leaders to bring the ark of the covenant to Jerusalem (2 Chron 2:5).

The main point: there are expanding, concentric circles with what we think of as a family at the center. In Israel, the individual house was never isolated, because some kinsman-redeemer from a larger group was always there to aid, redeem or make reparation (Lev 25; Num 5:6-10; 35). No matter how large Israel became, it remained an extended family, the sons of Israel.

This unity has a unique Hebrew flavor. There is unity not only between the individual members of a home, and between one house and the larger units (such as a tribe or the whole nation), but there is also unity with past generations. When a man died, he was gathered to his people.[18] Josiah is told he will be gathered to his fathers and to his grave in peace (2 Kgs 22:20). The two phrases are parallel ways of saying the same thing. To die in peace is to be gathered to the assembly of the fathers who have gone before: a large peaceful throng of his ancestors welcomes him. While the passage may primarily refer to being buried in a common family grave, more is implied. Anyone not buried with his fathers is under a curse (Jer 8:2; 25:33; Ezek 29:5). This generational unity is seldom present in our Western thinking.[19]

Though ancestor worship in Eastern religions is a perversion of generational unity, Western Christians would overcome individualism, isolation and existential thinking if they adopted a biblical concept of the family. The New Testament culture, though unlike Israel's, still held the concept of the family as an extended household (Eph 5:22 - 6:9; 1 Tim 5:1-16). The extended family, and the family of God—not a welfare state—took care of its own members.

3. The Womb of Major Institutions

As we saw in earlier chapters, the family is the womb, literally and morally, of the godly individual. Timothy is one notable example of what godly families can do. Timothy's father was not a believer, yet his mother and grandmother overcame this pagan influence.

The family is also the womb of the two other institutions that God ordained: the church and the state. Each of these three has governmental authority and power. Before God commanded His family, Israel, to engage in centralized worship, godly worship developed in the home. Altars were set up by households. Also, 1 Timothy and Titus make clear that the family is the training ground for church leaders. Good government also grew out of the family. Household leaders became the political and economic leaders.[20] The older men or elders of households became the leaders of nations.[21] When Joseph went to bury Jacob in Canaan, he was accompanied by dignitaries: Pharaoh's servants, the elders of Pharaoh's house and the elders of the land of Egypt (Gen. 50:7). The elders from important households also became the elders or leaders of the nation in Israel.[22] Examples include the seventy special rulers who received the Holy Spirit (Num 11:16-30); the twelve representatives, one from each tribe; and leaders of thousand-man units.

Several implications are clear. The family could still be the womb for these institutions today. Only one family would have to survive a nuclear holocaust for the human race to start again. Worship and government could develop out of a family unit. Also, the family has original and primary jurisdiction and should be protected before any other institution. For example, at certain times family life took precedence over war (Deut 20:7; 24:5). Finally, the family has a profound formative impact upon these two institutions even today. The more biblical family life is, the stronger the church and state will be. In many ways, Puritan New England was closer to Israel's model than we are today.

4. *The Family and its Relationship to the other two God-Ordained Authorities*

The family has original governmental jurisdiction and power over its own functions and those of the individuals in it. The father has executive authority over his wife, as do parents over their children. For example, the husband had executive administrative control over the vows of his wife and children (Num 30), and parents had executive control over the marriages of their children (Ex 22:16-17). These powers, however, were not unlimited. The church and state were involved in family life and, when exercising their legitimate authority, sometimes limited a family's power.

As noted in previous chapters, once formed, the church regulated worship, not the family, even though some worship was still in family units. In the old covenant, the priesthood controlled the tabernacle and the temple; in the New Testament, participation in the sacraments and membership in the covenant community is controlled by the elders. Under the old covenant, the state regulated the exercise of authority in certain family issues (e.g., in certain divorces, Deut 21:10-14; legitimate inheritance by the firstborn, 21:15-17; rebellious children, 21:18-21). The New Testament gives no indication that this view changed, although Greek and Roman law possibly ignored it.

The Bible designates the family as the basic authority unit in God's plan, granting to it vast, though not absolute power. While in many aspects it is an independent institution, it is not totally independent; rather, it is interdependent with the state and the church. All three must work together for good or for ill (Neh 9:32, 34, 38).

Biblical structure protects the family's independence and authority. When family authority is curtailed, the church or the government will rush to fill the gap (Matt 15:1-9; 2:1-23), and tyranny will flourish. Instead, both the church and state should protect and promote healthy families that are independent and self-sufficient. So protected, the family can recognize the legitimate exercise of ecclesiastical and governmental authority. Without protection that nurtures the development of godly families (who guard a biblical sense of internal unity and external connectedness to larger units), unity among churches and nations will remain an unfulfilled utopian desire. The centrality of family life is highlighted in God's decalogue: the first human institution protected is the family (Ex 20:12), mentioned directly in the fifth, seventh and tenth commandments. Reverence for God and family authority are inextricably bound together.

God's Definition of Marriage

A life-long marriage covenant between one man and one woman is God's irreducible minimum definition of a family unit. To understand His definition of the family, we must start with His definition of marriage.

1. Marriage is a ***covenant.***[23]

In Malachi 2:13-16, God stands as a legal witness against the men of Israel. In response to their complaint that God has ceased to hear their prayers, He calls them covenant breakers. The men have dealt treacherously or deceptively with the wives of their youth (v14), by illegitimately divorcing them (v15). God calls these divorces spiritual violence against these women (v16), since the wife is a wife by covenant. What is a covenant and what significance does it have? O. Palmer Robertson defines a covenant as a "bond in blood sovereignly administered."[24] These men had made solemn vows and covenanted before God to husband these women but now were breaking covenant and divorcing their wives: they rejected their lifelong commitment to their wives. God considers divorce a serious sin.

But marriage is a covenant in another sense, a twofold covenant. In Prov 2:16-22, Solomon urges his son to avoid the adulterous woman who leaves her husband and forgets or ignores the covenant of her God. She has broken the marriage covenant, but her treachery is viewed as also breaking her covenant with God. God views the marriage covenant as a subset of the covenant with Him; therefore, to break covenant with a spouse is also to break covenant with God.

How serious God is about the marriage covenant can be seen in the type of covenantal vows people took when promising something in His presence (Ruth 1:15-17). Note also the punishment prescribed for breaking marriage vows by adultery (Lev 20:10; Deut 22:22). Spiritual adultery against God's covenant and adultery against the marriage covenant are both capital offenses.

2. Marriage is a covenant of ***companionship.***

In Prov 2:17, the adulteress' husband is called the companion of her youth.[25] From her youth, she has been his intimate friend. In Mal 2:14, the wife of the deceitful divorcer is called his wife by covenant and his companion.[26] She is united to him and she, too, has associated with him since his youth. The heart of a marriage covenant is a lifelong, life-and-death promise to provide companionship in fellowship—a deep intimacy, not superficial contact. This intimate union is equivalent to becoming one flesh[27] (Gen 2:24), an act that is accomplished by the process of leaving parents and cleaving to each other.[28]

Companionship means completing the other spouse. Adam was not complete without Eve (Gen 2:18-25). Everything else but Adam's aloneness was good. The wife is the companion, complement and crown of the husband (Prov 4:9);[29] refreshing him like fresh water from a fountain (Prov. 5:18). This kind of companionship brings no shame or confusion (Gen 2:25), rather, it brings trust (Prov. 31:11).

3. Marriage is a covenant of companionship ***between equals.***

Man and woman, both individually and corporately, are the image of God (Gen 1:26-28). Therefore, anyone who states or implies that a woman is not made in God's image is totally incorrect. To imply that a woman is inferior in being or personhood is a pagan perversion of the equality of the sexes. Scripture views no one as subhuman. Later, we will examine the roles of men and women, but note that subordination does not destroy identity: wives, children, subjects, and slaves are all fully and equally human.

4. *Marriage is a covenant of companionship between equals* ***that results in unity.***

We have noted already that marital unity comes out of companionship (Gen 2:2-3). In the Bible, "flesh" can mean a people, a group of blood kindred or all human beings. The unity in marriage is that of a unified body or group, very similar to the unity enjoined upon the body of Christ (Eph 4:1-6; Phil 2:1-4). This unity does not obliterate distinctions between the husband and wife, but allows them to function as a cooperative, coordinated tandem, like a pair in figure skating. That Adam and Eve were naked but not ashamed highlights this unity.[30] No division or confusion existed between them, as well as no embarrassment. Tragically, sin marred this unity. The good news is that Christ can heal the fractures (Eph 5:22-33).

5. *Marriage is a covenant of companionship between equals that results in unity* ***for the purpose of dominion.***

Man "images," or reflects God. God blesses Adam and Eve, commands them to have dominion, and tells them how.[31] Man is to be fruitful and multiply. Children are not, therefore, culturally but covenantally defined, as part of dominion. Also, man is to subdue or make the earth subject to him.[32] As a result, he is to rule over the earth.[33] Marriage creates other families who will extend man's rule. This extension is not to be confused with the perversion of this God-given mandate—exploitation.[34] Marriage and children are not for the sole purpose of fun or recreation, but for godly dominion.

6. *Marriage is a covenant of companionship between equals that results in unity for the purpose of dominion* ***under God.***

God creates, rules, and rests (Gen 2:1); man is to work, rule, and then rest in worship (Gen 2:3). The work, rule and rest must be for and under God's dominion and His claim to our loyalty and love is above the family's claim (Deut 13:6-11; Luke 14:25-27; 18:26-30). Therefore, intermarriage with non-covenantal people breaks continuity with our very purpose of existence and is spiritual, covenantal adultery (Gen 6:1-8).[35]

The concept of covenant is not common today. Marriage is viewed casually, or even humorously, certainly not in life-and-death covenantal terms. Companionship is reduced to romantic feelings. Equality is reduced to identity without distinction. Unity is rejected for individualism and self-realization. Dominion is viewed as crass exploitation. Birth control and abortion make children obsolete. Is it any wonder that marriages do not last?

Marriage did not evolve any more than man did (Gen 2:24; Matt 19:6). God not only ordained the institution of marriage, He designed it: one man and one woman—Adam and Eve, not Adam and Steve; Adam and Eve, a pair, not a pair with spares. God assigned roles. The very nature of God, reality, society and redemption are all tied to this structure and its roles, which are not reversible (1 Cor 14:34-38; 1 Tim 2:8-15). As a result, serious consequences accrue from attempts to alter these roles (Matt 19:3-12). Modern scientific speculation cannot alter God's norms. Evolutionary views of primitive promiscuity progressing to polygamy and eventually to monogamy are false. Marriage is larger than the individuals in it, the couple, the families involved, and even the culture at large. It is creationally and covenantally ordained, not culturally determined for the convenience of society. One man and one woman who covenant together before God for life is the *only* acceptable definition of marriage. All other "forms" are degenerate devolutions from the God-created directive (1 Tim 3:2; Titus 1:6).

God makes marriage the norm, therefore several things follow. *First*, marriage is good (1 Cor 7:2; Heb 13:4) and not to be forbidden (1 Tim 4:3). *Second*, it is a covenantal duty (Gen 1:26, 27; Deut 25:5-10). *Third*, it is assumed, even under adverse conditions (Jer 16:1-4; 1 Cor 7:1-7; 25-26). *Fourth*, it is for the purpose of kingdom service in this age (Matt 22:30; 1 Cor 7). *Fifth*, it is a model of the mystery of grace (Eph 5:22-33).

The Fall mangled marriage: blameshifting, role reversal, abuse, bigamy, incest and other perversions entered history early (Gen 3 - 50). Praise God that Christ's blood and the Holy Spirit's power can reverse this perversion. Only Jesus can restore marriage to what it should be (Eph 5:22-33). He alone gives realistic hope for the family.

Notes:

Chapter 5

1. For the best down-to-earth explanation of why we need the Bible and theology, see chapter 1 of J. Adams, *A Theology of Christian Counseling: More than Redemption* (Grand Rapids: Zondervan, 1979).

2. But why a systematic theology? Adams helps to clarify the necessity:

> In its simplest form, theology is nothing more or less than systematic understanding of what the Scriptures teach about various subjects. Biblical passages concerning any subject—let us say, the teaching of the Bible about God—are located, exegeted in context, placed into the stream of the history of redemption and their teachings classified according to the several aspects of that subject (God's omnipotence, omniscience, omnipresence, for instance). Within each classification, these teachings are compared to one another (one passage supplementing and qualifying another) in order to discover the total scriptural teaching on this aspect of the doctrine. Each aspect, likewise, is compared to other aspects in order to understand the total scriptural teaching about that question (and various subjects also are studied in relation to each other for further amplifications and modifications according to the light that one subject throws upon another). Thus, simply stated, theology is the attempt to bring to bear upon any given doctrine (or teaching) all that the Bible has to say about it. Biblical theology also notes the development of special revelation particularly in relationship to the redemptive work of Christ. And the individual theologies of the various writers of biblical books must be studied and related to one another too. All of these elements are of concern to us in this book.

Ibid., 11. All of chapter 2, "Theology and Counseling" is very helpful in understanding this task. What he says is true not only of counseling in general, but specifically of marriage and family counseling.

3. The word family comes from Latin *familia* which means the servants in a household. It comes from *famulus*, a servant.

4. The Hebrew *bayit* means a house or its contents. The Greek *oikos* has the same meaning. These words also can be used to mean household, or the people who dwell in the building.

I used the following lexicons:

W. Gensenius, *A Hebrew and English Lexicon of the Old Testament*, trans. E. Robinson (Boston: Houghton Mifflin, 1854); L. Koehler, W. Baumgartner, *Lexicon in Vetris Testament Libros* (Grand Rapids: Eerdmans, 1951); F. Brown, S. R. Driver, C. A. Briggs, *Hebrew and English Lexicon of the Old Testament* (Oxford: Clarendon, 1978); W. F. Arndt, F. W. Gungrich, *A Greek-English Lexicon of the New Testament and other Early Christian Literature*, 2nd edition revised and augmented by F. W. Gingrich; F. W. Danker (Chicago: University of Chicago, 1957).

5. G. W. Bromiley, ed., *The International Standard Bible Encyclopedia (ISBE)*, vol 3 (Grand Rapids: Eerdmans, 1986), 262.

6. Abram and Sarai, Elkanah and Hannah, and Zacharias and Elizabeth stand out as examples.

7. *ISBE*, vol 3, 262. Abram had Lot with him.

8. Idem. See also G. J. Botterweck, H. Ringgren, eds., *Theological Dictionary of the Old Testament (TDOT)*, vol 2, rev. ed. (Grand Rapids: Eerdmans, 1977), 114. The perfect example is Abraham's household which at times included wife, son, concubine and son, dependent relative Lot, servants, and sojourners.

9. Ex 22:21-24; Deut 24:17-22; 2 Kgs 4; 1 Tim 5:1-6.

10. R. L. Harris, ed., *Theological Wordbook of the Old Testament*, vol 1 (Chicago: Moody, 1980), 105.

11. *TDOT*, 114.

12. *ISBE*, 773.

13. Idem.

14. *Mispahah* means a larger family, clan, or circle of blood relatives.

15. The term in Josh 7:16 is *sebet* which means 1) rod, staff; 2) tribe. The second usage comes from the rods carried by the leaders as signs of authority and rule (Num 17:2,3). In Ex 31:2 the term is *matteh* which means 1) rod, staff; 2) tribe. Both terms can be a literal rod or one of the tribes represented by the rod.

16. *'Am* means 1) people; 2) peoples, nation; 3) people, citizens, inhabitants.

17. *Goy* means 1) swarm, people; 2) people, nation, and most often is used of the gentile but it can be used of Israel.

18. Gen 25:8; 25:17; 49:29,33; Num 20:24,26; Deut 32:50; Judg 2:10; 1 Kgs 2:10; 2 Chr 16:13,14.

19. Someone will claim that this should be different today: times are different, cultures are different. But we need something more substantial than such claims to invalidate this model. Jesus lived in a different time and culture. Are we to ignore His life, death, resurrection and ascension as irrelevant for these reasons? Surely not. You would have to argue that the new covenant negates this extended family concept upon which so much of the life of God's people was built in both testaments.

Covenantal unity and units ought to be a part of our thinking. Sadly, they are not—and we suffer for it.

20. Gen 10:5, 10, 20.

21. Gen 21:22-34; 26:1-33; 36:15, 19, 30, 31, 40.

22. Ex 3:16, 18; 4:29; 12:21; 24:1, 9-16.

23. *Berit* means 1) treaty, alliance, league; 2) constitution, ordinance; 3) agreement, pledge.

24. *The Christ of the Covenants* (Phillipsburg: Presbyterian and Reformed, 1981). Chapter 1, "The Nature of the Divine Covenants," 3-15, is helpful.

25. *'Allup* means 1) tame, docile; 2) friend, intimate. It comes from a verb that means "cleave to," "learn," "become familiar with."

26. *Haberet* means 1) associate; 2) companion; 3) wife or consort. It comes from a verb that means "to unite," "be joined to" or "tied to."

27 *'Ehad* means 1) one, same, equal to; 2) one of a kind; 3) one in a list of several things. Here it means "the same" or "one of a kind." *Basar* means 1) the flesh on the body; 2) the body; 3) male organ of regeneration; 4) kindred, blood-relations; 5) men as contrasted to God; 6) all living people, mankind. Here it means "person" or "one being" with a primary physical reference to sexual union.

28. *'Azab* means to 1) leave, abandon; 2) let go free; 3) leave behind, desert. Here it means "to abandon" or "leave parents behind". This is cutting the apron strings. *Dabaq* means to 1) glue or weld to; 2) cleave, adhere to; 3) attach to. Like a welded joint, there is a strong bonding that cannot be broken easily.

29. Prov 12:4; 16:31; 17:6; Isa 62:1-5.

30. *Bos* means to 1) feel shame; 2) be ashamed of, disconnected, disappointed by reason of; 3) confounded, confused. This can even be used in a military context to mean "deadly failure," or "rout."

31. *Radah* means to 1) tread, trample down; 2) walk, go; 3) have dominion, rule; 4) break off, tear away.

32. *Kabas* means to 1) tread upon, trample under; 2) subdue, make subject to.

33. See footnote 31.

34. Often romantic eastern mystical ecologists blame Christianity for all our ecological woes. For an answer to this attack, see F. Schaeffer's *Pollution and the Death of Man* (Wheaton: Tyndale, 1970).

35. Ex 34:10-17; Deut 7:1-11; Josh 23:1-13; Judg 12:9; 1 Kgs 3:1; 11:19; 2 Chr 18:1; Ezek 9-10; Neh 13:23-31.

CHAPTER 6

The Family: God Looks at Marriage

If God started the first family with a couple, a married man and woman, what did God expect from their relationship? What components does God require for a godly marriage? Two major areas stand out: companionship and cooperative dominion.

Necessary Components for a Godly Marriage

Components of Companionship

1. Roles in Marriage

This vast subject arouses heated controversy (see Appendix 4). Detailed discussion of this crucial issue is beyond the scope of this book. However, a quick overview of biblical texts will be helpful. The Old Testament defines the husband-father as the highest authority in the home: men have greater responsibility than women in worship (Ex 23:14, 17; Deut 16:16) in dedicatory vows (Lev 27:1-8); and have authority over wives' and children's vows (Num 30:1-15). Men receive honor in battle (Judg 4:8-10); and in their own household as its head (1 Sam 25; 2 Sam 6). This hierarchical arrangement does not negate the ontological equality of the husband and wife. This is seen in Proverbs, where the father and mother are spoken of as joint authorities to instruct the children (Prov. 1:8, 9)[1] and a mother gives canonical instruction to her son (Prov 31:1-31).

The New Testament upholds this authority, extending it to include the church. It takes pains to point out that such an extension parallels the Old Testament pattern of women's exclusion from the priesthood. Key points stand out concerning sexual roles. There is an authority structure in husband-wife relationships. In 1 Cor 11:2-16, Paul praises the Corinthians for holding to his teachings exactly as he had passed them on because no other practice exists in any of the early churches. There is no room for individual, corporate, or cultural relativity in Paul's statement. There is a chain of authority: God, Christ, the man, the woman. Paul uses the word *kephale* which means head, or authority over.[2] In 1 Tim 2:9-15, Paul instructs Timothy what to teach women in church and that they are not to teach or have authority over men. In fact, they are to use the home structure to learn (1 Cor 14:35). In Ephesians 5, Colossians 3, Titus 2 and 1 Peter 2 and 3, the husband-wife relationship involves authority and submission. That it parallels parent-child and owner-slave relationships on this authority issue cannot be denied, unless there is a bias to do so.

Authority means sacrificial love and loving submission. The husband is to live in an understanding way by honoring his wife (1 Pet 3:7)[3] and to lay down his life for his wife just as Christ did for the church (Eph 5:25). She is to submit to and obey her husband,[4] which is taught in many places.[5]

Finally, there are four specific reasons given for this structure of authority and submission: first, Paul says that Adam was created first, then Eve who was taken out of him (1 Cor 11:8; 1 Tim 2:13). Pre-Fall history demands this structure. Second, God's purpose and direction in creation demand it (1 Cor 11:7-10). The subordinate one complements or crowns the superior in a glorious way. Man does this for God as woman does for man, which is God's purpose. There is no chance or accident about it. Third, Paul says Eve sinned first (1 Tim 2:14). The details of the Fall demand this structure as does pre-Fall history. Paul treats both as real time-and-space history. Fourth, the order and peace of society depend on this structure of authority (1 Cor 14:33). Social units, families, churches, and society in general, must have this order if there is to be peace and harmony.

It is not enough to accept biblical marriage roles. We need to understand them. What does it mean in practice for a husband to have authority? If biblical roles are a crucial component of a godly marriage, what are these roles? The husband's role is that of a loving leader. He must love because Jesus Christ is his *model.* Jesus is the *soter*, savior, redeemer, deliverer, and defender, like Joshua, or the judges (Eph 5:25-33). Jesus' self-sacrifice is his *method.* While all Christians are to love one another (John 13), a husband's love is unique. He is to pattern his love after Christ's life-giving sacrifice. That sort of loving leadership differs radically from the methods of the world's leaders (Matt 20:20-28). The symbols of Christ's love are the towel, basin and cross; the world's are the scepter and sword. One day He will return with both, but, for now, the sufferings of Christ still are being finished by His body (Col 1:24). The *means* a husband must use to express his love are example and exhortation. Like Christ, who was a prophet, priest and king to His people,[6] the husband teaches, intercedes for and protects his wife.

As he leads her, a husband must present his wife to God the Father in all her purity (Eph 5:26,27). Again, his means are priestly prayer and prophetic teaching; but he also leads by doing other things. He must manage (1 Tim 3:4,5; Titus 1:6).[7] He must stand and lead the family like a flock. He must care for them as the bishop or overseer of his home.[8] Also, he must plan and provide for his wife (1 Tim 5:8).[9] He should cherish his wife as he would himself (Eph 5:28, 29), and give her food, clothing, and sexual comfort (Ex 21:7-11; 1 Cor 7:3-5). Finally, he must understand his wife, living with her according to knowledge (1 Pet 3:7). He is to know God's requirements for her as well as her individual requirements and requests. If he fails, his prayers could be hindered.[10] He is to provide her with honor, respect, and understanding. His high and holy calling is to be like Christ.[11]

The husband's authority does not exalt him over, make him better than, or render him independent of his wife. No, he is interdependent, does not stand alone, and is incomplete without her.[12]

What is her role? The wife's role is that of a suitable helper. She is a counterpart to her husband (Gen 2:18).[13] She completes, complements and crowns him and he is incomplete (Gen 2:18; 1 Cor 11:11), lacks glory (1 Cor 11:7), and is naked without her (Prov 12:4). Her *model* is the church (Eph 5:22). Her *method* is submission to her husband's commands (Eph 5:22-24, 1 Pet 3:1, 2). Her *means* is a godly character, not cosmetics (1 Pet 3:2-4). Nothing else in all creation is suitable for him (Gen 2:19, 20), and only his equal can complete him (Gen 1:27).

The wife is a helper in the task of dominion.[14] Her goal is to bring glory to her husband in his dominion-seeking and she helps in many ways (Prov 31:23). Primarily, she manages the household and has special care for young children (Prov 31:10-31; 1 Tim 2:15; Titus 2:3-5).

Also, she helps in economic dominion (Prov 31:16, 18, 24). She takes economic initiative as an auxiliary to the husband's provision.[15] She has *real* authority, even if it is subordinate to her husband's. Moreover, she helps with diaconal or social work (Prov 31:20). In the midst of this, she gives wise instruction to those around her (Prov 31:26), including personal refreshment to her husband (Prov 5:15-19; 31:28-31). Finally, she brings fame to her husband (Prov 31:23, 31). Like the church, she brings glory to her lord, not to herself; yet she shares in his glory (Eph 1:22, 23; 3:21). If she is a widow, she has new responsibilities (1 Tim 5:11-16).

These biblical roles differ from traditional worldly hierarchies and from modern democratic feminism. Respecting these roles brings peace and harmony to homes. Neither oppressive, worldly leadership, nor egalitarian non-leadership works. When either of these faulty patterns dictates the husband-wife relationship, not only will that union suffer, but the children will find it difficult to grasp their God-given sexual roles. In order to pattern their own marriages according to God's design, they need godly models.

2. Communication in Marriage

Communication is important in any human activity. Unity comes from truthful communication that constructively encourages the other person (Eph 4:25, 29-30). Though most of the biblical data about communication is not specifically directed to marriage, several key points apply.

Speech is a human characteristic that reflects God's image. Man communicates because God does. Sadly, speech was affected by the Fall. Adam and Eve blameshift and hurt each other.[16] God later curses man's speech to limit his evil because communication gives power to unify and accomplish things.[17] God says He hates evil speech,[18] and will judge it.[19] Mercifully, Jesus Christ redeems speech and saves through words.[20] The Holy Spirit seasons speech,[21] which can build others up in the faith.[22] Pentecost and the miracle of tongues reverse the curse of Babel.[23] Speech has value and power:[24] it can hurt[25] or it can heal.[26] Also, speech has discernible connections with other areas of life. Attitudes affect speech[27] which in turn reflects and affects heart attitudes.[28] Therefore, God regulates speech. Here are just a few biblical principles that govern speech:

- Style and timing are as important as content.[29]
- Thinking should precede speech.[30]
- Godly speech takes wisdom and work.[31]
- Manipulative speech (e.g., lies and slander) is forbidden.[32]
- Words and vows are regulated.[33]
- Economy of speech helps avoid sin.[34]
- Active listening is required.[35]

Consequently, clear, objective speech can be described and is desirable.[36]

I recommend two passages for study on the godly attitudes and mechanics of communicating to achieve unity: Ephesians

4:1 – 6:20 and James 3:1 – 4:12. Each contains a wealth of instruction that apply to this crucial area of marital union.

Some biblical data relates directly to communication in marriage— both its breakdown, and its repair:

- Communication should refresh and help (Prov 5:15, 19).
- Sin prevents communication and quarantines couples (Gen. 3:7-13; Lev 15).
- Communication needs regularity (1 Cor 7:3-5).
- Communication breaches can be dealt with in a godly way (1 Pet 2:18–3:7). Those caused by jealousy can be solved with the help of God and church leaders (Num 5; Matt 18:15-35; Luke 17:1-10).
- God models good communication for us. We see this in His relationship with Israel (Jer 3:12-20; 4:1, 2; Ezek 16; 23:22-35; Hos 4:15-19).

(For very practical help on communication, read "Communication Comes First".[37]) Without godly communication, marital unity is impossible. Without unity, growth and joy are impossible.

3. Sexuality in Marriage

Sexuality is another form of communication in marriage. Intercourse both culminates and revitalizes communication between spouses. Much has been written on this subject, but little from God's point of view. The Bible teaches that *the body* was created good,[38] cursed by sin,[39] and redeemed in Christ.[40] The Bible teaches that *sexual gender* is good (it is part of being in the image of God[41]), cursed by sin,[42] and redeemed in Christ.[43] The Bible teaches that *sexual gratification in marriage* is good,[44] cursed by sin,[45] and redeemed in Christ.[46] God never views sexuality apart from its function of reflecting His nature. Its legitimacy in marriage comes only from the contribution it makes toward enabling a couple to fulfill God's calling in life. Several principles of sexual union stand out.

Sexual intercourse is always *a covenantal act* (remember that a covenant is a legal, binding agreement between two people, between nations, or between God and human beings). As noted, marriage is doubly covenantal: person-to-person and person-to-God. Sexual union is part of covenantal life in both regards and is, therefore, joyous but serious business—not casual pleasure to be pursued out of physical lust or romantic whim. While not sacramental (a God-ordained physical sign of His spiritual commitment to us, such as the Lord's supper and baptism), sex is solemn and holy (Gen 2:24; Heb 13:4). Sexual union is *built upon knowledge of one's spouse.* In Genesis 4:1 the word for intercourse is *yada*', to know or learn; 1 Peter 3:7 has a similar idea. Many couples feel that sexual union is a mystical, wordless affair. But the Bible places sexual union in a context of communication. Communication precedes communion; talking and agreement are the foundation of sexual union. The spiritual union created by rich verbal communication is at the heart of sexual union (1 Cor 7:5). This union in turn leads to greater knowledge of and deeper union with one's spouse (Gen 2:24). One-fleshness, or a unified "personality of the couple" should result, because sexual union heightens unity. It is not an end in itself. In the following list, you will find biblical principles that govern a couple's sexual union:

- Forgiveness *is preliminary to true union (Gen 8:21; 1 Cor 6:6-9).*

Knowledge of God's grace is foundational to good sexual intercourse. How can two people become one flesh, an expression of loving unity if they are angry and resentful of each other, if they carry a grudge, refusing to forgive their spouse?

- *Sexual desire is* commended and commanded *(Prov 5:15-23; Heb 13:4).*

Sex in our society is often seen as a natural appetite, an instinct— like hunger—that needs satisfying. The Bible teaches that sexual intercourse should be focused exclusively upon one's spouse (Prov 6:24, 25; Matt 5:27-32; 1 Cor 7:2; 1 Thess 4:6). Far from being an uncontrollable appetite, it is to be consciously incorporated into a couple's life. Whatever problems exist, sexuality is not an expendable part of marriage and may not be ignored. How to communicate sexual desires is modeled in Song of Solomon. This book should not be allegorized away. Though it reflects deep spiritual truths, it also expresses the Bible's persistent affirmation of the joy of sexuality.

♦ *The* motivation *behind sexual duty is* love *(1 Cor 7:3, 5).*

The heart of good marital sex is loving service, not self-satisfaction. Sexual service to one's spouse is a *mutual obligation.* The wife is not the only member of the couple responsible for satisfying her partner (Song of Solomon; 1 Cor 7:4, 5). A husband must learn to satisfy his wife and surrender his desires for her sake.

♦ *Sexual union is to be* frequent and regular *(1 Cor 7:5).*

Only an agreed-upon, short separation for the sake of prayer provides a valid reason for infrequent sexual union.

♦ God regulates *this area of life.*

No adulterating of the marital union is permitted, and no person or thing should come between a husband and wife (Ex 20:14). God also tells couples when not to have sexual union: during menstruation (Lev 15:19-30) or immediately after child birth (Lev 12). God is Lord of our sex life as well as over other areas of our life.

♦ God's presence *is necessary for truly satisfying sex.*

Self-control and contentment are mandated (1 Cor 7:5; 1 Thess 4:5), and are fruits of the Holy Spirit's work in a believer. To obey and enjoy God's laws in general and His instruction on sexuality in particular, one needs the Holy Spirit. Sex, salvation and sanctification fit together.

- *Marital union is to be* honored—*not just tolerated (1 Tim 4:1-5; 1 Thess 4:4; Heb 13:4).*

Forced celibacy is sin and voluntary celibacy is not a higher state than marriage. See *The Westminster Larger Catechism*, question and answer 138-139.

The purpose of sexuality, like other forms of communication, is to enhance the marital relationship and to increase companionship and unity so that the couple's activities will produce godly dominion under God, which includes having children. Christian marriages should neither denigrate nor deify sexuality. Christians avoid worldly lust while skirting asceticism. Sex is neither sleazy nor sacramental. It is sanctified, a blessing. Honor God in this and your marriage will be enriched. For some very practical help in the area of sexuality, read Ed Wheat's *Intended for Pleasure*.[47]

4. Forgiveness and Reconciliation in Marriage

The Bible does not say much specifically about forgiveness in marriage although Paul warns of the need for it by commanding husbands to love their wives and not become embittered against them (Col 3:19).[48] The husband must work at forgiveness and reconciliation or the root of bitterness can cause trouble and defile a marriage just as it can defile any interpersonal relationship (Heb 12:14-15). He must live with her in knowledge and treat her gently (1 Pet 3:7).

Why is forgiveness necessary in marriage? People are sinners and will sin against God and each other. An old Puritan preacher said that just as you cannot rub flint and iron together without getting a spark, so you cannot put two sinners together without having sparks. If this is true in ordinary human relationships, it is doubly true in the intimacy of marriage. Forgiveness covers a vast area of Scripture and is the heart of the gospel: we can be forgiven and reconciled to God, (2 Cor 5:11-21), and to one another (Eph 4:1-13; Col 3:1-17). Several passages give us the major principles of forgiveness.

- Look at yourself first.

You are a hypocrite if you want to rid your brother or spouse of his or her sin, and have not dealt with your own (Matt 5:21-26; 7:1-5). Your sin is serious—it may even involve murder of the heart. Before coming to God to worship, you must examine your own heart.

- Take action.

Seek forgiveness and make restitution if necessary. Once you have identified and confessed your sins, you can go on to another action—that of seeking others who stray. Matthew 18:15-35 gives you a method for handling those who sin against you.[49] You must work hard at reconciliation (Luke 17:1-10). While you must be patient and not make a federal case out of every offense (Prov 10:12; 1 Pet 4:8), you have an obligation to turn people from sin and death (Gal 6:1, 2; Jam 5:21).

- Forgive daily.

You must have daily forgiveness for your marriage to succeed (Eph 4:25-27). If love is the fuel that keeps the engine of marriage running, then forgiveness is the oil that keeps the friction and heat at a minimum. (For very practical help in this area, see Jay Adams, "The Reconciliation/Discipline Dynamic"[50] and *From Forgiven to Forgiving*.[51])

5. Problem Solving in Marriage

Even after people forgive, problems remain and must be solved, including the sinful habit which gave occasion to the particular sin. What is to be done? The Bible does not talk about the particulars of problem-solving in marriage, although allusions arise in the wisdom literature: Song of Songs and Proverbs mention problems between husbands and wives and the need to solve them (Prov 12:4; 19:13, 14; 31:10; Song 1:6; 2:15). Several principles govern problem-solving:

Unified Hearts

The husband and wife must have their *hearts together*. They must be reconciled to Christ and to each other. Many couples forget that they are on the same team, fighting an enemy that wants to destroy their unity. If couples could only remain united to face the common enemy of their marital soul, namely sin, I would see a lot less counseling and I might have more time to spend with my own wife!

Holy Habits

Christian couples must develop biblical *habits* by which to handle conflict *God's way*. We may generalize about how people approach problems and conflict resolution.[52] Some people solve problems by *winning*. They coerce, manipulate, fight, and flatten anyone in their paths, including their spouses. Every conflict is a Super Bowl from which they must emerge victorious. Some solve problems by *ignoring* them. Such people coexist, ignore, dodge, hold their breath, etc., hoping time will change the situation so they won't have to face it. Like an ostrich with its head buried in the sand, they hope it will go away if they ignore it. For them, nothing is too big to be ignored. They never hurt their spouse directly, they just kill with not-so-benign neglect. Neither of these two methods is biblically acceptable. Some people solve problems by *yielding*. They conciliate, appease, give in and avoid conflict. This can be biblically acceptable, *if* the motives are correct (Phil 2:1-11). If the motive for such behavior is God's glory and the good of the other person, yielding is not wrong (Matt 22:34-40), though it is often maligned in our society. A godly attitude of conciliation views the other person as important. However, there are possible dangers: if one spouse always yields and the other tries to win, the former may struggle with frustration and bitterness, the latter with pride and stubbornness (Jam 3:13 - 4:3).

Also, they may not find the best solution if they do not seek God's wisdom to solve their problem creatively, in faith (Jam 1:2-8).

The best problem-solving is *creative compromise*. Those who have learned this art prayerfully seek God's wisdom. They win the war with sin in their own hearts and they triumph over sin that attacks the unity of their marriage. They seek to serve God, their neighbors, and the kingdom. For these wise, stable Christians, problems are God's discipline tools that perfect their holiness and their faith (Heb 12:1-13; Jam 1:2-4).

Team Strategy

The husband and wife must have their heads in gear. Five rules of thumb help:

- *Defeat* the problem, not each other.

Once a couple's hearts and habits are under control, they can approach problems. They must not even try while sinful hostilities exist and the first two general principles are uncompleted.

- *Define* the problem biblically.

Personal attitude issues need to be distinguished from objective problems. What is sinful? What is not? Problems can involve biblical principles, practical consequences, and personal preferences, all of which must be distinguished from each other. Principles must not be compromised—to do so is sin. Practical consequences that have serious effects cannot be ignored—to do so may create more problems. Personal preferences are not essential, though they do color thinking. In my experience, too much effort is expended on defending personal preferences. This effort wastes energy and often degenerates into a childish attitude of one-upmanship. You had the window seat last time, so I get it this time.

- *Detect* the biblical solution or solutions.

Spiritual maturity and wisdom (Heb 5:11-14), knowledge of the Bible (2 Tim 3:15-17), and active Bible study are all necessary (Heb 4:12, 13). Many couples read the Bible without ever reflecting on its implications in their everyday marital conflicts.

♦ *Delineate* a step-by-step application of the biblical solution.

Prayer, perhaps prayer and fasting, and hard work are involved. (Jam 1:2-8). How many Christian couples do you know who have fasted in order to solve a family problem, or who have taken a day off together to search the Scriptures about their financial situation, or whether to buy a new house?

♦ *Demand* a covenantal commitment to change.

Commitment to each other and accountability to others in the church press you to keep your word (Heb 10:19-25).

(For the best help in solving problems see Wayne Mack, *Your Family God's Way*[53] and Ken Sande, *The Peacemaker.*[54])

You need God's wisdom and grace to pull together these components of companionship. (See Jay Adams, *Christian Living in the Home*[55] and R. C. Sproul, *The Intimate Marriage.*[56])

Components of Cooperative Dominion

1. Family Worship

Since man's purpose is dominion under God (Gen 1:28), the family must build upon worship of Him. As mentioned in Chapter 3, the family gave birth to the church. Biblical data yields several key ideas. *Worship started in the family.*[57] The family was *the only church until national Israel emerged.*[58] Family worship is *now limited by God.*[59] Family worship is *still permitted and needed.* Family worship accomplishes three major purposes: it focuses the family on God in a personal way; it focuses the family on biblical principles; it trains the family members for public, corporate worship in the church.

Practical issues need to be addressed. Proper fear of God's holiness and humble joy for His grace must fill the heart (2 Cor 5:6-21). Elements of worship include prayers (praise, adoration, thanks, repentance and petition), Bible reading, catechism and instruction, singing, and setting aside money for God's causes. The atmosphere must be peaceful, not rushed. The time should be regular, when all family members can attend. The content and length needs to be adjusted for children. Practical help can be gleaned from godly pastors,[60] including your own.

2. Church Membership

The family needs the church and sacraments. The close tie between family and church will be seen in Chapter 10, but note that in order for the family to grow in grace, it must be under the authority of a local church. The Bible teaches that individuals and families should be part of a local church (see Appendix 5).

3. Economic Dominion

The cultural mandate (Gen 1:28), has never been rescinded; in fact, it was reissued after the Fall and after the flood waters of God's judgment. As noted in Chapter 3, the family is the womb of economic growth and development. For the Christian family, this work must include obedience to the Great Commission (Matt 28:16-20). As the Christian couple faces work, they do so as servants of God and therefore need the biblical view of work and finances that focuses on the kingdom of God. Pietistic indifference or laziness do not honor God. Several biblical principles stand out.

Money can be a *dangerous temptation*.[61] God must be *the Lord of one's financial life* since there can only be one master.[62] Money must be *used for the eternal goals of the kingdom of God*.[63]

The tithe is the start of financial responsibility.[64] *Wise godly management is rewarded.*[65]

Practical help is available. Wayne Mack[66] and Ron Blue[67] offer useful resources for the Christian family that seeks to have godly dominion over and through its finances. Cottage industries or family businesses are still viable means of dominion.[68]

4. Governmental Dominion by Leadership in Societal Groups

Christians have a responsibility to help the needy, whether through the family[69] or the church.[70] Because the home and the family are the keys to voluntary diaconal ministries[71] and nothing in the world can match them—especially no institutionalized setting[72]—they are the keys to helping the church take up its diaconal duties.[73] Couples must be kingdom-oriented and diaconally minded. Only as the godly family, in conjunction with a godly church, works at being salt and light are we going to see a reversal of humanistic, collectivistic statism.[74] The Holy Spirit creating such couples and churches is our only hope of real reformation in society.[75]

5. Political Dominion by Participation in the Political Process

The Bible teaches us to submit to God-ordained authorities as a godly duty,[76] and to serve in a position of governmental leadership as a divine calling.[77] Each particular culture and country will have its differences. However, in the United States of America each citizen is part of the government and a godly family that remains faithful to its Christian calling will participate in the political process. Families should work to have a unified approach to political issues and involvement.

6. Goals in Marriage

God is a God of order (1 Cor 14:33, 40) and works everything according to the pattern of His will (Eph 1:11; 3:11; Heb 6:17). Man, as His image, must do the same. Individuals and couples will give account to God for their lives (Matt 12:36-37), and need to redeem their time in order to be faithful to Him (Ps 90:12; Eph 5:15-16; Col 4:5). The pure heart focuses on the Lord because He is its treasure and seeks first His kingdom and righteousness (Matt 5:8; 6:19-34). The pure heart prays with thanksgiving, thinks properly and practices obedient Christian living (Phil 4:4-9). The pure heart has priorities, plans according to them, and then practices godly discipline. This is true for individuals and should be true for couples also. Couples ought to have kingdom priorities, and plans to carry them out. I counsel a lot of couples and very few have clearly delineated goals for their marriage and family. If couples are to honor God, they must plan their work and work their plan, one that includes all the necessary components of a godly marriage.

Without the components of companionship, marriages and families will fail. Without the components of cooperative dominion, couples will build some other kingdom rather than Christ's. Without the kingdom of God, Western families and culture will fail.

Notes:

Chapter 6

1. Prov 10:1; 15:20; 17:25; 19:26; 20:20; 23:22-25; 28:24; 29:15; 30:11-12.

2. J. Hurley, *Man and Woman in Biblical Perspective* (Grand Rapids: Zondervan, 1981), 163-168; W. Grudem, "The Meaning of *Kephale* (Head): A Response to Recent Studies," *Recovering Biblical Manhood and Womanhood: A Response to Evangelical Feminism*, J. Piper, W. Grudem, eds., (Wheaton: Crossway, 1991), 425-462.

3. He is to *aponeo* her, "to assign," "show," "pay honor."

4. *Hupotasso* means 1) to subject, subordinate; 2) attack, apprehend. It is composed of two words: *hypo* which means "under"; *tasso* which means 1) to place or station; 2) order, fix, determine, appoint.

5. 1 Cor 14:33-34; Eph 5:22-33; Col 3:18-19; 1 Tim 2:9-15; Titus 2:3-10; 1 Pet 3:1-6.

6. For a classic expression of the theology of Christ's earthly work, see *The Westminster Larger Catechism* questions and answers 42–45, or *The Westminster Shorter Catechism* questions and answers 23–26.

7. *Proistemi* means 1) be at the head (of), rule, direct; 2) be concerned about, care for, give aid, and is a combination of two words; *pro,* which means "before" or "in front of"; and *istemi*, which means "stand." *Epimeleomai* means "care for" or "take care of."

8. *Episkopos* means "overseer" or "bishop" and comes from a combination of *epi,* which means "over" or "to"; and *skopeo,* which means "to look (out) for," "notice," "keep one's eye on." The idea is to keep an eye on something until it reaches a goal.

9. *Pronoeo* means to "think of beforehand" or "take care of," which is a combination of *pro,* which means "before"; and *noeo,* which means "to think of." The idea is to think of things ahead of time and to get the provisions ready.

10. *Egkopto* means to "hinder" or "thwart."

11. For an excellent, brief, popular presentation of his duty, see J. Adams, *Christian Living in the Home* (Phillipsburg: Presbyterian and Reformed, 1972), Chapter 7, "Loving Leadership".

12. Gen 2:18, 23-24; 1 Cor 11:11-12.

13. *Kenegedo* means "over against," or "opposite him." The root meaning of *neged* means "in front of," "before," "in the presence of," "in the sight of." The picture is of a face-to-face, exactly fitting counterpart.

14. *Ezer* means "helper" or "help." This word is used of God's help to Israel, Deut 33:26-29; Ps 20:2; 33:20; 115:9; 121:1.

15. The wife is primarily responsible for the household but has freedom to pursue economic ventures. The home seems to be the center, but to

absolutize the home as the *only* possible center of economic endeavor goes beyond the text. The balanced approach would be to emphasize the household first, especially children, then if the house does not suffer, outside work would be possible. It is prudent not to go outside the home until the children are grown and on their own or at least in school if they are not home-schooled. Of course, home industry is the best option, if it can be managed, since it puts the family together.

16. Gen 3.

17. Gen 11.

18. Prov 6:16-19; 12:22.

19. Prov. 10:13-14; Matt 12:36-37.

20. John 1:1; Jam 1:18-20; 1 Pet 1:13-25; Heb 1:1-2.

21. Eph 4:15-5:21; Col 4:6.

22. 1 Cor 14:3, 9-25.

23. Acts 2.

24. Prov 18:21; 25:15.

25. Prov 12:18; 25:18.

26. Prov 12:18; 15:4.

27. Prov 18:8, 23; Rom 14:4; 1 Cor 4:1-5; Jam 4:11-12.

28. Prov 10:20; Matt 12:22-37; 1 John 3:18.

29. Prov 15:1-2, 23; 16:21, 23-24; 18:23; 25:11-12; 1 Cor 2:1-5; 1 Tim 5:1-2.

30. Prov 15:28; 17:24; 20:25; Jam 1:19-21.

31. Prov 22:17-21.

32. Ex 20:16; 23:1-3; Lev 19:15-18; Deut 5:20; 13:6-11; Prov 14:5; 24:28-29.

33. Num 30; Matt 5:33-37; Jam 5:12.

34. Prov 10:19; 11:12; 13:3; 15:28; 17:14; 21:23; 23:9; 25:8-10; 27:2; 1 Pet 3:1-7.

35. Prov 18:15, 17; 21:28; Jam 1:19-21.

36. Prov 20:5; 1 Cor 13:7; 14:3; 9-25; 1 Thess 2:3-12; 1 Pet 1:19-21.

37. Adams, *Christian Living in the Home*, Chapter 3.

38. Gen 1:31; 2:7; Col 2:9.

39. Gen 3:16-19; Rom 1:18-25; 8:18-25.

40. 1 Cor 15.

41. Gen 1:26-27, 31; 2:7, 18-25; 3:22-23.

42. Gen 2:25; 3:8-10, 21; Deut 22:5; Rom 1:26-27.

43. 1 Cor 11:2-16; Gal 3:26-29; Eph 2:11-22; Col 3:11.

44. Gen 2:24-25; 1 Cor 7; Heb 13:4.

45. Gen 3:7; Rom 1:24-47; 1 Cor 6:9-11.

46. Song; 1 Cor 6:9-11; 7. For a fuller presentation, see my article on "The Biblical Ethics of Transsexual Operations," *Journal of Biblical Ethics in Medicine*, vol. 4, no. 2 (1990), 30-37.

47. E. and G. Wheat, *Intended for Pleasure*, revised edition (Old Tappan: Revell, 1981).

48. *Pikraino* means "to make bitter" and can be used literally or figuratively as in "to embitter." Here, it is in the passive voice, meaning "to become bitter" or "embittered" against someone.

49. For the best treatment of this divine methodology, see J. Adams, *Handbook of Church Discipline* (Grand Rapids: Zondervan, 1986). The neglect of church discipline is one of the greatest deficiencies in the modern church.

50. Chapter 8 in Adams, *The Christian Counselor's Manual* (Grand Rapids: Zondervan, 1973).

51. J. Adams, *From Forgiven to Forgiving* (Amityville: Calvary Press, 1994).

52. Dr. John F. Bettler, director of the Christian Counseling and Educational Foundation, Laverock, Pa., and Professor of Practical Theology at Westminster Theological Seminary in Philadelphia, is credited with these basic categories. John is a gifted teacher and preacher and has been my pastor, teacher, mentor, boss and friend.

53. W. A. Mack, *Your Family God's Way: Developing and Sustaining Relationships in the Home* (Phillipsburg: Presbyterian and Reformed, 1991).

54. K. Sande, *The Peacemaker: A Biblical Guide to Resolving Personal Conflict* (Grand Rapids: Baker, 1991).

55. Op. cit., see note 11.

56. R. C. Sproul, *The Intimate Marriage: A Practical Guide to Building a Great Marriage* (Wheaton: Tyndale, 1986).

57. Gen 3:3-5; 4:26; Deut 4:7; 1 Sam 12:1-7; 1 Kgs 18:24-27; Ps 34:15-18.

58. Gen 4:3f; 8:20; 12:7-8; 13:4, 18; 22:9; 26:25; 33:20; 35:1-7; Ex 12:1-11; 17:14.

59. He always regulated worship (Ex 20:22-26). The altar of burnt offering for sin (Ex 22), and the altar of incense for praise (Ex 30), are both dictated by Him. Worship is to be led by ordained men (Lev. 8). Worship is to be centralized (Deut 12:20-28). Some worship and fellowship meals could be at a distance in the family context. However, the main ones were to be corporate and centralized even though in a family context. In the New Testament the ordained priesthood is replaced by the ordained elders who control corporate, centralized worship, especially the sacraments (Heb 10:19-31; 13:7-8, 17-18). No family should perform baptisms or celebrate the Lord's Supper.

60. J. H. M. d'Aubigne, *Family Worship: Motives and Directions for Domestic Piety in the Family* (Dallas: Presbyterian Heritage Pub., 1989). Also J. W. Alexander, "Thoughts on Family Worship" in *The Family* (Harrisonburg: Sprinkle, 1981).

61. Prov 11:28; 15:6, 17; 23:4-5; 27:23-24; 38:25; 1 Tim 6:6-10; 17-19.

62. Prov 30:7-9; Matt 6:19-34.

63. Prov 3:9-10; 8:18-21; Luke 16:9-13.

64. As pre-Mosaic, it cannot be tied to the worship of Israel that has since ceased (Gen 14:17-24; Deut 26:1-11). It flows out of a grateful, redeemed heart.

65. Prov 10:15, 16, 22. The lives of Job, Abraham, Isaac, Jacob and Solomon make it clear that success is not inherently sinful as do the economic activities of the godly wife of Proverbs 31. See also R. J. Rushdoony, *The Institutes of Biblical Law*, vol 1 (Phillipsburg: Presbyterian and Reformed, 1973). Chapter 8 on the eighth commandment and Chapter 10 on the tenth commandment deal with dominion and economic matters. Much of what is said is helpful; all is thought-provoking. This is a good theological base from which to think through economic dominion.

66. W. A. Mack, *Strengthening Your Marriage* (Phillipsburg: Presbyterian and Reformed, 1977), Unit 5, "Unity Through Financial Agreement."

67. Ron and Judy Blue, *Money Matters for Parents and their Kids* (Nashville: Nelson, 1988).

68. See Chapter 3, note 8. Also see "Should Mom Get a Job?" in *Home School Court Report*, Summer, 1990, available from the Home School Legal Defense Association, P.O. Box 3000, Purcellville, VA 20134. This little article points out the diminishing returns for a working mom as reported by the House Democratic Study Group of Washington, D. C.

69. Lev 25; Deut 15:1-11.

70. Deut 14:27-29; 26:11-13; Gal 6:9-10.

71. 1 Tim 5:16.

72. For the serious problems of institutionalized help, see D. J. Rothman *The Discovery of the Asylum* (Boston: Little, Brown, 1971); *Conscience and Convenience: The Asylum and its Alternatives in Progressive America* (Boston: Little, Brown, 1980).

73. For a grasp of this subject and its power to witness to God's grace, see David R. Rupprecht, *Radical Hospitality* (Phillipsburg: Presbyterian and Reformed, 1983).

74. For a grasp of the church's proper ministry versus the improper governmental usurping of this ministry, see George Grant's *The Dispossessed: Homelessness in America* (Westchester: Crossway, 1986); *Bringing in the Sheaves: Transforming Poverty into Productivity* (Brentwood: Wolgemuth and Hyatt, 1988). These excellent works lack a sufficient emphasis on the family or household as the basic unit needed to accomplish this task.

75. My own family's halting efforts to minister through our home are an example. We have had people live with us. While the dangers are real and the mistakes have been many, we have ministered to people with the following

concerns: physical handicaps, pregnancy out of wedlock, singleness, marital conflicts, and suicidal desires. We have had in our home: newlyweds, people off the street, ex-inmates, mental patients and foster children. Such radical hospitality is a powerful tool in training children for ministry. In spite of all the difficulties involved, any healthy Christian family can exercise effective hospitality if properly trained. Of course the encouragement of a church body makes such a ministry lighter.

76. Rom 13:1-7; Titus 3:1; 1 Pet 2:13-14.

77. Joseph, Moses, Joshua, the judges, the kings of Judah and Israel, Daniel and his three friends, Esther and Nehemiah are all examples.

For a sound, balanced view of the Christian's involvement in political activity, see C. Gregg Singer, "Covenant Theology, Social Action and the Great Commission," *The Bulletin of Greenville Presbyterian Theological Seminary*, vol 5, no 4 (Nov/Dec, 1992, Class paper no 2, insert). Available from the seminary at P. O. Box 690, Taylors, SC 29687.

CHAPTER 7

The Family: God Looks at Children

Our Western culture views children schizophrenically. On the one hand, a romantic idealism deifies them as innocent, noble savages, the quintessence of purity and power, who must bravely fight the pressures of corruption in the family and society. *Coming of Age in Samoa* is replaced by coming of age in San Diego! Praise the teens, and pass the condoms. We establish defense funds and encourage police protection to prevent child abuse. We celebrate the miracles of modern medicine that can save the life of a one-pound, three-month premature baby.

On the other hand, children are pains in the corporal and corporate anatomy. We suck another premature (or not so premature!) baby to bits and discard him in the trash—tissue to be aborted at the will of a mother. We relegate those who are born to daycare centers or to the blue-box baby-sitter. If we want to cut through this dialectical cultural idolatry, we need to hear God's definition of a child.

God's Definition of Children

God creates children who reflect their parents.

Man is the image of God.[1] A son is the image of his father.[2] The parallel between the "imaging" of divine creation and that of human procreation or imaging is important. Children do not *become*, but *are* the image-bearers of God. Likewise, children do not *become* like their parents only through teaching and modeling, but *are* like them by virtue of conception. Obvious ethical implications flow from the fact that children are fully human. This chain of "imaging," from parent to grandparent, all the way back to God, appears in Luke 3:23-38, which traces the expression "the son of" all the way back to Adam, "the son of" God.

God gives children as a blessing.

God gives children—conception is not a mechanical, naturalistic phenomenon.[3] A closed womb is a curse and a childless couple suffers.[4] Childlessness does not negate a marriage, but is a burden[5] which God's kindness overcomes.[6] God views children as a good gift, a blessing that He gives to His people.[7]

God tells us that children are sinners.

Children inherit sin by virtue of being made in the image of their parents. They are sinners in thc womb[8] and are under God's wrath as evidenced by Canaanite children under the ban for destruction,[9] and Babylonian children who experience the same end.[10] As sinners, children, like adults, need to be regenerated by the Holy Spirit.[11] Biblical Christians cannot accept the idea that a child is innocent until he reaches a mythical "age of accountability." Naturally, this truth has great implications for raising children.

God requires parents to have children.

Part of man's dominion under God is to be fruitful and multiply.[12] God expects a godly seed.[13] Though this duty is now cursed,[14] God promises to redeem it.[15] The childbearing duty is not to be laid aside.[16]

God owns the children of believers.

God has a concern for all people and is kind to people who do not believe. He has bestowed general, non-saving blessings on children of unbelievers.[17] However, He sustains a special relationship to children of believers.[18] For a fuller treatment of this issue, see my article, "Who Owns the Children of Divorce?".[19]

God expects His children to train their children in His righteous ways.

God forbids you to corrupt your children by dedicating them to another god, law system, and lifestyle,[20] or by allowing pagans to influence them, especially by marriage.[21] God demands that you train them,[22] and not sinfully ignore them.[23] We will examine the process of parenting later, but note: training in righteousness is not optional, and failure is a serious sin that leads to the destruction of the church and state as well as the family.

God's Word has ethical implications for reproduction and child-rearing.

Birth control may be the issue most obviously affected by a Christian view of children. However, sterilization, artificial insemination, surrogate motherhood, *in-vitro* fertilization, and choices based on amniocentesis all affect the family and its view of children. Dealing with each of these questions would enlarge this book to unmanageable proportions. To wrestle with such issues, you might begin with the books mentioned in endnote 16, and in the Annotated Bibliography.

The Biblical View of Maturity, Growth and Aging

Modern thinking about children incorrectly defines growth and maturity. In the multiplicity of modern culture, who man is and what he should strive to become is not clear. Most people hold a vague humanistic idea that man should actualize his potential from within and evolve towards some future omega point. Western humanism fits nicely with Eastern mysticism: John Dewey, Carl Rogers, and Pierre Teilhard de Chardin would jump for joy at the trends they helped to create.[24] (Since they have died, however, they now know better.)

God's goal for men is to make them His disciples and to conform them to the image of Jesus, His Son.[25] The goal and passion of a disciple of Jesus is to be like his teacher[26] and to glorify and enjoy God forever.[27] All human growth should move a person closer to this goal of being like Jesus.[28] While not indifferent to skills useful for general cultural activities,[29] God emphasizes character development and godliness.[30] Just as a child develops day by day through proper nourishment and by trusting his parents' direction in his life, so we mature by abiding in Christ and His love, obeying God's commands, dying to self, and producing much fruit.[31] Aging should advance a Christian towards Christlikeness.[32] The sinful rebel's goal, on the contrary, is to avoid maturity by usurping God's authority and defining his own path of wisdom.[33]

Since a sinful man's goal for himself differs from God's goals for him, he also develops methods appropriate to his goal. These sinfully-designed methods for man's growth are as plentiful and as varied as the clinical psychologists who espouse them. Though seemingly varied (even contradictory), such methods are all naturalistic and humanistic. God's "miracle-grow" method to reach maturity—the new birth, sanctification, participation in the life of a church, etc.—is excluded from modern thinking in general, and from clinical psychology in particular.

Social scientists approach human development the same way they examine non-personal elements of creation.[34] They define human development in precise stages, which are as inaccurate as they are dangerous. Whether tight, mechanical, deterministic stages (Freudianism or behaviorism), or loose, romantic, evolutionary stages (humanistic or transpersonal psychology), secular stage theories do not capture God's design for us.

To break human growth into distinct, developmental stages is a modern phenomenon. Philippe Aries's work indicates that our distinct phase "childhood" is new.[35] The medieval view, which differed from the conception in the ancient world, viewed a child as either an infant or a lad moving into adulthood. After a brief infancy, a child reached six or seven and entered the adult world.

From the fourteenth century on, a new idea emerged: children have a *special nature* different from adults.[36] This thinking culminates in the romantic view of children developed by Rousseau: the child, the noble savage, innocent, pure, spontaneous, fragile, to be "coddled" and kept in a different family setting away from adult life. Some moralists and pedagogues react and call for discipline, not coddling, and add that childhood lasts for a protracted period. Aries says coddling arose from the family, discipline from churchmen; both differ from the medieval view and methods.

He examines the effects of this new view on education and claims that the moralists invented the modern concepts of childhood and education, including grades by age groups. The schoolboy or scholar was to the sixteenth, seventeenth and eighteenth centuries what adolescence is to the nineteenth and twentieth centuries. Slowly, the medieval view died: the precocity of the entry into adult life ended and an altricial view of childhood development took over.[37]

After he analyzes changes in family life that redefine childhood,[38] Aries draws conclusions that capture the modern idea of childhood.[39] He points out that the change from the medieval approach to the modern preoccupation with children[40] helped to shift the focus from the family to the school.[41] As a result, this new concept of childhood matured and transformed society.[42] This transformation molded childhood and society profoundly, and we live with that change today.[43] While Aries's conclusions may be questioned,[44] the data he amasses show how the concept of teenager and the tolerance-for-rebellion-as-natural idea developed.

What does God say about all of this? The biblical model of growth, based on God's truth, is accurate and therefore adequate. It is more flexible and favors godliness, the goal of human development. Let's examine biblical terminology and its implications.

The Old Testament talks of *nursing infants*.[45] These are often contrasted with a child or toddler who is able to get about on his own[46] (see the next term below). This period lasts from birth to approximately two years, although it might be longer.

Toddler or *child* is used for children from approximately two up to twelve.[47] As noted above, this child is contrasted with the infant. In Numbers 14:29-31, the numbered men are contrasted with children *(tap)*. The *Theological Wordbook of the Old Testament* says that it is the remaining group in God's people after men and women are singled out.[48] In Ezekiel 9:6, a series of groups is mentioned. The first is old men; the second, young men and virgins; the third, women and children. The contrasts are between old age with wisdom and weakness, postpuberty youth with strength, and women and children with limitations and weaknesses. Therefore, this period is postweaning and prepuberty with its physical immaturity and limitations. But remember the Old Testament terms are flexible in their usage, not fixed.

Lad or *young man* is used for older children or young adults from approximately thirteen up to twenty.[49] Since the Hebrew term for "lad" can be used of children as young as newborns, it also is flexible (2 Sam 12). Usually, it refers to the physical vigor of postpuberty and most often to persons who are physically and sexually mature (i.e., in postpuberty, but not yet married or of the fighting age of twenty). Young men are contrasted to older men, but all are physically mature.[51] Ishmael is approximately sixteen or seventeen,[52] Isaac grown, but not married,[53] the Shunamite woman's son grown, but still able to be on his mother's lap.[54]

A *man* or full adult is from approximately twenty up to sixty years of age.[55] A man is eligible for military service between the ages of twenty and fifty.[56] The age of Levitical service is from twenty-five to fifty,[57] and from thirty to fifty for Levitical military service during the period of the tabernacle.[58]

An *elder* or mature old man is from fifty or sixty years upwards.[59] A gray grandparent is a gracious gift from a good God.[60]

In Leviticus 27:1-8, Moses places people into age groups: one month to five years, five years to twenty, twenty to sixty, sixty and up. The Lord groups people for us: newborns, children, youth, adults, elders. The Old Testament uses flexible, overlapping terms which give general categories that emphasize functions more than distinct chronological stages. Let's summarize:

I. *Childhood*

A. Newborn: *birth to one month.* The newborn struggles to live and is incorporated into the family, the church and the nation by circumcision and dedication.

B. Infant: *one month to five years.* The infant is nursed and learns to walk, talk and be independent of his mother by weaning.

C. Youth: *five to twenty*

1. *Child: five to twelve.* The child develops physically until it reaches physical maturity at puberty.

2. *Lad or youth: twelve to twenty.* The physically mature child learns wisdom to prepare for marriage and military service.

II. *Adulthood*

A. Man: *twenty to sixty.* The man exercises dominion in the family by marriage, in the church by worship especially at the feasts, and in the state by military service.

B. Elder: *sixty and above.* The elder exercises dominion in the family by rule and advice, in the church by teaching future generations, and in the state by judging and advising.

New Testament terms clearly parallel those in the Old. The New Testament talks of a *nursing baby*[61] which can refer to a living yet unborn infant[62] or a newborn.[63]

It uses the word *infant*[64] for very young children who are nursing[65] or who are legally minors.[66] The little child or infant is contrasted to wise and intelligent adults[67] and is viewed as foolish, or uninstructed.[68] The infant is not an adult[69] and is legally not able to make his own decisions.[70] The infant is immature, easily deceived[71] and incomplete.[72]

The New Testament talks of a *little child*[73] which can be a *newborn*[74] or *recently born,*[75] thus overlapping with *infant.* A *child* may be a little older than the infant and also can refer to a more advanced young child.[76] *Child* also refers to a legal minor who is under discipline.

The New Testament talks of *young man* or *youth.*[77] In Acts 2:17, youths are contrasted with *elders*. Again strength and vigor are the central ideas. The New Testament talks of a *man* who is an *adult*, as opposed to a *child.*[78]

Finally, the New Testament talks of *elders*, or older men and women.[79] In conclusion, the New Testament almost parallels the Old Testament in its flexible use of age definitions, its emphasis on functions and its actual age groupings.

Remember, the biblical writers are not technically precise—deliberately so. They view growth within a covenantal framework and perspective and report real history as they convey God's will. We must draw our conclusions in the light of God's Word.[80]

Aries correctly recognizes modern Western culture's obsession with the problems of childhood. Teen years are canonized as the pinnacle of freedom and spontaneity. What comes out of teens is good: everyone wants to go back to those days. The teen years have been expanded into the young adult period because people want freedom from responsibility up to thirty or, perhaps, forty. With enough vitamin supplements, enough aerobics, and proper food we can push it up to fifty. With facials and liposuction, maybe we can reach sixty. With a frozen body, who knows what the future holds? If all else fails, we can place our sperm in a sperm bank and come back in the form of a future teen. If we don't take the Nobel Prize, at least we might get in the National Basketball Association. Let's all become eternal Bart Simpsons.

The biblical view of maturity and growth is not popular, but it is necessary for the survival of the family, the church, the state and Western civilization. Instead of holding up Bart Simpson in all his animated rebellion, hold up Christ in His glory, crucified on the cross and exalted to the throne at the Father's right hand.

Secular suggestions fail. While some see the problems with our children, their analysis and solutions do not go to the core of the problem. D. Elkand's *The Hurried Child* is a case in point.[81] In part, he understands what Aries has shown and sees some of the pressures our children face from parents, schools, and the media. Yet he analyzes data from a speculative, psychological perspective and leans on social science concepts that are secular to the core. He does not view the child as a sinner, but has a quasi-romantic view of children and fails to see that the goal of the maturing process is Christlikeness, not what Epictetus and Marcus Aurelius deem proper. "Altruistic egotism" via Hans Selye and Elkand will not enable teens to love God with everything they have, or their neighbor as themselves.

Though flawed, the medieval concept may have been closer to a biblical concept of childhood. Of course children are not adults, but they *are* adults in training. Christ, the goal, is not a baby any more. Jesus is no Peter Pan, who desires to keep his subjects in eternal infancy. We are all like little children, dependent on His goodness and His fatherly care, but His intention is that we all "grow up into Him, who is the Head" (Eph 4:15). Luke 1:80 and 2:41-52 show that the measure of growth is whether or not a child, like John the Baptist, or Jesus Himself, is growing in stature and wisdom, strong in body and spirit.

The biblical goal of parental instruction is Christlikeness. Parents are responsible for the education of their children and although the church, the state, economic entities and voluntary organizations all have vested interests in the education and skills of children, God does not give the responsibility to anyone other than the parents. God instructs parents about raising their children and assumes they will. If the goal of maturity is Christlikeness and the parents are the God-mandated agents, then what does that say about schools? Obviously, home schooling is not only permissible; it is the ideal. Parents may, for other godly reasons, look to a private school that is under parental board control. Less viable are church-run schools and the public educational system. The church's job is to preach the gospel, not to teach general technical skills. While there are acceptable church schools, they often permit and may inadvertently encourage parental cop-out. The public educational system is a rival to parental control of children and has always been anti-family, anti-Christian, and favorable to statism in general and socialism in particular.[82] Yes, there have been godly teachers who are salt and light in the system, but they are the exceptions. Parents need to use ecclesiastical and governmental schools with extreme caution.[83] The goals and methods of governmental schools are antithetical to godliness. Too often, the goals and methods of ecclesiastical schools are no different.[84] Parents must not renege on this responsibility.

But what should responsible parents do? First, Christian parents must see their child's heart as the Bible describes it, as easily perverted.[85] Proverbs and other passages show this. Young people lack the maturity to be adults.[86] The ability to behave, reason and speak as a man not only needs development, it is affected by the child's sin. Children are sinners, in need of godly, gracious instruction and correction.

The Bible describes what children need: authoritative control. In Galatians 3:23-4:7, Paul uses (and thus validates) a cultural practice as a model. The child needs the custody of a tough disciplinarian who gives orders, just as God dealt with His child Israel. Additionally, there is the need for discipline.[87] Childhood discipline, including the rod and reproof,[88] is to the end that the child will take correction as an adult and live.[89] Finally, there is the need of gentle patience[90] when dealing with the child.

How should we summarize the implications of this biblical data on childhood and the process of growth? First, the *goal* of growth is Christlike maturity by Christ's power. As the pioneer and perfecter of faith,[91] Jesus Christ is our model. Second, our *method* is to be discipleship, which the next section will discuss. Third, *parental control* of the process is crucial. The school, church and state should be involved *only* as the parents deem proper, or when parents have sinfully abused their authority. Fourth, "teenager" and "rebel" are not acceptable *categories* to describe Christians. Fifth, the age of majority (about twenty) should be determined not only chronologically, but also by quality of character.[92]

This is the biblical view of children and childhood. How are we to see children become like Christ? For that we must examine God's view of parenting.

Notes:

Chapter 7

1. Gen 1:26-27; 5:1.

2. Gen 5:3.

3. Gen 4:1; 29:31-35; 30:2, 6, 8, 20.

4. Gen 15:2; Lev 20:20-21; Judg 13; 1 Sam 1:1-8, 11; 2 Sam 6:23; 2 Kgs 4:14-16; Jer 22:30.

5. Gen 11:29-30; Judg 13:3; Luke 1:5-7.

6. Ps 113:9; Isa 54:1-3.

7. Deut 28:4, 11; Ps 127; 128.

8. Gen 6:5-8; 8:21; Ex 20:5; Deut 5:9; Ps 51:5; 58:3; Isa 53:6; 58:8; Jer 17:8-10; Rom 5:12-21; Eph 2:1-3.

9. Num 31:13-20; Deut 7:1-5; 20:10-18.

10. Ps 137; 149.

11. Rom 2:28-29; Col 2:10-12; Titus 3:4-7.

12. Gen 1:26-28; 9:1, 7; Ps 127:3, 5.

13. Ruth 4:12; 1 Sam 2:20; Mal 2:15.

14. Gen 3:16.

15. Gen 3:15; Rom 16:20; 1 Tim 2:15; Rev 12.

16. For most people today, including most Christians, limiting the number of children is assumed. Modern fears of overpopulation, plus the severing of sex from biblical companionship and dominion, allow most people to see children as something to be avoided completely or conceived according to personal preference. Though many Roman Catholics believe birth control to be wrong, and there is a growing interest in the question on the part of "homeschool" style families influenced in part by Christians such as Mary Pride, most Christians have not wrestled through this issue. Jeremy C. Jackson's "The Shadow of Death: Abortion in Historical and Contemporary Perspective" in R. Ganz, ed., *The Christian Case Against Abortion: Thou Shalt Not Kill* (New Rochelle: Arlington House, 1978), traces the ideas behind birth control as well as abortion. J. J. Davis, *Evangelical Ethics: Issues Facing the Church Today* (Phillipsburg: Presbyterian and Reformed, 1985), chapter 2, tracks the history of Christian thought on contraception. Dr. F. E. Payne's *Making Biblical Decisions* (Escondido: Hosanna House, 1989) helps to sort out the ethics of contraception. His *Biblical Medical Ethics: The Christian and the Practice of Medicine* (Milford: Mott Media, 1988) is excellent.

Davis, op.cit., 49, says:

> In summary, then, it would appear that there is no explicit endorsement of artificial contraception in either Testament. The Old Testament is clearly pro-natalist in its general outlook. The New Testament, though allowing for voluntary celibacy, does not envision permanent

childlessness as a matter of choice for married couples. It would appear that the burden of proof rests on those who advocate contraception, given the general drift of Scripture.

The Bible gives no indication of the propriety of limiting the number of children, therefore the case for contraception is much harder to make. Perhaps there is an analogy with marriage which is the mandated norm (Gen 1:26-28; 2:18-24). However, Jesus and Paul indicate that there may be exceptions (Matt 19:10-12; 1 Cor 7:1, 7, 8, 25-28). Notice, the exception is *only* for the sake of the kingdom of God. Perhaps, on analogy, there are two reasons for no children: physical incapacity, and personal choice in order to serve God. Personal preference, or personal ease would not be acceptable and a violation of the first great commandment. More exegetical work is needed on this subject. See the debate in *Antithesis* 1:4, July/August 1990, "Issues and Interchange: Is Birth Control Morally Permissible?", 46-49. The best help yet is D. Doriani, "Birth Dearth or Bring on the Babies? Biblical Perspectives on Family Planning," *The Journal of Biblical Counseling*, Vol. XII, No. 1 (Fall 1993), 24-35. One thing can be stated clearly: any contraceptive that is abortive is not acceptable because it involves taking human life.

17. Gen 16:7-14; 21:18-21.
18. Deut 14:2; Ezra 9:2; Ezek 16:20-21; 1 Cor 7:14.
19. *Journal of Pastoral Practice*, 8:3 (1986), 39-42.
20. Lev 18:21; 20:1-5; Deut 12:29-31; 18:9-13; Ps 106:24-39.
21. Ex 34:12-17; Deut 7:1-5.
22. Deut 4:9-10; 6; 21:18-21; Ps 78:1-8; Prov; Eph 6:4; Col 3:21.
23. 1 Sam 2:22-36; 8:1-9; 2 Sam 13-15; 1 Kgs 1:5-6.
24. Heb 9:22.
25. Matt 28:16-20.
26. Matt 10:25; 1 John 3:2.
27. This is the answer to question 1 of the Westminster Shorter Catechism.
28. 1 Pet 2:21.
29. Ex 28:3; 31:1-11; 1 Kgs 4:29-34; 7:13-14.
30. 1 Cor 11:1; 1 Tim 3:1-13; Titus 1:5-9; Heb 13:7-8.
31. John 15:1-17.
32. Eph 4:17-23.
33. Gen 3:4-5, 22; 11:4; Ps 9:19-20; Isa 14:14; Ezek 28:2.
34. For a general historical overview of the dangers of the model of physical science being used in social science and the dangers of positivism and socialistic sociology, see F. A. Hayek, *The Counter-Revolution of Science: Studies in the Abuse of Reason* (Indianapolis: Liberty, 1952). For the dangers in psychology, see M. S. Van Leeuwen, *The Sorcerer's Apprentice: A Christian Looks at the Changing Face of Psychology* (Downers Grove: InterVarsity, 1982).
35. P. Aries, *Centuries of Childhood: A Social History of Family Life*,

trans P. Baldick (New York: Random, 1962). Few modern writers disagree with Aries.

36. Ibid., see "Conclusion: The Two Concepts of Childhood," 132-133.

37. Ibid., see "Conclusion: School and the Duration of Childhood," 329-336.

38. Ibid., "Conclusions: The Family and Sociability," 405-409. Later, when we come to Zimmerman's work, we will understand what Aries observes. He is not quite accurate when he says that the family triumphs, not the individual, 406. He rightly sees that as the old medieval society broke up, much was lost—neighborly relationships, friendships, and traditional contacts. Modernization is not all good. He does see a change from extended families to isolated units, although his terms are not those of Zimmerman.

39. Ibid., 411-415.

40. Ibid., 411.

> In the Middle Ages, at the beginning of modern times, and for a long time after that in the lower classes, children were mixed with adults as soon as they were considered capable of doing without their mothers or nannies, not long after a tardy weaning (in other words, at about the age of seven). They immediately went straight into the great community of men, sharing in the work and play of their companions, old and young alike. The movement of collective life carried along in a single torrent all ages and classes, leaving nobody any time for solitude and privacy. In these crowded, collective existences, there was no room for a private sector. The family fulfilled a function: it ensured the transmission of life, property and names, but it did not penetrate very far into human sensibility. Myths such as courtly and precious love denigrated marriage, while realities such as the apprenticeship of children loosened the emotional bond between parents and children. Medieval civilization had forgotten the *paideia* of the ancients and knew nothing as yet of modern education. That is the main point: it had no idea of education. Nowadays our society depends, and knows that it depends, on the success of its educational system. It has a system of education, a concept of education, an awareness of its importance. New sciences such as psychoanalysis, pediatrics and psychology devote themselves to the problems of childhood, and their findings are transmitted to parents by way of a mass of popular literature. Our world is obsessed by the physical, moral and sexual problems of childhood.

This preoccupation was unknown to medieval civilization, because there was no problem for the Middle Ages: as soon as he had been weaned, or soon after, the child became the natural companion of the adult.

41. Ibid., 412.

The great event was therefore the revival, at the beginning of modern times, of an interest in education. This affected a certain number of churchmen, lawyers and scholars, few in number in the fifteenth century, but increasingly numerous and influential in the sixteenth and seventeenth centuries when they merged with the advocates of religious reform.

42. Idem.

Henceforth it was recognized that the child was not ready for life, and that he had to be subjected to a special treatment, a sort of quarantine, before he was allowed to join the adults. This new concern about education would gradually instill itself in the heart of society and transform it from top to bottom.

43. Ibid., 413.

Family and school together removed the child from adult society. The school shut up a childhood which had hitherto been free within an increasingly severe disciplinary system, which culminated in the eighteenth and nineteenth centuries in the total claustration of the boarding-school. The solicitude of family, Church, moralists and administrators deprived the child of the freedom he had hitherto enjoyed among adults. It inflicted on him the birch, the prison cell—in a word, the punishments usually reserved for convicts from the lowest strata of society.

44. Aries sees the restrictive nature of modern education but fails to assess the problems accurately because he is a secularist. He believes in the innate goodness of man in general and children in particular and sees the family and church as enemies of the freedom of the child and does not believe that the book of Proverbs is correct.

45. *Yanaq* means "to suck." See 1 Sam 15:3; 22:19. *Ul* means "suckling child." The *Theological Wordbook of the Old Testament*, R. L. Harris, ed. (Chicago: Moody, 1980), vol 1 and 2, says that it is a synonym of *yanaq* and comes from the verb *ul,* which means "to suck."

46. 1 Sam 15:3; 22:10; Ps 8:2; Jer 44:7; Lam 2:11; Joel 2:16.

47. Various terms are used for weaned children. *Olal* or *olel* means "little one," "child," "babe." *Tap* means "infant" or "toddler," and comes

from the verb *tanap,* which means "to trip," or "to take quick steps." The *TWOT* says that *tap* is used for humans from birth to twenty, but with the emphasis on the younger ages. Notice the flexibility. *Walad* means "offspring" or "child," and comes from *yalad* which means "to bear," "bring forth," or "beget." *Zera* means "sowing of a seed," and comes from *zara,* which means "to sow," "scatter seed."

48. Deut 20:14; Josh 8:35.

49. *Na ar* means "boy," "lad," "youth," "servant." According to the *TWOT,* it comes from the verb *na ar,* which means "to grunt," "cry," "scream," or "bellow." (Do you think the Hebrews had rock music?) It can be used of individuals all the way from weaning up to marriage. Obviously, it is used flexibly.

50. Females before marriage are called *betulah,* "virgin," i.e., a grown woman who has not had sexual intercourse. Young men of this period are not only called *na ar*, but *bahur*, which means "young man," and comes from *bahar,* which means "to examine," "choose," "prefer." It is often used of picking warriors. This time is the chosen or preferred time because of the vigor of youth. See Ezek 9:6; Gen 14:24.

51. Gen 19:4.

52. Gen 21:12-20.

53. Gen 22.

54. 2 Kgs 4.

55. Lev 27:3.

56. Ex 30:14; Num 1:20.

57. Num 8:23-36.

58. Num 4:3; 42-49.

59. *Zaqen* means "old man," and comes from a verb *zaqan,* which means "to grow old," "be bearded."

60. The biblical view of aging is vastly different from most modern western ideas and has several elements. Old age is a *blessing*. One result of sin is a shortened life (Gen 6:1-4). Renewed blessings include length of days (Ex 20:12, Deut 5:16; Ps 37:25; Isa 46:3-4; 65:20; Zech 8:1-4). The gray beard is a badge of honor (1 Sam 12:2; Hos 7:9). Since old age is an honor from God, *we should honor the aged* (Ex 20:12; Lev 19:32; Prov 16:31; 20:29; 23:22-23). Old age is *usually a prerequisite for leadership*. In the Septuagint, the ancient Greek translation of the Old Testament, *presbuteros* is used to translate *zaqen*. It is the word used to describe the leaders of the Sanhedrin and later, of the church. See chapters 3 and 5 for thoughts on governmental functions developing out of the family clan eldership. Old age has special covenantal teaching responsibilities (Ps 33:11-12; 48:13; 71:18; 73:15; 102:18). Note especially Ps 78:4; 145:4, and Titus 2:2. Old age *demands godly support*. The family has the primary responsibility (Matt 15:1-9; John 12:25; 1 Tim 5:4, 8, 16). The church has the secondary

responsibility (Acts 6:1; 1 Tim 5:16). Only after these resources are exhausted should the state become involved. Social security is a non-biblical system which violates the separation of family, church, and state.

Obviously, there was no youth culture in Israel. Most attempts to trust youth lead to disaster (1 Kgs 12:1-11). We should desire to be elders (1 Tim 3:1-7), not to stay young, irresponsible teenagers. Proverbs 17:6 captures this biblical view.

61. *Brephos* means "sucking one." *Theladzo* means "to give suckle." Both are used. *Theladzo* is used in the Septuagint (Job 3:12; Song 8:1; Joel 2:16) to translate *yanaq*. See note 45.

62. Luke 1:41, 44.

63. Luke 2:12; 18:15; Acts 7:19; 1 Pet 2:2; Matt 24:19; Mark 13:12; Luke 21:23.

64. *Nepios,* meaning "infant" or "minor," is used in the Septuagint to translate *olal.* See note 47.

65. Matt 21:16; Heb 5:13.

66. Gal 4:1.

67. Matt 11:25; Luke 10:21.

68. Rom 2:20.

69. 1 Cor 3:1.

70. Gal 4:1.

71. Eph 4:14.

72. Heb 5:13.

73. *Pais* means "child," "boy," "youth," "servant." Note related terms: *paidion* means 1) very young child, infant, newborn, 2) child, 3) smallest *pais*; *paidarion* means 1) little boy, boy, child, youth (no longer a child), 2) young slave; *paideia* means 1) upbringing, training, instruction including discipline, correction, 2) training; *paideuo* means to 1) bring up, instruct, train, educate, 2) practice discipline; *paideutes* means instructor, teacher; *paidagogos* means attendant (slave), custodian, guide, literally boy-leader. The Septuagint uses *pais* to translate *na ar* or *yalad*. See notes 45 and 47.

74. John 16:21.

75. Matt 2:8, 11, 13-14, 20.

76. Matt 18:2, 4; Mark 9:24.

77. *Neaniskos* means 1) youth, young man; 2) servant. *Neanias* means "youth" or "young man." The age was probably approximately twenty-four to forty in Greek usage. *Neaniskos* means little *neanias*. Therefore, it is a younger category. In the Septuagint, *neaniskos* is sometimes used to translate *na ar*, but most often *bahur*. See notes 49 and 50. Also see Matt 19:20, 22; Luke 7:14; Acts 2:17; 5:10; 1 John 2:13.

78. *Aner* means "man." This can be in contrast to a "woman" or a "boy." See 1 Cor 13.

79. *Presbutes* means an "old man," "aged man." *Presbutis* means "older woman," an "elderly lady." A leader is a *presbuteros,* which can mean "aged" as well as an "elder" or "presbyter."

80. See the chart on the following page.

81. D. Elkand, *The Hurried Child: Growing Up Too Fast Too Soon* (Reading: Addison-Wesley, 1981).

82. S. Blumenfeld, *The N.A.E.: The Trojan Horse in American Education* (Boise: Paradigm, 1984); *Is Public Education Necessary?* (Boise: Paradigm, 1985). Blumenfeld is intriguing. He is Jewish, and recently converted to Christianity through reading Calvin's *Institutes* while doing historical research on the American educational system. As an educator, he has taught in both public and private school contexts.

83. Nowhere in Scripture do we see godly parents sending their children off for non-covenantal education. Abraham does not send Isaac to Ur College. The kings of Judah do not send their sons to Assyrian State or Babylon U. Joseph, Moses and Daniel had secular, statist educators, but not by choice. Tertullian's question, "What does Jerusalem have to do with Athens?" is always important to ask. See Appendices 6, 7. Secular education should be seen for what it is: heresy. This fact should force us back to the Scriptures to see more clearly God's mind on education for our children and force us to work hard at applying truth in the marketplace.

84. For a stimulating challenge on this issue, see J. E. Adams, *Back to the Blackboard: Design for a Biblical Christian School* (Phillipsburg: Presbyterian and Reformed, 1982). I know of no one who has refuted Adams's case. I know of no school that has had the courage and wisdom to implement fully this biblical approach. I have heard of some attempts, but do not know of them personally.

85. Prov 1:22.

86. 1 Cor 3:1-2; 13:9-12.

87. Prov 3:11-12; 13:1, 24; 15:5; 19:18; 20:30; 22:6, 15; 23:13-14; 29:17.

88. Prov 29:15; Eph 6:1-4.

89. Prov 12:1; 13:18; 15:10, 31-32; 16:22; 17:10; 19:20, 27; 23:12; 29:1.

90. Eph 6:4; Col 3:21; 2 Tim 2:22-26.

91. Luke 6:40; Heb 2:10; 5:8-14; 12:1-13.

92. See chart on the following page.

Overview of the Biblical View of Age

1. Time

-9 months	0	1 mo.	5-6 yrs.	12-13 yrs	20 yrs	60 yrs	
Conception	Birth	Legal Status	Weaning	Puberty	Legal Adult	Retirement to Elder	Death

2. Biblical Contrasts

	IMMATURITY			MATURITY		
	Infancy		Youth	Adulthood		

Biblical Categories	Newborn	Infant	Child	Lad	Man	Elder
Biblical Terms	יָנַק עול βρέφος θηλαζω	עוֹלֵל νηπίος	טַף παῖς παιδάριον	נַעַר בָּחוּר νεανίσκος	אִישׁ ἀνὴρ	זָקֵן πρεσβύτερος
Developmental Task	Becoming part of the family, church and state	Learning to walk, talk and be weaned from mother	Developing physical sexual maturity	Developing wisdom to overcome foolishness	Developing through marriage, familymanagement, ministry in worship, military service	Advising & training the younger generation of leaders
Developmental Goal	A living member of God's covenant people	A functioning person	To be physically ready for adulthood	To be morally ready for adulthood	To be ready to perpetuate God's covenant	To be capable of raising up a third generation of leaders

CHAPTER 8

The Family: God Looks at Parents

One area remains in our mini-systematic theology of the family—parenting. Most of us are ill-prepared for this most difficult and demanding human activity. A plethora of books—both secular and religious—offers us advice.[1] Some are helpful, but none of them can show us more than God has already told us. He gives us instructions in His Word for this high and holy calling.

Before we look at a few practical applications of Scriptural parenting, let's remember the basic principles. I am not writing a parenting manual. My readers, as guided by their own study of the Scriptures through the insights that the Holy Spirit gives them, will see how these principles will affect their own family life. However, I will mention several areas in which I feel our society has wandered far from the Biblical patterns. What are those principles?

Biblical Principles for Parenting

Parenting imitates God.

God is our Father and rock[2] and our parenting should follow His pattern of parenting His children.[3]

The goal of parenting is godliness.

The goal of parenting is to perpetuate the covenant and relay God's truth. Godly parenting will produce Christlike covenant keepers who show beatitudinal characteristics,[4] produce the fruit of the Spirit[5] and live lawfully.[6]

Parenting uses God-given tools.

God gives parents the tools to do the job:[7] the rod of discipline[8] and the reproof of the Scriptures.[9]

Parenting follows a covenantal pattern (Deuteronomy 6–7).

As we think of parenting, consider these covenantal principles about which the Lord teaches us so much in both the Old and the New Testament:

- Parenting is a covenant responsibility **mandated by God** (6:1-3). There is no such thing as optional parenting. When God gives children to a couple, He gives them the responsibility to teach those children to love the Lord their God with all their heart.

- Parenting requires a personal covenant **commitment to God** (6:4-5). You need to listen to God and to have a total love for Him. Without such dedication, you will never convince your children that God is the number one priority for your life and for theirs.

- Parenting requires a **knowledge of the Bible** (6:6). Parameters of parental authority and conduct are limited by Scripture. Parents are given divine but limited authority to rule their children. Parents cannot murder them;[10] change their birthright or inheritance; sell them into permanent slavery;[11] execute capital punishment against them[12] or make them suffer for parental sins.[13] Parents must know the Bible if they are to teach their children biblical truth.

- Parenting requires **time and an ongoing relationship** with the children (6:7-9). Life context teaching is required. Our children learn as much by watching us deal with a flat tire or betrayal by a friend as they do from a Sunday School lesson. If we place God's glory ahead of our own pleasure in such circumstances, we will reinforce our children's respect for God. Discipleship requires constant contact and provides the only way for all of God's word to be applied to all of life.

- Parenting requires constant **vigilance and covenantal faithfulness** (6:10-19). Complacency and forgetfulness are surreptitious enemies. As time passes, well-intentioned parents sometimes ease off. Energy and watchfulness slip. Parents need to guard against both theoretical enemies—Dr. Spock, P.E.T., New Age thinking—and against practical enemies—other parents with different standards, peer pressure, or even church youth leaders who want groupies instead of disciples.

- Parenting requires **answering children's questions in the light of the history of God's redemption** (6:20-25). Parents must be able to answer questions that children ask and must be able to relate them to the reality of God's salvation. An answer that ignores all God has done in His kingdom will reinforce a child's idea that only he counts, and that he can decide his course of action on the basis of his own circumstances.

- Parenting requires **oversight of children's marriages** (7:1-5). Parents cannot allow their Christian children to marry pagan partners. God feels so strongly about this that He has destroyed families, churches and nations over this issue. The message is clear: no compromise—no covenants with pagans.

- Parenting God's way **pays off** (7:6-26). That God has chosen Christian parents (both in the sense of having chosen them for salvation and having selected them to parent particular children) means that prayer and obedience to God's commandments will bear the fruit God has promised, namely the fame of God's name and of His grace. The parent who bears God's name and follows His plan for parenting will have God's presence and pagans will notice this grace.

A friend of mine with seven children once had a non-Christian cleaning lady. One day as she kicked off her good shoes and slipped on her work shoes, she sighed contentedly and told my friend, "I love coming here. It's so peaceful!" "Peaceful?" my friend replied, as her two-year old broke out crying from a fall and the rice began to burn in the kitchen. "You know what I mean," answered the cleaning lady.

Godly parents teach their children the peace, love and grace of God every day. Anyone who gets close enough will feel it. Do I have to point out how radically this biblical view of parenting deviates from secular views and even from the parenting habits of most Christians?[14] For some practical help in applying these principles, see Bruce A. Ray's *Withhold Not Correction*, and Tedd Tripp's *Shepherding a Child's Heart*.[15]

Parenting does not end until the children are in godly marriages.

Our society assumes that a young person ceases to be under the authority of his parents as soon as he decides he doesn't want their advice anymore. This can sometimes occur before a child has even finished his schooling or taken a job. The Bible gives parents and their children no such leeway.

Some Practical Effects of Biblical Parenting Principles

The Biblical View of Contracting a Marriage

The Western European view, especially in the United States, approaches dating, courtship and marriage in an individualistic, romantic way that resembles a heightened form of mating. With "researchers" like Kinsey and Masters and Johnson pushing a sexuality that is purely evolutionary and mammalian, people "fall in love," which really amounts to falling in lust. The dating scene in singles bars reminds me of leks (mating sites for certain terrestrial birds). The male struts in front of the females until one (or several) of them chooses to go off and mate with him. Christians try to sanctify this approach, sanitizing its grosser aspects. While arranged marriages may not be the answer, Christians need to think hard about how their children choose a marriage partner.

Parental control in this area is not optional. God requires parents to influence this final step in the parenting process. It is one of the most crucial for the sake of Christ's body, the church. Appendix 3 reviews the devastation that mixed marriages have caused in the history of God's people and the world. Satan's stratagem must be resisted.

Marriage is not primarily an individual choice: the choice of a partner influences the family, the church and the state, as well as the individual. If marriage is not seen as a covenantal act, it becomes a matter of pure choice, on a par with a preference for chocolate-chip-mint ice cream. Unfortunately, couples think they can take a lick or two of the ice cream cone, and throw it away if they don't like the flavor they chose. It might be fair to argue that the more whimsical the choice of marriage partners becomes, the higher the divorce rate will become.

Modern marriages are contracted by dating, a cultural custom that stems from the pagan influences of enlightenment romanticism. Feelings of attraction are the measure of true love.[16] Romanticism's sexual overtones and primitivism are evident in the life of J. J. Rousseau and enshrined in *Coming of Age in Samoa.*[17] Such a romantic notion naturally despises the arranged marriages mentioned in the Bible. Our society elevates autonomous sexual or romantic excitement, holding it up as an ideal to children who are all too often independent of the family and church, scarcely influenced by either. Our Western view of childhood and teenagers, combined with that wonderful invention, the automobile, have highlighted the romantic model of mate selection and of contracting a marriage. Couples can elope to Las Vegas and get married at a drive-up window!

Marriage God's way demands a covenantal approach because religious commitment is at the heart of marriage.[18] Although parental control is assumed,[19] personal preference is factored into the decision.[20] However, rebellion against God's covenantal requirements should not motivate partner selection.[21] Christian young people need to consider the economic as well as the religious consequences of their decisions, refusing to be ruled by crass selfishness.[22]

Parents must take the responsibility of teaching these views and implementing them. Of course, if parents fail to follow the biblical approach to parenting in general, they will not be able to teach this particular view of contracting marriage. As we will see later, the church can be a great aid in this regard.[23]

The Biblical View of Finances and Inheritance

— *Money*

Biblical Christianity is not a Gnostic, ascetic dualism that denigrates the physical, material world. The Bible teaches both by example and precept what our attitudes and actions should be about money and finances. The Bible speaks of finances and inheritance (see Appendix 3) and tells us that Abraham gave portions of his goods to his children, leaving the inheritance to Isaac. Moses received legislation from the Lord relating to finances and inheritance. Several principles can be culled from the Scriptures.

- Material possessions and money can become temptations. To focus on this world as it is and to love money is a deadly danger.[24] Our treasure and hope cannot be material.[25] The love of money is covetousness and idolatry,[26] which only love for the Lord can prevent.[27] God made you for only one loyalty and you can have only one master. As Bob Dylan paraphrased the Word, "You gotta serve somebody: it may be the devil, or it may be the Lord: but ya gotta serve somebody." You cannot serve God and mammon.

- Money must be used for the sake of the eternal kingdom of God.[28] The tithe is the start of financial responsibility. This pre-Mosaic practice[29] acknowledges that God is the giver of every good gift.[30] There are at least two motivations for tithing. The first is that the tithe represents our acknowledgment that all we have comes from God. We symbolically return to Him what is His. We respond to God's grace.[31] The second purpose of the tithe is to capitalize the next two generations so they can serve God.[32] God cares about how we manage the finances He gives us. He promises to reward wise, godly management.[33] Much practical help is available from sound Christian authors.[34]

— *Inheritance*

We must also go straight to the Scriptures to find principles of inheritance. In His Word, God Himself is the model for the notion of inheritance. The Bible shows us that *God's people are God's inheritance*. God calls Israel His family, His inheritance.[35] The *Theological Wordbook of the Old Testament*[36] points out that as a great King, *God also gives His children an eternal inheritance*[37] (portions of the land).[38] This inheritance is so important that God gives two key portions of the law as specific legislative guidance in case problems arise about inheritance.[39] The first is the levirate law which insures the perpetuity of the inheritance.[40] The second prohibits parents from canceling the firstborn's inheritance rights because they prefer another child.[41]

We might wonder why the Bible gives so much place to such material concerns. Though these practical matters have their own significance, God also uses them to teach us spiritual lessons. He wants us to understand that the land belongs to Him[42] and that the firstborn child has a crucial typological importance.[43] We need to understand how important it is for us as Christians to accept our wealth as a gift from God and to use it humbly for Him.[44] The Old Testament stories always point us to the bigger and better things God will bring about. And even in the Old Testament (often seen as negative and judgmental), we find resounding examples of God's grace. Levi, for example, committed a murder and should have been cursed by having his family scattered. Instead, God graciously turns the curse into a blessing and He becomes their portion or inheritance. Imagine—God Himself is the gift! The Levites no longer own land, but the tithe (God's portion) becomes their livelihood.[45] This picture points to the inheritance in God's final kingdom. All the wealth of the nations will belong to God's people[46] as an eternal inheritance that will never be taken away.[47]

Of course the imagery makes even more sense when we read the New Testament, which reveals Jesus as the true King. Jesus is the eternal firstborn who inherits His Father's name as the Messiah.[48] It is He who inaugurates the eschatological kingdom and earns the Christian's eternal inheritance[49] on the cross. Risen and glorified, He gives us God the Holy Spirit as the down-payment of our eternal inheritance.[50] The Spirit seals us by His word until the day of redemption.[51] This inheritance, though founded on grace, not works,[52] is not received without the fight of faith or the pain of perseverance.[53] Hypocrites[54] cannot inherit the true eternal kingdom.[55]

In the New Testament, the reality of the kingdom of God changes everything. The emphasis shifts from the physical inheritance of land for the twelve tribes to the spiritual inheritance of "land" in the eternal kingdom. Members of God's final kingdom inherit eternal life, defined as the knowledge of God Himself.[56]

The Levites were only a representative substitute for the whole nation. In Christ, the whole people of God live as Levites.

In our daily lives, our "levitical" family takes precedence over our birth family.[57] We are redeemed from the futile lifestyle of our familial forefathers because we are born by the Holy Spirit and adopted into the family of God (good news for those with terrible family backgrounds!). Some Christians use this as an excuse to abandon their biological family, or to renege on family responsibilities. They may argue that since they and their offspring have a treasure kept in heaven, they don't need to provide an inheritance for their children and grandchildren. Jesus warns that the Pharisees' neglect of family duties is sin and that to pietize away your family obligations does not impress God.[58] Therefore, you must care for your family both now[59] and in the future.[60]

Significantly, inheritance is a concern of God's heart.[61] Because of this, He gives us the duty to care about it, too.[62] Nevertheless, ungodliness on the part of the children can limit or eliminate their inheritance[63] because wisdom flowing from a godly heart is necessary to use the inheritance properly.[64] Finally, the inheritance is a God-given trust or stewardship. It is not to be squandered selfishly, but used with an eye to future generations.[65]

Many steal from their future to live luxuriously today. The bumper sticker expresses it nicely: "We are spending our children's inheritance." In our consumer society, built on theft, people don't even care about their own future, let alone that of future generations. We don't even seem to mind if there *are* future generations. If we don't kill them in the womb, we borrow so heavily or vote for so many bond issues that they are doomed to economic slavery.[66]

As Christians we are responsible not only to provide an inheritance for our own families, we must also contribute economically in order to move Christ's kingdom work forward. Our contributions to the kingdom leave a spiritual inheritance that stretches beyond the immediate impact we have on our family and friends. Any ministry of mercy, evangelism, teaching or discipling depends on two things: gifted, godly, Holy Spirit-empowered people to pray and do the work, and money to fund it. Capital is only dirty when it is invested in the wrong kingdom. The *love* of money is a root of all sorts of evil[67] because when we love it, we love the temporary kingdom it represents. The devil offered Jesus a kingdom. All he had to do was bow down. We, like Jesus, must not grab at the temporary pleasures the devil dangles before us. Rather we must invest in the permanent kingdom. Love for the King and His kingdom is the only effective way to launder money![68] Think this through biblically.[69] Take the time as a couple to discuss it and to pray about it. Practical advice on wills, estate planning, etc., is available from most Christian institutions.[70]

The Biblical View of Singleness

"If you're rich, I'm single," states one of our many California bumper stickers. The sentiment captures the economic responsibility that having a family entails. Singleness is a family issue. The Bible does not say much about singleness. Why? Because the Bible sees each individual as a part of a household. The Bible teaches the opposite of "happiness is being single." God tells us that it is *not* good for a person to be alone.

In the Old Testament, marriage is quite obviously the norm.[71] Young people were part of their father's household until they got married.[72] Marriage is everywhere present in the Bible, and we find examples of young people at home with their parents, as well as laws on the rape of a virgin.[73] Other laws lead us to believe that singles lived with their families: the laws concerning the death of an unmarried brother or sister imply that the single person is as much a part of the family as a husband, wife or child.[74] The laws concerning vows place a woman's vow under the authority of her father, if she is not married, or her husband, if she is.[75] The laws of inheritance highlight this tight relationship between singles and families.[76]

The New Testament confirms and expands this "family-oriented" view of singleness. As in the Old Testament, marriage is the norm. Paul recognizes that singles, widowers and widows, and divorced persons all have the natural desire to marry.[77] True singleness is an exceptional gift from God the Holy Spirit,[78] given to some for the sake of the King, His kingdom, and service to others.[79] Jesus gives three causes for singleness: congenital or birth defects; sinful mutilation by castration; singleness by choice for the kingdom's sake. The last possibility He describes as being "a eunuch for the Lord." Jesus Himself is the prime example of someone who chose singleness for the sake of the kingdom. This choice should not be made lightly. Biblical singleness requires a conscious evaluation of gifts, a conscious acceptance of the particular gift[80] of singleness, and a conscious choice to give up the rights and privileges of married life.[81] Perhaps more than any other, this gift involves the fruit of the Spirit, self-control.[82]

The biblical view of singleness is diametrically opposed to the world's view. Hedonistic, self-centered "happiness is being single" crumbles in the face of the truth, "happiness is knowing Jesus." Only in that context can you have sanctified singleness. Later we will see that the biblical views of the family and singleness have far-reaching, profound effects upon the church and society.[83]

The Biblical View of Care for Aging Relatives

God's view of the family is multigenerational. Parents are obligated to capitalize, as well as catechize, their children; older people, especially grandparents, need to catechize younger generations. But are there any obligations the other way? The world hates age and tries to cover it with a cosmetic veneer of youth. But God honors age, not youth. What is a family's obligation to honor age?[84]

The Old Testament commands us to honor parents.[85] Israelites who refused to do so faced severe punishment.[86] Jesus points out that to put aside these divine commandments and to substitute man's wisdom and commands is deadly hypocrisy.[87] Paul says to do so is to be worse than a pagan[88] and instructs families to care for their own dependent elderly so as to please God and not unduly burden the church.[89]

The world, in its mad, idolatrous worship of youth, tries to cover up the elderly, often killing them. Our society's recent push for "euthanasia" (a euphemism for murder) and our judicial approval of death machines and death pacts, grimly reminds us that some families do not want the elderly. The Christian family must act otherwise.[90] Christian families must make plans ahead of time concerning these God-given obligations.[91] Two other topics will round out our systematic theology of the family.

The Biblical View of Divorce and Remarriage

The tidal wave of divorce has caused Christians and non-Christians alike to react. Christians have tackled this topic *en masse*, and advocate extreme positions on both ends of the spectrum: on the one hand, some advise allowing no grounds for divorce and remarriage; at the opposite pole, other Christians recommend a sad acceptance of "any cause" for divorce and remarriage, since this is the pragmatic reality in which we live. Divorce is such a vast subject that I can only summarize the texts relating to the issue and then summarize the biblical data. For the best extended treatment, see Jay Adams, *Marriage, Divorce and Remarriage*.[92]

Old Testament passages that relate directly or indirectly to divorce are as follows:

Genesis 2:18-25: Jesus uses this norm in His discussions of divorce (Matt 19:4-6).

Exodus 21:7-11: This legislation protects a slave wife from certain abuses. It allows divorce and financial freedom for the wife if her husband has refused her food, clothing or sexual rights.

Leviticus 21:1-15: The priests have a higher standard of spouse selection than a layman. They may not marry a divorced woman or widow.

Leviticus 22:1-16: A daughter of a priest who is divorced or widowed comes back to her father's home because her divorce is real, changing her family and legal status. She is no longer part of her husband or his family: death and divorce are equated.

Numbers 30:9-15: The vow of a widow or divorcee stands because she is no longer under her husband's rule. Death and divorce are legal equivalents.

Deuteronomy 21:10-14: Pagan war brides are protected. If the Israelite divorces her, he has afflicted her and she is free to go wherever she wants and to contract any obligations she wants. She is legally dead to him and he to her. The divorce is real, the legal equivalent of the death of the spouse.

Deuteronomy 22:13-21: A man who unjustly accuses his wife of not being a virgin when they married is fined (with the fine going to her father whose reputation is at stake) and the husband loses the right of divorce. Sin may restrict one's right to exercise the option of divorce.

Deuteronomy 24:1-4: Serial divorce and remarriage pollutes the land. This statute is preventative in nature and limits foolish divorces in Israel. Note that the law does *not* encourage or permit divorce on the grounds of a husband's dislike of the "indecent thing," but the law limits sin. Remarriage to a former spouse after the spouse has been married to someone else is totally forbidden and sickens the Lord.

Ezra 10 and Nehemiah 13:23-31: National repentance included divorces which are viewed as godly, necessary courses of action. Therefore, divorce *per se* cannot be sin.

Esther 1:10-22: Divorce among pagans is most often arbitrary.

Isaiah 50:1: God divorces His bride, Israel. Therefore, divorce *per se* cannot be sin or we would have to say that God sins.

Jeremiah 3:1-10; Ezek 16:1-63; 23:1-49; 44:15-27: the same picture as in Isaiah 50.

Hos 1:2-9; 2:1-23; 3:1-5: God tells Hosea to remarry Gomer, an act which seems to violate Deuteronomy 24. Here again we see a picture of the amazing grace of God, who can turn the curse of our sin into glory for His name. On the basis of this passage, some argue that remarriage may not be sin in every case.

Malachi 2:10-16: God hates divorce. He gets nauseated by it because it is treachery to Him and to the spouse—a form of violence or covenant breaking *par excellence*. Unrighteous divorce shows that the divorcer's heart is devoid of the Holy Spirit's presence and activity and is, at root, treacherously disloyal to God, spouse, and everything covenantal.

In the New Testament, passages that relate to divorce are as follows:

Matthew 1:18-25: Joseph is righteous, yet he is considering divorcing Mary, therefore, biblical divorce is not sinful.

Matthew 5:31-32: Jesus corrects the Pharisees' false view of Deuteronomy 24:1-4, making clear that, among believers, *porneia* is the only grounds for divorce.[93] Jesus clearly assumes that remarriage will follow most divorces. Unlawful divorce involves all parties in sin.

Matthew 19:3-12 (Mark 10:1-12): The famous Hillel and Shammai debate is discussed and Jesus shows they both are wrong because they do not understand Deuteronomy 24:1-4. Improper divorce results in adultery because Jesus expected remarriage.

You cannot commit adultery unless you form an improper relationship. Jesus bases everything on the Genesis account. The Mark passage, addressed to Gentiles, adds that the same is true for the woman.

Luke 16:14-18: Jesus adapts His preaching to focus on the sins of the self-righteous Pharisees. The exception clause is not mentioned because these men are openly mocking Jesus and He is not going to give them an inch.

Romans 7:2-3: Remarriage after the death of a spouse is permissible.

1 Corinthians 7:10-40: Paul is repeating the Lord's teaching on divorce and remarriage and adding new revelation in the context of the gospel coming to the Gentiles. Paul affirms the Lord's teaching (10-11), and reaffirms Deuteronomy 24:1-4 by commanding not to compound the sin of a sinful divorce by remarriage. He goes on to address a new situation in which Gentile converts have mates who are not yet converted (12-16). The Christian must not seek to get out of the marriage, but rather to win the spouse. However, if the spouse insists on breaking the relationship, the Christian is free. Paul allows for remarriage of properly divorced people.[94]

1 Timothy 5:11-15: Paul positively encourages remarriage for young widows and even though this does not speak of divorce *per se*, it has implications that will become apparent later.

Christians must work through the detailed arguments about these texts, always keeping in mind the entire thrust of Scripture and its fulfillment in Christ. Jay Adams is a faithful guide through the maze, so I will content myself here with a summary of the biblical data. Note the following:

- Divorce was not part of God's design.[95]

- Divorce is a result of the fall. It is man's sinful heart that devises divorce,[96] which God hates.[97]

- Divorce is not always sinful. God divorces Israel, as seen in Isaiah, Jeremiah, Ezekiel and Hosea. Righteous men divorce righteously, as demonstrated in Ezra, Nehemiah and in Joseph's thoughts. Divorce is even commanded in one case (1 Cor 7:15).[98]

- God regulates the grounds for divorce. Neither the family or the state has ultimate authority in this realm.[99]

- Divorce is a real, legal severing of a marriage covenant. Spouses are legally dead to each other.[100]

- Divorce on biblical grounds carries the right of remarriage. The innocent party is free to remarry after a righteous divorce.[101]

- Unrighteous divorce is sin and causes more sin.[102]

- Unrighteous divorce can be forgiven.[103]

The Biblical View of Adoption

The Old Testament does not talk of adoption *per se*, but the New Testament shows us that both God and man adopt. Something close to adoption is seen in the life of Abraham who pleads to the Lord to accept his household servant Eliezer of Damascus as his heir.[104] After God had graciously comforted Abraham and reissued the covenant to him, He promised Abraham a son. Even though Lot was his relative, Abraham preferred to give his wealth to Eliezer. In effect, Eliezer was an adopted son. (At least Abraham didn't have to contend with the state! He could dispose of his possessions as he wished.) God, too, adopts. He chooses Israel from among the nations to be His firstborn son.[105]

In the New Testament, adoption takes on great significance. John tells us that the sons of Israel rejected the Messiah, but God gives the right to become sons to those who believe so that divine adoption and divine new birth are mentioned in the same verses.[106] Paul develops this line of thinking fully and tells us that the Holy Spirit is the Spirit of adoption who enables us to cry, "Abba, Father," as we await His power to resurrect our bodies.[107] We are already adopted sons, heirs of God, joint-heirs with Jesus Christ. Paul goes on to mention that God had adopted Israel.[108] The sonship we have is not some mystical deification. Rather, we are adopted into God's family, just as Israel was.[108] God sends the Holy Spirit into our hearts so He can adopt us into His family and give us an eternal inheritance.[110] This inheritance is no afterthought, but a part of God's eternal plan.[111]

Thus God is our justification and model for adoption of human children into our covenant homes. The Old Testament has a theme of care for the Levite, stranger, widow and fatherless[112] and the tithe was the major way of providing this care.[113]

Adoption is a primary way in which the family can be the focal point of diaconal ministries of mercy. Other ways include foster care and hospitality on a short-term or long-term basis. Adoption is a model of God's hospitality and grace and is a way of bringing people under the general blessings of God.[114] Obviously, the motivation is gratitude to God for His unspeakable gifts of His Son and His Spirit so we could be adopted into His family and be His heirs. No other organization—orphanage, group home, etc.—can match a real family setting for ministry. No other family-based ministry can so powerfully witness to God's grace as adoption, which should be considered by families with children as well as childless husbands and wives. After all, God did not *need* children—Jesus was enough. Much needs to be done theologically and pastorally to focus on this ministry.[115]

Summary

My mini-systematic theology is not comprehensive. However, it is a framework for our thinking. Obviously, God's views are radically different from the world's; it just so happens that He is correct and everyone else is wrong.[116] You may be saying to yourself, "Do all these biblical views make a difference in individual families, churches, and cultures? Can you prove that they make a difference in time and space?" I thought you might ask. Let's look at history since biblical times to see if there is any evidence that God's view does make a difference. Let me say that even if the evidence were lacking (which it is not), God's views would still be true. Whether I can prove them and convince you or not is beside the point.

Notes:

Chapter 8

1. For an example of nonreligious materials, see *Effective Parenting,* a newsletter for sponsors of parent training (American Guidance Service, 4201 Woodland Rd., Circle Pines, MN 55014-1796). For an example of religious materials, see M. Yorkey, ed., *The Focus on the Family Guide to Growing a Healthy Home* (Brentwood: Wolgemuth and Hyatt, 1990).

2. Deut 32:1-18; Isa 30:29; 44:6-11; 51:1-3.

3. A study of God's methods of discipline for training His people needs to be done in a systematic fashion. No doubt, this would help transform our approach to education.

4. Matt 5:1-12.

5. Gal 5:22-25.

6. Ex 20; Deut 5.

7. Prov 19:18; 22:6; 29:15; Eph 6:4.

8. Prov 13:24; 20:30; 22:15; 23:13-14.

9. Prov 3:11-12; 13:1; 15:5; 19:18; 29:17; 2 Tim 3:15-17.

10. Deut 12:31; 18:10.

11. Deut 21:15-17.

12. Deut 21:18-21.

13. Deut 24:16; Ezek 18.

14. Typical is H. C. Trumbull's *Hints on Child Training* (Brentwood: Wolgemuth and Hyatt, 1989). While much of his advice makes sense (which is more than can be said for many modern writers), there is little biblical content. Writing in 1890, he gives his wisdom. However, while most of his advice falls within general biblical parameters, there are a few things that do not square with the Scriptures. Much of what is written today falls into this category, but is far worse than Trumbull. Read the plethora of books on parenting with discernment.

15. B. A. Ray, *Withhold Not Correction* (Phillipsburg: Presbyterian and Reformed, 1978); Tedd Tripp, *Shepherding a Child's Heart* (Wapwallopen: Shepherd Press, 1995).

16. One popular Christian title is *Love Is a Feeling to Be Learned.*

17. M. Mead, *Coming of Age in Samoa: A Psychological Study of Primitive Youth for Western Civilization* (New York: Dell, 1928, 1955, 1961).

18. Ex 34:10-17; Deut 7:1-5; 2 Cor 6:14-18. See chapters 6-7.

19. Gen 24:2-3, 51; 23:1-2; Ex 21:1-11; 22:16-17; 1 Cor 7:25-38.

20. Gen 24:57-58; Judg 14:1-4.

21. Gen 6:2; 26:24-25; 28:6-9.

22. Gen 24:22, 53; Ex 22:16-17.

23. Wayne A. Mack, *Preparing for Marriage God's Way* (Tulsa: Hensley, 1986). This is an excellent tool for use in premarital counseling which can be used by a counselor and a couple, a teacher and a class, a parent and a child, or by a couple themselves. For a mother's teaching and plea in this regard, see D. Voshell's *Whom Shall I Marry?* (Phillipsburg: Presbyterian and Reformed, 1979). Jim West's *Christian Courtship vs. The Dating Game* (Palo Cedro: Christian Worldview Ministries, 1992), is an excellent booklet and can be obtained from CWM at P. O. Box 603, Palo Cedro, CA 96073-0603.

For the best treatment of biblical preparation for marriage, see "A Biblical Pattern of Preparation for Marriage," an unpublished paper by Dr. Hendrik Krabbendam, a professor at Covenant College, Tennessee. Copies are available from him at 1301 Aladdin Lane, Lookout Mountain, TN 30750.

24. 1 Tim 6:6-10.

25. Prov 23:4-5; 27:23-24; 28:25; 1 Tim 6:17-19.

26. Eph 5:5.

27. Prov. 30:7-9; Matt 6:19-34.

28. Prov 3:9-10; 8:18-21; Luke 16:9-13.

29. Gen 14:17-24; Heb 7:4.

30. Jam 1:16-18.

31. Deut 26:1-11; 2 Cor 8:8-9; 9:6-15.

32. Prov 13:21-22; 19:4.

33. Prov 10:15-16; 22; 2 Cor 9:6.

34. See chapter 6, notes 66-67. Larry Burkett is another author who gives practical help on finances: *Answers to Your Family's Financial Questions* (Pomona: Focus on the Family, 1987).

35. Deut 7:6-11; 9:26, 29; Ps 106:40.

36. R. L. Harris, ed., vol. 2 (Chicago: Moody, 1980), 569-570 and also the chapter titled "Inheritance."

37. Num 26:55; 2 Sam 14:16; Ezek 47:21-23; Acts 7:5; 13:19.

38. Ps 37:9, 11, 18, 22, 29.

39. Num 27:6-11, 36.

40. Deut 25:5-10; Ruth 4:5-6.

41. Deut 21:15-17.

42. Lev 25:23.

43. Ex 4:22; 11; Rom 8:29; Col 1:15, 18; Heb 1:6; 12:23; Rev 1:5.

44. 1 Cor 4:7-21.

45. Num 18; Deut 10:6-9; 12:12; 14:27-29.

46. Isa 14:2; Zeph 2:9.

47. Ps 37:18; Rev 20-22.

48. Heb 1:4.

49. Matt 3:1; 4:17.

50. Rom 8:16, 23; 2 Cor 1:22; 5:5; Eph 1:14.

51. Matt 5:5; Acts 20:32; Rom 8:12-25; Eph 1:13-14; Col 1:12-14; 1 Pet 1:3-5.

52. Gal 3:18.

53. Col 3:24; Heb 6:12; 1 Pet 3:9; Rev 21:7.

54. 1 Cor 6:9-11; 15:50; Eph 5:5.

55. Heb 9:15; 1 Pet 1:4.

56. John 17:1-3.

57. Matt 10:37-39.

58. Mark 7:9-13.

59. 1 Tim 5:7-8.

60. 2 Cor 12:14-18.

61. Gen 31:14; Prov. 19:14; Mic 2:2.

62. Prov 13:22; 2 Cor 12:14; 1 Tim 5:7-8.

63. Gen 48:5-6; Deut 21:18-21; Ps 69:25; Prov 20:21; Luke 12:10-15; 15:11-13.

64. Ecc 7:11; Isa 57:13.

65. Gen 25:32-34; Num 27:26; 1 Kgs 3-4.

66. 1 Cor 15:32; Phil 3:17-21; 1 Tim 5:6; Jam 5:5.

67. 1 Tim 6:6-10.

68. Matt 6:19-24.

69. R. Rushdoony on inheritance is very helpful. See "The Eighth Commandment," *The Institutes of Biblical Law*, vol. 1 (Phillipsburg: Presbyterian and Reformed, 1980), 448-541; vol. 2, 171-224.

70. Help is available from a worthy institution, Westminster Theological Seminary in California, 1725 Bear Valley Parkway, Escondido, Ca. 92027. Phone (760) 480-8474. Contact Robert den Dulk, who is an expert in this field.

71. Gen 2:18-24.

72. Gen 24; 29.

73. Ex 22:16-17; Deut 22:28-29.

74. Lev 21:1-4; Num 6:5-8.

75. Num 30:1-16.

76. Num 27:1-11.

77. 1 Cor 7:9-11; 1 Tim 5:11-15.

78. The Greek word is *charisma* and is the same term used in Rom 1:11; 5:15, 16; 6:23; 11:29; 12:6; 1 Cor 1:7; 12:4, 9, 28, 30-31; 2 Cor 1:11; 1 Tim 4:14; 2 Tim 1:6; 1 Pet 4:14. Rom 5:15-16; 6:23; 11:29 talk of the gift of salvation through Christ and His blessings on His people. In every other case, Paul refers to a "charismatic" gift of the Holy Spirit which is given for service to others. Paul's usage in 1 Cor 7:7 indicates that singleness is a gift of the Holy Spirit. When was the last time you heard anyone call singleness

a gift, let alone a charismatic gift?! The state of singleness is not the same thing as the gift of singleness.

79. Matt 19:11-12.

80. Rom 12:1-8.

81. Luke 2:36; 1 Cor 7:9, 26, 37-39; 9:3-6.

82. 1 Cor 7:8-9; 1 Tim 5:11-16.

83. I am not aware of much from a biblical perspective on singleness. This was not a focus of my research. One helpful book is Elizabeth Elliott's *Passion and Purity* (Grand Rapids: Revell, 1984).

84. See Appendix 9, V.

85. Ex 20:12; Deut 5:16.

86. Ex 21:17; Lev 20:9.

87. Mark 7:6-13.

88. 1 Tim 5:7-8.

89. 1 Tim 5:3-4.

90. While no book is perfect, including this one, the typical evangelical book does not even address the issue of aging parents or grandparents and their care, e.g., *The Focus on the Family Guide to Growing a Healthy Home* (Brentwood: Wolgemuth and Hyatt, 1990).

91. See Jay Adams, *Wrinkled, But Not Ruined: Counsel for the Elderly* (Woodruff: Timeless Texts, 1999). Also, see Appendix 9, V.

92. Adams, *Marriage, Divorce and Remarriage* (Grand Rapids: Zondervan, 1989). See also, J. Murray, *Divorce* (Phillipsburg: Presbyterian and Reformed, 1981).

93. The term means prostitution, unchastity, fornication and is used of every kind of unlawful sexual intercourse. While it is used literally and figuratively, here it can only be literal. See W. Hendriksen, *The Gospel of Matthew* (Grand Rapids: Baker, 1973), 304-306.

94. Adams, *Marriage, Divorce and Remarriage*, 49-91.

95. Gen 2:24; Matt 19:1-9.

96. Matt 19:8. Adams, op. cit., 27.

97. Mal 2:16.

98. *Choridzestho* is in the imperative mood. This means that it is a command. It means, "you (singular) let him go."

99. Deut 24:1-4; Matt 19:1-9.

100. Ex 21:7-11; Lev 22:1-16; Num 30:9-15; Deut 21:10-14.

101. Ex 21:2-11; Deut 21:10-14; 1 Cor 7:27-28.

102. Deut 24:1-4; Matt 5:31-32; 19:3-12.

103. Since this has not been covered, see Adams, op.cit., 92-96.

104. Gen 15:1-6.

105. Ex 13; Deut 7:6-11.

106. John 1:10-13.

107. Rom 8:12-25.

108. Rom 9:4.

109. Deut 7:7-11; 8:1-5.

110. Gal 3:26 - 4:7.

111. Eph 1:4.

112. Ps 68:5; 82:3; 146:9; Prov 23:10; Ezek 22:7.

113. Lev 18:21; Deut 14:22-29.

114. 1 Cor 7:14 shows that nonbelievers may be blessed by association with believers. Of course, this does not mean they are regenerated.

115. For a good start, see S.and M. Olasky, *More Than Kindness: A Compassionate Approach to Crisis Childbearing* (Wheaton: Crossway, 1990). Chapter 7, "Different Issues in Adoption" and Appendix A, "Bethany Christian Services Responds to Bill Gothard."

Also see S. D. Doe, "Not from the Flesh but from the Heart," and D. E. Longacre, "Decreed for Adoption," in *New Horizons in the Orthodox Presbyterian Church*, vol 14, no 1, Jan 1993, 4-7.

116. Rom 3:4.

Section 3

~

IS THE WEST BEST?

~

CHAPTER 9

The Family in Western Culture

If Christianity is true and its view of the family is correct, we would expect to see the effects on societies that apply the Christian model. Does history highlight and underscore the biblical data? Yes.[1]

Although a thorough history of the family in Western culture is beyond the scope of this book, a summary of the monumental work by the distinguished sociologist, Carle C. Zimmerman (1897-1983)[2] should suffice. His research on the family and its history has no equal. His five major books on the family remain the most extensive and complete work to date.[3]

A Historical Overview of the Family

In Zimmerman's work we discover eight major conclusions:

1. Sociology can be done in different ways.

He proves that different sociologies are different ideologies of the family in academic garb. He systematically destroys mainstream sociology's dual tenets of evolution and the unqualified linear progress of the family's development: Compte defined sociology by building on J. J. Rousseau's romanticism and by rejecting religious values and ideas. Mainstream sociology and anthropology are anything but value-neutral (Appendix 6).

Zimmerman also argues that the great civilizations, both East and West, are the proper objects of study, not primitive tribes, unless these bear enough similarities to our civilization that we can draw valid conclusions.[4] While touching on Eastern cultures, he is comprehensive in his study of Western societies, from the ancient Greek and Roman families, through the Middle Ages in Europe, to present-day European and American culture.

2. The family is the key entity in shaping Western culture.

He builds on F. de Coulanges and T. Mommsen's observations that the early Greek and Roman families contained the roots of religion, law and government within their bosoms; it shaped their histories.[5] Capitalizing on F. LePlay, the pioneer family researcher, he notes how all the individual and corporate structures of society are in the family in germinal form.[6] He argues strenuously, along with LePlay, that the study of the family is no mere academic exercise because societal stability and growth hinge on the family and its strength.[7] No other entity in society has such foundational and formative influence. Change the family and society will change.[8] Though Zimmerman does not mention the Bible, his data supports the thesis of chapters 5-8. The family is foundational and pivotal in shaping a culture as the womb of religious, governmental and cultural growth.

3. Changes in family structure are cyclical.

The historical data do not support theories of linear, evolutionary growth that undergird collectivistic or socialistic values but support cyclical changes between three family types.[9] Modifying LePlay's patriarchal, stem, and unstable family types,[10] he describes three family types.[11] The trustee family is characterized by clan loyalty, power, law and prerogatives: the individual family is a trustee for the clan which is of utmost, often eternal, importance. The opposite type is the atomistic: the individual member is paramount and is more important than the family as a whole, the husband-wife relationship, the parent-child relationship, or society itself. The domestic type is intermediate between the other two and has characteristics and strengths of both, yet without many of their limitations. Within each era of Western history, the predominant family type changes resulting in cultural strength or weakness.

As Zimmerman studied, he came to believe that through all these cyclical ebbs and flows there was gradual progress in the delineation and structure of the Western family.[12] Though Zimmerman lacks a view of divine providence, agnostically describing what was and is, his descriptions help us grasp cultural change. He does not accept an evolutionary model, but sees a gradual shaping and reshaping of the family. What Zimmerman could not see from his agnostic position is that God is in heaven shaping and molding history, which follows the counsel of His eternal will, not a mechanistic cycle. As the domestic family developed, it became a crucial force in cultural continuity and growth. He also came to believe there is growth and change within individual family units as they age.[13] The family is a dynamic, not static, unit, both on the individual and cultural levels.

4. The family is the key to the reconstruction of American society and to the survival of Western civilization.

Very early in his career, he observed severe problems in American society and believed the resultant crisis demanded a new approach to social theory building and societal solutions that would proceed from it.[14] Only a return to familism held hope for Western culture.[15] As time passed and American urbanization accelerated, he tenaciously held to this view and insisted that the family remains the absolutely necessary vehicle of procreation, economic progress, and cultural continuity.[16] He vehemently disagreed with Huxley's solutions in *Brave New World:* "Family life means more now than it ever did and we need it more."[17]

5. The atomistic family type results in cultural decay.

He traces the signs of such decay in Greece, Rome and modern Europe:[18]

The symptoms of these periods are all the same—widespread popularity of divorce, feministic movements, great development of social life outside the family, youth problems, revolt of children against the parents, childlessness, great expansion of positive law about the family increasing rights of men, women and children to have and control their own incomes and property and all the other marks which indicate that husband-wife and parent-child relations are the opposite from the trustee type.[19]

The results of this phase come back to threaten the family with tragic results: the family weakens and loses control over itself and its destiny.

The final culmination of the atomistic family results in rapid, easy divorce, childlessness, limited conceptions of love (largely of the purely sexual nature) and the tendency of a loose organization to break up. This is the age in which the state has to step in and do what it can to hold the family together and protect the weak from the strong.[20]

Though Zimmerman proves that the family is a key to affect cultural change, he misses something central that his own work proves. Before strong families can regenerate a society, they must themselves become regenerate. For families to be regenerate, the individuals in them must experience personal regeneration by the Holy Spirit. Such a reformation of individuals and families leads to revival and, finally, to reformation.

Zimmerman misidentifies the signs of atomistic decay, ignoring the description in Romans 1 and 2 of the bitter fruit produced when individuals, families and cultures set aside God's biblical law. This diagnostic failure is clearly seen in his proposed solutions to save the family.

6. The family battles for its life as the state attempts to control it.

Historically, as noted above, the atomistic family phase accelerates the state's attempts to control the family in order to save both.[21] The family, weakened by its own selfishness, now has another enemy. The twentieth century gives savage examples.

We have seen since that the German state, far from freeing people, was the first in the twentieth century to assume absolute control over the family, to organize and supervise it with full intention of using the family for the furtherance of its designs. From marriage to the grave, from birth to senility, the individual was made a slave of the state. He became merely a tool, an instrument for achieving the state's purpose.[22] Zimmerman helps us understand the French Revolution, the Russian Revolution, German Statism and other attacks on the family by the state. However, he misses the spiritual reality behind the battle. Without such spiritual realism, the Christian family in America will not know how to defend itself from an ever-encroaching state.

In the United States of America, the battle rages as different pro- and anti-family groups vie for the power to control the family and its future.[23] The battle against the family is fierce.

7. *The domestic family type is necessary for cultural growth.*

Family structures other than the domestic family stifle or destroy societal growth:[24]

> Thus, we see that, in all stages and levels of civilization, the domestic family institution is basic to society. No civilization can proceed without it. No great civilization has endured for any length of time without paying considerable attention to the organization, promulgation, and protection of the domestic family.[25]

8. *Christianity defined, developed and dignified the domestic family.*[26]

At two different times in the history of Western civilization, the church promoted the domestic family concept which, along with other biblical doctrines, helped to salvage Western culture. The first was at the end of the Roman Empire. Pagans looked to man for salvation through the power of the state; Christians looked to God for salvation through the protection and promotion of the family.[27] As the Empire declined, the old family system failed. The Church bound society together during the decline, decay and invasion of the civilization.

The moral agent in the revision of the family was the Christian Church. There are probably few subjects more thoroughly discussed in our literature than the collapse of the Roman Empire and the rise of the Christian Church. The empire did break up. The Church rose first as a moral force and later became a combined spiritual and secular power. The Church was against social decay, whether in Rome or among the barbarians, whether within the Church (the heretics) or without (among the pagans). Without quoting at length from the Church Fathers, we can give their attitude toward the Roman decay in a few words.[28]

The Church held up the domestic family against barbarian trusteeism and Roman atomism.[29] Thus, the Church was the necessary link between the past and the future and accomplished this feat primarily through the teaching and preaching of men like Augustine.[30]

Zimmerman says:

> The evidence given here is sufficient. The reforms seeking to keep the Roman family from decaying, and thus undermining the empire, most probably delayed the end of this society. But by the time the Christians took up the task, the foundations of the social system were already shattered. The barbarian system was the only one which could control the rampant dissolution and even this could not do it very well. The barbarian chief or tribal group brought the trustee family system into the empire. The feudal manors, which became the next chief focal points of social organization, found that they also had to adopt this system.
>
> Family organization in Europe again returned to the condition of Homeric and early Roman times, when the world of the individual became kin, clan, lord, and fidelitas. The only thing carried over from the past was the Christian Church, with its conception of decency, moral virtue, and the ultimate dignity of the individual.

> The Christian idea was that the social system of the Romans could be recreated and saved by the development of the domestic family social organization. Within the family there were no such things as "others," because they conceived a lifelong unit of husband and wife, parent and child as furnishing a family personality with common aims and interests. Between these domestic units they conceived "all men as neighbors" and the maxim "do unto others as you would have them do unto you." But the Christian movement developed too late in the scene for it to attain the necessary control to restore the Roman Empire. Thus, in a large sense of the word, the return to trustee familism in the Middle Ages was an historical accident. No one wanted true familism as a permanent system of family organization; rather, it was accepted as a necessary compromise. The church had a remedy which demonstrated in time that it could hold society together without a complete return to blood responsibility and blood feud. Its ultimate development, beginning with the tenth century, required four centuries of constant effort on the part of the church. Thus, the church furnished the fundamental historical continuity between the Roman Empire aspect of western civilization and modern western civilization. Disregarding all else that may be said about it, the church was an institution molded in the Roman Empire. It brought to us the fundamental conceptions throughout the ages of the proper relations between man and man, as developed in the best thinking of Greece and Rome.[31]

The second period when Christianity and its emphasis on the domestic family type helped to salvage the culture was the Protestant Reformation. As Zimmerman puts it:

> Most writers praise or blame the Protestant leaders for the philosophical steps which led to the modern atomism of the family. Neither praise nor blame is deserved. The original Protestant leaders, from Hus through Luther and Calvin to those of the eighteenth century, really wanted a stricter and more puritanical family than actually existed in the Middle Ages. The founders of the modern philosophy that the individual is God were not the religious leaders but the intellectual sophists. The Reformation leaders were profamilistic.[32]

Zimmerman notes that most of the Reformers were biblical in their theology, not humanists, deifying reason.[33] Through the years, his research only uncovered more proof of this position.[34] The facts are incontrovertible: With Christianity comes a strong domestic family that blesses and stablilizes a society.

These eight points summarize Zimmerman's prolific work.[35] His accurate assessments of Western history bear out our biblical study. His domestic family model, with some biblical exegetical modifications, is the type of family necessary for proper cultural growth. While some common-grace vestiges of such a family type exist in non-Western cultures, the East has only recently begun to achieve the cultural productivity of Western Christianity. At the same time, the Western family may be losing its Christian roots. The West must return to a biblically defined domestic type, if society is to remain strong and our culture is to improve.[36]

Christianity teaches, promotes and exalts the proper view of the family. More importantly, God empowers families to live according to this model. Zimmerman is blind to what he has proven. Never once does he point to a revival of orthodox biblical Christianity. But this makes his findings all the more powerful:

> That the family of the immediate future will move further toward atomism seems highly probable. Except for the Christian Church—which at present is not popular among the directive forces of western society—no agency or group of persons seems fundamentally interested in doing anything other than facilitate this increasing atomism. New names for the decaying atomistic family, seeking to give it the prestige of improvement or progress are constantly being invented. No matter what it really means, every slogan which now commands prestige is attached to the atomistic family. It and its extension toward further atomism are called liberal, humane, democratic, free, etc. Anyone who even suggests that the preservation of the familistic system is desirable is simply considered out of his head by the modern Plutarchs.[37]

Although he never mentions God or His gospel as the solution, Zimmerman has collected the evidence of post-biblical history: Christianity is necessary for the proper family structure, and that proper family structure is necessary for permanent cultural growth. The history of Western civilization illustrates the truth of the Bible. Without a return to Christianity, we will continue to sink into neo-paganism.

Zimmerman is neither antagonistic nor overtly favorable to Christianity. Today, the academic intelligentsia scoffs at Christianity and its domestic, biblical view of the family. As a result of this blindness to biblical truth, academic research on the family and its history, though vast, has failed to define, defend or direct the family.[38] Antagonism, agnosticism or indifference to truth will not help the family or save Western civilization.

Many studies have even damaged the family, encouraging it to follow practices that will produce misery and division. In spite of their antagonism, however, such studies tend to vindicate Zimmerman's eight points. In spite of the cataracts that cloud the eyes of anti-Christian academia, scholars see a shadowy form of the truth about the history of the family.

James Casey, *The History of the Family*,[39] reflects on the last century of academic study about the family. Chapter 1 analyzes the changing approaches to the study of the history of the family. He warns of two prominent dangers. The first is specialization.[40] Analysis of the family has sometimes been too narrow, isolating the family or one of its aspects from the cultural context: religious ideas, political structures, etc. The data are often distorted. The second is the danger of substituting quantitative statistical precision in examining the data for true methodological rigor.[41] Casey claims that while statistics have their place, they often miss the richness of human life in general and of historical data in particular. The historian is a novelist, not a mathematician. Casey tries to avoid both pitfalls.

In spite of his non-Christian bias, Casey sees that reformation Calvinism and New England Puritanism have had salutary cultural effects. Their view of society and work were foundational for the modern view of the family and of industrial growth.[42] Thus, Casey confirms Zimmerman.[43] So does the highly touted series, "Family, Sexuality and Social Relations in Past Times."[44] The first book, *Western Sexuality*,[45] is blatantly anti-Christian, openly attacking Christian sexual and familial practices. Some of the historical essays rise above the vitriolics, citing sources for the attacks.[46]

In the second book, *The Explanation of Ideology*,[47] E. Todd builds upon P. Laslett's and A. MacFarlane's concept of relative constancy of family forms in a given culture.[48] Using F. LePlay's family typology,[49] Todd delineates eight existing family types. He gives compelling evidence that the family structure dictates the ideological and political structures of the society in which it exists:[50] ideas and political structures are extended expressions of the basic family type. Todd's conclusions are all the more remarkable because of his openly anti-Christian stance.[51] While Todd's irrational mechanism is not rich enough to explain his observations of historical data, he demonstrates a remarkable correlation between family type and ideology. Without extended argument, we may conclude that the family gives birth to governmental and social structures that reflect its structure whatever the culture may be. Biblical revelation would lead us to expect this.

The third book in the series is Todd's *The Causes of Progress*,[52] a sequel to his first. His family types are slightly altered, though complementary to those in his first book. His major thesis: specific family types favor cultural development; others do not.[53] Todd defines progress in terms of ideas and literacy, not industrial growth[54] and this explains for him why the economic and cultural growth of England and North America are declining, while those of Germany, Japan and Korea are rising.[55]

Todd's explanations are, again, too simplistic for his fascinating data. However, his observations are revealing. He argues that Comte was wrong: the family type sparks modernization; modernization does not transform the family.[56] The family is foundational to the culture. Todd also supports Weber's observation that Protestantism is more productive than Catholicism. However, he claims that the dominant family type in Protestant Europe was the authoritarian family. According to him, this authoritarianism was what gave birth to cultural potential.[57] He says:

> History defined as a general movement of mankind in a given direction is usually considered to be a central theme of Judeo-Christian inquiry. With Judaism, the concept that history was linear supplanted the ancients' view of a cyclical Time. Progress is one possible direction this linear history can take as it leads Man onwards—not necessarily to Paradise, but at any rate to somewhere else, to a different world, one that is transformed by his intelligence at work. Strictly speaking, progress confers *direction* upon history; it sets up movement. Strikingly, at the very cradle of this 'historic' conception of mankind's future we discern an authoritarian family structure, the solidest and longest-lasting of them all: that of the Jewish people.
>
> The first five books of the Bible, the Pentateuch, recount at one and the same time both the birth of a faith and the birth of a people. To the analyst of family structure they make up an extraordinary essay focused upon the authoritarian type of family, defined as having the principle of primogeniture as its fundamental structural element—the obsessive theme that runs through Genesis, Exodus, Leviticus, Numbers and Deuteronomy. Jacob, who becomes Israel—simultaneously an individual and a people—uses his "mess of pottage" to buy from Esau his whole birthright as eldest son and heir. As the story unfolds, the greater part of the religious subject-matter is a symbolic representation of the right of eldest sons, from the death of the First Born of Egypt to the redemption of the First Born of the Hebrews through the institutionalization of the priestly power of the Levites.

> With its authoritarian family saga the Bible dramatizes the succession of one generation to another and the continuity of hereditary lineage. Thus it elaborates a lineal concept of time as embodied in father-son-grandson succession. This earliest perception of Time as a dimension that is continuous and, in the mathematical sense of the term, oriented, thus consists of an enormous collective genealogy of families and lineages.
>
> The picture of historical movement as incarnated in the history of families was rediscovered in the sixteenth century by the Protestants of northern Europe, who avidly seized upon the Bible precisely because they saw themselves mirrored in it. Most of those countries that adopted Protestantism have an authoritarian family tradition not very different from the Jewish family tradition. One main difference does exist, however: northern Europe quite strongly disapproves of marriage between cousins, whereas the Jewish tradition very readily tolerates it.[58]

Zimmerman was right: the biblical view of the domestic family is what allows for continual cultural growth. Pagans will see the beauty of God's wisdom and ways (Deut 4:1-9). It shouldn't surprise us that history illustrates what the Bible teaches: the family is primary and pivotal in shaping and developing culture.[59] Also, the family structure revealed in the Bible maximizes the growth of a culture's economy, church and government. Only a biblical family structure can prevent the excesses of either trustee tribalism or of atomistic individualism. History illustrates what the biblical books of Deuteronomy, Judges and the major and minor Prophets teach. When a culture ignores God's pattern for the family, whether out of sinful, willful ignorance (as in Greece or Rome, Rom. 1:18-32); out of self-satisfied, smug hypocrisy (as in Victorian England, Rom. 2); or out of a visceral, doglike return to its autonomous enlightenment vomit (as in Nazi Germany, or in present-day USA, 2 Pet. 2:22), God judges. Like Lady Wisdom in Proverbs 1-9, history calls out loudly for all to hear: the union of vital, biblical Christianity and a strong biblically defined domestic family is the formula for cultural blessings and growth.[60]

If Chevrolet is the heartbeat of America, the biblical family built on biblical Christianity is the heartbeat of Western culture. May God grant us revival and reformation before we die of a cultural coronary.

Notes:

Chapter 9

1. Biblical history differs from other history in some important respects. While both deal with what happened in the real world, biblical history is infallibly recorded. Thus, you have an inspired, inerrant, objective account of history. Also, the modern despair over the fallibility of the reader that destroys any hope of definitive objective truth is overcome, to a large degree, by the Holy Spirit's work in the regenerate reader (Ps 19:7-14; 119:97-112; 1 Cor 2; Heb 5:11-14). The same is not true for other historical data. Writers and interpreters *are* fallible. (See Appendix 6.) However, you can evaluate things biblically or theologically and have hopes of something of value. See C. Gregg Singer's *A Theological Interpretation of American History*, 2nd ed. (Phillipsburg: Presbyterian and Reformed, 1981). The modern existential despair over, and denigration of, objective historical reality must not paralyze Christians.

2. *Contemporary Authors*, rev. ed., says that Zimmerman got his Ph.D. in 1925 at the University of Minnesota. He taught at the University of Minnesota, 1923-30; Harvard University, 1931-63; University of Istanbul, 1963-4; North Dakota State University, 1964-7; University of Sasketchewan, 1967-8; University of Calgary, 1968-70; University of Rome, 1954-55; and lectured at universities in Peru and Mexico, 1959-60. He advised governments on rural economics in Thailand, Cuba, Canada, and the USA. He wrote over 500 articles and reviews on sociology and actively corresponded with sociologists worldwide, with the exception of South Africa and the Iron Curtain nations.

3. *Family and Society: A Study of the Sociology of Reconstruction* (London: Williams and Norgate, 1933) was coauthored with Merle E. Frampton. This 600-page book emphasizes the importance of correct methodology for sociological studies and champions LePlay's approach to the family. Zimmerman proves that the reshaping and salvaging of American society rests on the family and its strength. *Family and Civilization* (New York: Harper and Brothers, 1947), an 800-page tome, is his major work. He expands and clarifies his views in *Family and Society.* He traces the history of the family in Western civilization from Greece to the present and also touches upon Islamic, Indian and Chinese cultures. *The Family of Tomorrow: The Cultural Crisis* (New York: Harper and Brothers, 1949), a 250-page book, builds on the others. His major thesis is that its family system affects the continuity of a culture. *Marriage and the Family: A Text for Moderns* (Chicago: Regnery, 1956), was coauthored with L. F. Cervantes. Zimmerman wrote part one "The Present Crisis" and "Differences of the Sexes." Zimmerman basically reaffirms and expands the findings of *Family and Civilization.* Cervantes deals with the differences between the sexes as found

in the social sciences. *Contemporary Authors*, 1st revision, says that Cervantes is a Jesuit who received his Ph.D. from St. Louis University in 1947. He has written extensively in the areas of sociology, marriage and family, and theology. *Successful American Families* (New York: Pagent, 1960), a 218-page book, is coauthored by L. F. Cervantes. This is the summary of a study of 60,000 American families. He believes this is empirical validation of his other works.

The study included high school students, their families, and families of their friends from eight cities: three older cities, east of the Mississippi; three new western cities; and two semi-rural cities. The criteria for "successful" were (1) the avoidance of family disruption by divorce or desertion; (2) the avoidance of interference by the police; and (3) keeping the children in school. Successful families met all these; good families met two out of the three criteria; ordinary families were defined by the child who drops out before finishing school, but gets a job; poor families had dropouts who drifted afterwards. The survey works with successful and good families. The hypothesis of the study is: successful or good families associate with other families with similar values to protect the family's value system, which allows cultural continuity.

4. While basically correct in his criticism of main line sociology's dependency upon studying primitives only, Zimmerman has a serious flaw. He says that it does not matter which form of marriage came first or that there was even one type to begin with (*Family & Civilization*, 328). He ignores creational norms and biblical history; in effect, there is no right and wrong. This also blinds him to the fact that *something* can be learned from primitive cultures, even if the evolutionary hypothesis is wrong. He argues this way in *The Family of Tomorrow* and *Marriage and the Family*. Zimmerman's thinking parallels that of A. Bloom, *The Closing of the American Mind: How Higher Education has Failed Democracy and Impoverished the Souls of Today's Students* (New York: Simon and Schuster, 1987). Both scholars analyze astutely, understand causal connections, share a great love for Western culture, believe that the academic, literary elite have power to change society, depend on some form of rational cultural law, and are vilified by contemporary colleagues. They also share the fatal flaw of ignoring God's Word, which causes them to choose wrong solutions for the problems they so poignantly observe. Bloom is a far better writer and more enjoyable to read. I doubt that *Family and Civilization* will ever hit the best seller list!

5. F. DeCoulanges, *The Ancient City: A Study on the Religion, Laws and Institutions of Greece and Rome* (Garden City: Doubleday Anchor Books, n.d.); T. Mommsen, (quoted in *Family and Civilization*, chapter 14, 325-358).

6. *Family and Society*, 122.

7. Ibid., 129.

8. *The Family of Tomorrow: The Cultural Crisis.* According to Zimmerman:

> In this chapter we wish only to emphasize, and reemphasize, that the main function or necessitous cause for the existence of the family is the transmission, preservation, and enlargement of culture. Consequently, great changes in the culture occur in periods of violent antagonism to the family (73). Thus it arises inevitably that rejections of familism are also rejections of culture—nihilism, the denial of society itself (74).

9. *Family and Civilization*, 572:

> There were numerous attacks upon various doctrines, but fundamentally, the nineteenth century saw the rise and acceptance of the evolutionary conception of the family. They gave us instead of history, imagination. Instead of the constant struggle between familism and individualism, they gave us various evolutionary pictures. These have been reviewed in chapters 2, 3 and 4.
>
> The evolutionary cultists were shortly joined by the adherents of the school of linear progress. This is illustrated in outstanding detail by the works of Herbert Spencer. With the exception of a very few thinkers, from that time to the present these dogmas and schools of thought have to a remarkable degree dominated thought on the family. Since then, books on the family (except relatively few by religious writers and conservative clergymen, both Protestant and Catholic) have become works on evolution, the progress and rise of individualism, or adaptations advisable in the family to bring about improvements, rather than works on the family. Frederick LePlay was the only real exception to these schools during the whole nineteenth century.

10. *Family and Society*, 51-69; 97-98.

11. *Family and Civilization*, chapters 1, 6–9. *The Family of Tomorrow* and *Marriage and Family* follow this structure.

12. *The Family of Tomorrow*, chapters 2–4.

13. Ibid., chapters 9–10.

14. *Family and Society*, chapters 1–2.

15. *Family and Civilization*, 810.

16. *The Family of Tomorrow* holds to this strenuously.

17. *Marriage and Family*, 65.

18. *Family and Civilization*, chapters 13, 15–16, 20.

19. Ibid., 161. See also Plutarch's detailed descriptions, 409-411.

20. Ibid., 210.

21. Ibid., 305, 396.

22. Ibid., 569. He makes similar observations for the USSR.

23. *The Family of Tomorrow* traces many of these cultural conflicts over control of the family. Chapter 12 gives details.

24. See *Marriage and Family*.

25. *Family and Civilization*, 735.

26. I do not believe that Zimmerman is trying to prove this. He honestly reports things as he finds them. Ironically, Zimmerman ignores biblical Christianity as a means of saving Western culture!

27. *Family and Civilization*, 735.

28. Ibid., 422.

29. Ibid., 444-5.

30. Ibid., 462-3. While Zimmerman is correct in noting the classical influence on Augustine, he gives too little credit to biblical thought; he does not understand the godly genius of Augustine. Zimmerman's natural law rationalism makes him too favorable to Greek and Roman thought as opposed to biblical thought, which is absent from his thinking.

31. Ibid., 459-60.

32. Ibid., 790.

33. Ibid., chapter 21, "Philosophy and Familism in the Nineteenth Century." Sadly, Zimmerman is trapped in this rationalism. Though a Congregationalist, he does not turn to biblical data. On 369 he says:

> It must be said at the beginning that the "origin" of any social institution such as the family can never be found. If it could, we might claim from parallels with other forms of animal life—as in the case of the ant colonies found imbedded in Baltic amber, which show identity of basic social organization among them for over two million years—that the original type would be surprisingly like that we see about us today. In other words, there is no reason to suppose that familism was fundamentally different several hundred thousand years ago from what it is at present. (This statement can neither be proved nor disproved, but is of no importance [in this particular work]). Social time, or what we reckon with in human history, is the only conception of life that can ever be of any significance to us.

34. *Marriage and Family*, 61-63, for example, covers the sexual reforms by the jurist Tribonium issued at the behest of Emperor Justinian's wife Theodora, a converted prostitute. *The Family of Tomorrow* thoroughly covers the contribution of the Protestant Reformers. While his analysis of Erasmus's

hatred of the Church, Milton's atomistic bent, and Luther's dependency upon the State are all very helpful, Zimmerman is not always accurate. Naively, he blames the Reformers for not being reconciled to the Council of Trent!

35. I want to be clear: these eight points are my distillation of Zimmerman. He might want more or less; they all are *his* points, not my speculations.

36. This is *not* to imply that Western civilization in general, or the USA in particular, is without sin. But it has been uniquely blessed because of Christianity in general and Protestant Christianity in particular. Francis Schaeffer and Herbert Schlossberg have proven this point.

37. *Family and Civilization*, 806-7.

38. *International Bibliography on Research in Marriage and the Family, 1965-1972*, vol II (University of Minnesota Press, 1974), references 12,870 titles of 7,500 authors, and limits itself to research only and omits popular and hortatory material: vol 1, which covers 1900–1964, has 12,850 references. The pace of research quickens. Although most 20th century empirical research would not cover biblical times or themes, the almost *total* dearth of research, historical or otherwise, touching on biblical issues is appalling. Most family research is devoid of references to God or His views of the family: it is both brain and heart dead and in the deepest sense pagan foolishness. Obviously, I could not research all of the material, but if the titles are clues, God and His views of the family do not exist. No doubt some Christian values creep into the work of Christian researchers. While bibliographical information stopped at 1972, I doubt subsequent research shows any significant change. What research I've read fits this pattern. Samples of the *Journal of Divorce: Clinical Studies and Research in Family Therapy, Family Mediation, Family Studies and Family Law* given to me by the publisher (Haworth Press, 75 Griswold St., Binghamton, N. Y. 13904), are good examples.

39. J. Casey, *The History of the Family* (Oxford: Blackwell, 1989). This is a book in a series entitled "New Perspectives on the Past." Casey lectures at the university level about European social history.

40. Ibid., 166. P. Aries, the French sociologist mentioned in chapter 7, also warns of this.

41. Ibid., 166-7.

42. Ibid., 161-5. He agrees to a degree with Max Weber's assessment. Although he sees this and values LePlay's work, he is blind to biblical truth. He claims that the family *cannot* be defined and in and of itself is *not* important, 168. Typical of many academics, he can accumulate data, but has difficulty in explaining what it means; he gives little or no help in defining, defending or directing the family.

For the Puritan view of the family, its biblical precision, and its salutary effects on culture, the following are essential. Edmund S. Morgan's *The Puritan Family* (cited in chapter 3) is the academic classic. Allen Carden's

Puritan Christianity in America: Religion and Life in Seventeenth-Century Massachusetts (Grand Rapids: Baker, 1990) is a positive evangelical evaluation. Chapter 11, "The Cycle of Family Life" shows the richness and joy of their biblical perspective. Carden captures the wealth of their tradition in our lives. J. I. Packer's *A Quest for Godliness: The Puritan Vision of the Christian Life*, (Wheaton: Crossway, 1990), chapter 16, "Marriage and Family in Puritan Thought" has the best theological evaluation of their views. Particularly helpful is his contrasting them with the non-biblical views of Aquinas and medieval Catholicism.

This view of the family is the quintessence of the biblical view. The popular pap that is fed to Christians today is tasteless and valueless compared to the rich feast fed to parishioners in Puritan times. Although not perfect, the Puritan view is the high water mark in defining, defending and dignifying the family.

43. I doubt that he holds to a conservative position like Zimmerman. However, this only makes the case stronger.

44. The general editors are Peter Laslett, Michael Anderson and Keith Wrightson. Basil Blackwell is the English publisher of these French works.

45. *Western Sexuality: Practice and Precept in Past and Present Times*, eds. P. Aries, A. Bejin; trans. A. Forster (Oxford: Blackwell, 1985).

46. The last two essays help to show the historical roots of modern attacks upon biblical sexuality in a family context: A. Bejin's chapter 15, "The decline of the psychoanalyst and the rise of the sexologist"; chapter 16, "The influence of the sexologists and sexual democracy."

47. *The Explanation of Ideology: Family Structures and Social Systems*, E. Todd; trans. D. Garrioch (Oxford: Blackwell, 1985).

48. Ibid., preface to the English edition.

49. Ibid., 6-7.

> With Frederick LePlay (1806-82), sociologist, Catholic, reactionary, as successful in empirical research as he was hopeless in political theory, the anthropological study of the family took a decisive step. It abandoned its universalist approach and began to analyze local variations. LePlay set out a typology which included three family forms, and studied their distribution throughout Europe, from Tangiers to the Urals. One is still surprised today by the quality of the monographs which this product of the Ecole Polytechnique, and his team, produced. Not one has been invalidated or even weakened by the most recent research, whether on England, Russia, Scandinavia, Italy, France or Hungary.

50. Ibid., 17-18.

> A universal hypothesis is possible: the ideological system is everywhere the intellectual embodiment of family

structure, a transposition into social relations of the fundamental values which govern elementary human relations: liberty or equality, and their opposites, are examples. One ideological category and only one, corresponds to each family type.

Ignoring all the accepted procedures of present-day social science and at the risk of being branded a positivist, I am going to test this theory and prove it in the same way as in any exact science: by exhaustively comparing the hypothesis and evidence, that is by a complete examination of the familial and ideological systems experienced by the settled human groups which make up at least 95 per cent of the population of the planet. Testing the theory involves two steps.

First, a general typology of family structure must be devised. It must be both logically exhaustive, starting from first principles and setting out all the possible family structures; and empirically exhaustive, that is to say taking into account and describing all the family forms which are actually observable on the surface of the planet.

Second, it must be shown that to each family form described there corresponds one and only one ideological system and that this ideological system is not to be found in areas of the world which are dominated by other family forms (in mathematical terms one would speak of a bijective relationship between family types and political types).

A further requirement is that secondary variations in family structure within each anthropological type must correspond to secondary variations in the political or religious forms within the corresponding ideological type.

51. Todd reluctantly praises LePlay whom he sees as a Catholic reactionary to the revolution and a hopeless political failure (endnote 49). Todd is indifferent to issues of ideology as truth; Christianity is no better than others (2; 167). History cannot teach us ideological truth, since a blind, irrational mechanism controls the universe and history (196). He loves Freud (38 and elsewhere), and approves of incest (176-177). One cannot accuse him of a biblical bias!

52. E. Todd; trans. R. Boulind, *The Causes of Progress: Culture, Authority and Change* (Oxford: Blackwell, 1987).

53. Ibid., x.

54. He does not give a full enough explanation for one to judge the merits of his definition of progress. Although his view has some merit, it may suffer from oversimplification.

55. Ibid., xi.

56. Ibid., 21-2. Reality is more complex than he allows. The family is basic and starts cultural change, yet it interacts with cultural changes. At least, Todd realizes his position on this is not as strong as his first work.

57. Ibid., 47. See also *The Explanation of Ideology*, 65-66, where he says that Lutheran, Presbyterian Protestantism and Judaism all have authoritarian family structure.

58. Ibid., 60-2. He goes on to conclude:

> The Weber-Sombart debate over the respective roles of Protestantism and Judaism in the development of capitalism at this point loses any significance it may once have had. Analogous family structures give rise to the same obsessive concern for education and for individual fulfillment, and hence the same cultural dynamic. This explains the very great role that adherents of these two religious faiths have played in Europe's economic development. But every people—and every culture—that possesses an authoritarian family structure displays this cultural and economic dynamic when circumstances permit it. In Latin America, for example, several nuclei of Basque settlements detached from traditional Catholicism act as local elites within an anthropological environment itself less authoritarian and less feminist than Basque culture.
>
> The varied codifications of family life contained within the Pentateuch probably go back to the ninth century before Christ (when they were put down in writing), a date not excluding the possibility they are much older still. The earliest evidence for authoritarian family structures thus predates the takeoff of northern Europe by 2,500 years at the least. Hence this same anthropological structure—a very stable one—appears to bring about historical advance at all stages of mankind's development, without itself being substantially modified by the passage of time.
>
> The authoritarian family is present when the concept appears for the first time of a lineal Time leading mankind in a given direction (ninth century BC, at the latest). Likewise, it provides the anthropological backcloth for the takeoff of northern Europe—first cultural, then economic (fifteenth to nineteenth centuries AD). Further, it constitutes the traditional model for the first industrial rivals to face Europe: Japan and Korea (twentieth century AD).

It is disturbing that beneath all this apparent change and progress this constant is to be observed ever present. But this must be considered as a more general phenomenon; examination of cultural takeoff in the Third World likewise reveals a persistence of very old geographical and ethnological factors.

This is an amazing statement from a non-Christian scholar!

59. Many historical studies on the family, limited to particular periods and places, complement Zimmerman's framework. However, a Christian reader must always discern the writer's presuppositions to avoid adopting a pagan view of history. The most comprehensive work is probably the series edited by Philippe Aries and Georges Duby, *A History of Private Life* (Cambridge: The Belknap Press of Harvard University Press). Volume 1, *From Pagan Rome to Byzantium* (1987), highlights the family and related issues in the Roman Empire, in later antiquity when the Augustinian west interacted with the monasticism of the eastern deserts, and in the early Middle Ages both in the West and Byzantine Empire. Volume 2, *Revelations of the Medieval World* (1988), covers the family in feudal times and shows how the trustee family replaced the atomistic Roman family. Volume 3, *Passions of the Renaissance* (1989), covers the family during the new quest for learning. The Protestant view of family life and worship are of special note. Volume 4, *From the Fires of Revolution to the Great War* (1990), records the development of the nuclear atomistic family in modern western Europe. Volume 5, *Riddles of Identity in Modern Times* (1991), highlights the twentieth century after the First World War.

Of particular interest in volume 5 is the last essay by Elaine Tyler May, "Myths and Realities of the American Family," a mixture of fact and conventional liberal social science wisdom to which Appendix 6 alludes. May's mainstream cultural analysis is biased towards liberal feminism. She assumes that sociological norms are statistically determined and that the toleration of new family arrangements is good. One can only suppose these arrangements would apply to any and all forms, including homosexual couples and homosexual adoptive parents. She denies that the family is the basis of society, approves of feminism, denigrates the neo-right's responses to it and sees the nuclear family as a product of Victorian myths, urbanization and industrialization. Her major use of movies to define cultural values is dubious at best. (See K. L. Billingsley, *The Seductive Image* [West Chester: Crossway, 1989].) Her trite recital of conventional wisdom on teenage pregnancy and abortion is expected but not accurate. (See S. and M. Olasky, *More Than Kindness* [Wheaton: Crossway, 1990].) She seems totally oblivious to Zimmerman and the history recorded in volumes 1-4.

60. Todd's research underscores the truth of LePlay and Zimmerman. Two critical issues need to be noted. First, Todd's work should hold true for

all cultures since it is based upon studies of 95 percent of the world's population (*The Explanation of Ideology*, 17). His data is more broad-based than Zimmerman's and includes many simple cultures. Second, like Zimmerman, Todd proves more than he realizes: the domestic type of family with the proper authority structure *must be* yoked together with biblical Christianity for cultural stability and growth. However, like Zimmerman, he myopically focuses on the proper family type to the exclusion of truth, religious values and faith. Therefore, he evaluates Germany's postwar economic growth and the USA's decline solely as functions of family type.

Germany is an example of the correct family type yoked to improper theology and ideology. Todd correctly notes that the Lutheran view of the family is the correct authoritarian type that is necessary for cultural growth. However, he fails to see the religious, ideological slide from Lutheran theology into liberal, Hegelian, dialectical idealism which results in Prussian, then Nazi Statism. Germany illustrates that the correct family type coupled with an improper faith commitment leads to a totalitarian state that tyrannizes and kills. Todd, in both books, sees the importance of family type but is indifferent to faith commitments. Thus he is only partially correct in his analysis of Germany.

The USA, on the other hand, is an example of the incorrect family type yoked to a pietistic Christianity. Todd sees in Puritan New England's Calvinistic view of the family the authoritarian type necessary for growth. Todd notes the shift to the atomistic type now prevalent in the USA. However, he fails to see the religious, ideological slide that resulted in a highly visible but weakened Christian moral base. Pietistic revivals and German liberal theology diluted Christianity in America. Progressive education modeled on Germany attacked the biblical content and parental control of education. As the moral base of the USA began to shake, both the family and the country suffered. The resulting society is a schizophrenic hybrid between pure atomistic individualism and a socialistic state. The USA illustrates that an incorrect family type coupled with a weak, but true, Christianity leads to a fragmented, weakened, dying culture. Todd, perhaps more than Zimmerman, proves that the domestic family type with its proper authority structure yoked to a vital, biblical, Reformation-based Christianity protects and stimulates cultural growth. God's Word and His providential dealings with Western culture confirm the necessity of this dynamic duo.

CHAPTER 10

The Family in Non-Western Culture

We focus on Western culture because God has caused the gospel to influence it for several millennia. However, we need to examine the family in other cultures for several reasons:

- Ethnic Europeans are a minority of the world's population.
- God controls the whole human race and its entire history.[1]
- Western culture interacts with many language groups and their subcultures [2](come to Los Angeles or New York if you need proof!).
- We live in the gospel age (Babel has been reversed by the cross of Christ and Pentecost[3]) and any help in understanding other cultures, family types and individuals will aid evangelism.
- We may live to see the center of Christianity and evangelism shift to the third world. Christianity is struggling in Europe and North America. Even though the gates of hell will not prevail against God, His anointed and His covenant people,[4] there is no guarantee that Western culture will survive.

What is life like in cultures devoid of the gospel and the proper family type? The Chinese culture is a prime case study.[5] Population size and cultural influence warrant examination of this example.

Ancient Chinese society was built on two key concepts: one, a trustee type of family. The family expanded in three concentric circles: family, kin, clan.[6] The father had enormous power and the oldest male member of the clan was the head who officiated in ancestor worship, marriage and funerals.[7] The clan held power over its families and the individuals in them through ancestor worship.[8] This system profoundly affected relationships within the family as defined by Confucianism.[9] Love and marriage had nothing to do with each other,[10] and women's lives were bitter,[11] as symbolized in the horrendous custom of bound feet. The clan owned the family and its individual members, in many ways tyrannizing and imprisoning them.[12]

The family existed solely for the purpose of keeping the society and state alive and healthy.[13] Confucianism and its emphasis on the five key relationships of filial duty bound people to each other and in turn to the society and state. The totalitarian state was fed by a totalitarian family.

As Chinese culture interacted with Western culture and eventually turned to Communism, the form of government changed but not its basic totalitarian cast. Chinese culture always has been built on and for a totalitarian state.[14] Chinese culture is an example of a major non-Western culture with the wrong trustee family type, and a false ethical, religious system that leads to tyranny and destruction.[15]

Indian society represents another large segment of the world's population. Although different from Chinese society, there are enough similarities to warrant parallel conclusions.

Ancient Indian culture was a result of the intermingling of Aryans and ancient Dasas. The culture's ideas, beliefs and family customs were captured in the early Vedic Hymns.[16] Three main structures shaped it:[17] linguistic regions, castes, a trustee type of family. The first two helped to reinforce the third. The patriarchal powers that typify a trustee system accumulated. In fact, there are enough similarities with other manifestations of trusteeism for Zimmerman and Unnithan to say:

> The family conditions and legends as well as its basic structure are almost identical in India, on the one hand, and in the regions adjacent to it both on the West and East. This applies on the East to the group of countries who have

> the Confucianist legends (such as China and Japan) as well as to Southeastern Asia where Polynesian, Indian and Chinese culture traits are mixed. It applies equally well to the European–Mediterranean area where the same legends and basic family organization appear under different names and guises.
>
> Thus, the family is the basic social institution and that form of social organization is, with minor variations, the same in both East and West. However, we add two ideas of importance. The joint family appeared in temporal relation to the rigid caste structure and to the derogation of the female. Insofar as that is important the joint family will weaken with the reduction of casteism and subjection of females. Further the joint family is largely antithetical to the problems of overpopulation and complete modernization of the economy and government of India.[18]

The Indians did not bind their wives' feet, but they did immolate widows on their husbands' funeral biers. The Indians did not have Confucian ethics, but their Hindu polytheism and Buddhist quietism led to a culture that denigrates man as the image bearer of God. Indians, who are humans, starve, as sacred cows eat their food.

Many more examples could be given. Strict Islamic cultures produce holy wars and treat women as nonpersons. The Mayan culture encouraged slavery and human sacrifice. Pagan culture devoid of the gospel and committed to the wrong family type leads to slavery and oppression.

Todd's two books raise another question: What happens to a culture devoid of the gospel that maintains a reasonably proper family type? Japan is a prime example.[19] The explosive growth of post-World War II Japan can be explained partially by its family structure. However, Todd ignores the totalitarian emperor worship that helped lead to World War II. Germany and Japan were totalitarian allies. The structurally proper family type alone, without Christianity, leads to tyranny.[20] Just as God's law cannot bring life without the Holy Spirit, so the formally correct family type without Christianity cannot breathe life into a culture.

The gospel, taken seriously in all its implications, will liberate not only individuals, but families and whole cultures. Too long we've heard that we must not export our value system into the third world. Leftist academics tell us not to impose our views: Coke, computers and Jane Fonda are O.K.; the Bible, Christianity, and the proper family type are not. Which God and which set of values will save man and society? Individuals, families, governments and cultures are lost without Christ.

Too many Christian academics teach the same prevarications—some consciously, some unwittingly. Of course we must be sensitive not to transfer our *sinful* distortions of Christianity into the third world. But under the guise of research, these Christian scholars have the hubris to denigrate conservative, biblical, God-centered views and to export ideas that are liberal, liberationist, and humanistic. Third world Christians do not need liberals condoning homosexuality; they have enough AIDS as it is. They do not need evangelicals pushing egalitarian marriage; they can destroy their families in their own time-honored ways. If the West has anything of lasting value, it is not movies, cars or Magic Johnson; it is the eternal gospel of Jesus Christ. Only as He sovereignly brings His whole counsel to bear on a people will its culture change.[21]

Notes:

Chapter 10

1. Deut 7:7-11; 1 Cor 1:26-31.

2. Even within Western culture, a variety of family types and sub-types exist: G. Barna, *The Future of the American Family* (Chicago: Moody, 1993), chapter 8, "Minority Families"; "The New Black Family," *Ebony*, vol XLVIII, no 10 (Aug. 1993).

3. Acts 2:1-42; Eph 2:11-22.

4. Ps 2; Revelation.

5. My primary sources are: one, Zimmerman's works (see Chapter 9); two, career missionaries ministering among ethnic Chinese; three, Olga Lang's classic *Chinese Family and Society* (New Haven: Yale University, 1946), xii. This is an excellent study from an avowedly pro-communist perspective.

6. Lang, op cit., 13.

7. Ibid., 26.

8. Ibid., 18-9.

9. Ibid., Part I, chapter 3.

10. Ibid., Part I, chapter 4.

11. Ibid., Part I, chapter 5; 332-3.

12. Ibid., 56.

13. Ibid., Part I, chapter 6.

14. Lang is too pro-communist to see the danger of dissolving the old Chinese family and society and replacing it with a modern collectivistic state. Todd, closer to reality, shows that the totalitarian tyranny of the family dictates the same in government but fails to see the inherent evil in this type of society.

15. Zimmerman, *Family and Civilization* (New York: Harper and Brothers, 1947), chapter 5, "The Family of Civilization" gives examples from ancient cultures: Egyptian, Eastern Mediterranean, Semitic as well as Islamic, Hindu and Chinese. His point is that they are basically the same. See also Zimmerman and Unnithan, *Family and Civilization in the East and the West: With Particular Reference to India and the USA* (Bombay: Thacker & Co., 1975), Chapter 5, "The Family is Fundamentally the Same in the East and the West." Unnithan, D. Litt., is an Indian scholar and researcher. He was educated in India, England (Cambridge) and Holland (Utrecht). He has taught at several Indian universities and lectured in many countries.

16. Ibid., 68-70.

17. Ibid., Chapter 6, "Studies in the Indian Family System," 67-87. Irawati Karve, *Kinship Organization in India*, 3rd ed. (South Asia Books, 1968) is credited for this observation, 70.

18. Ibid., 87.

19. Obviously the Japanese family type is not the biblically-defined

domestic type. However, there are some similarities even if they are only on the formal level.

20. In chapter 9 we saw this to be true in Western countries; it is true in the East as well. Again Zimmerman is correct: the West and East are similar.

21. As the gospel spreads, the transformation evidenced in Western culture may be repeated. Watch South Korea. Although Confucianism has tyrannized the family, the rapid spread of Christianity has the potential for transforming the Korean family, government and society. If so, Korea's growth will be long-lasting, whereas Japan's will fade if the culture continues to harden itself to the gospel. I must repeat that Western culture is not pure. The Reformation and the Enlightenment intertwined with each other to produce a hybrid culture. We must separate the biblical Reformation elements from the rebellious Enlightenment ones. Cultural agnosticism is no aid to the third world. They do not need a corrupt Romans 2 culture to replace their particular brand of Romans 1 culture! For some powerful, pithy ponderings on the centrality of the gospel to Western culture as it interacts with non-Christian religions and cultures, see A. Kayayan, "Tolerance or Betrayal," *The Outlook*, vol 42, no 11 (Dec. 1992), 10-11. Kayayan directs us to Christ in the midst of cultural conflicts but with historical perspective that most of us miss.

For an insightful analysis of how the gospel brings temporal, cultural and eternal blessings, see R. S. Greenway, "The Religion of Gravestones," *The Outlook*, vol 43, no 1 (Jan. 1993), 23. Brief, short-term mission work in Suriname and Uganda convinced me of how gospel-poor societies are impoverished by a lack of biblical input. Polytheism and polygamy are a deadly duo.

Section 4

~

WHERE'S THE BATTLE?

~

CHAPTER 11

The Family's Internal Battle

Joe is a hard-working owner of several lucrative businesses and is a former small college All-American in football and baseball who graduated with honors. Julie, his wife, was a cheerleader at his college and is now involved in several social clubs and civic organizations. Joe relentlessly presses his son Joe, Jr. to succeed athletically and scholastically. Julie tries to shield young Joe from the pressure. Joe Jr. dislikes school and detests sports, but loves the arts and theater. Dad yells, son rebels, fists fly, mom cries. All four now sit silent, brooding in my office as they wait for help. Families have battles—even Christian families.

A House Divided

Jesus put it plainly when He said a house, city or kingdom cannot be divided and stand.[1] Divisions start in human hearts as warring passions which pour out in open conflict, killing unity and destroying stability. The inward seeds of selfish ambition, envy and coveting sprout into a tangle of thorny weeds: disorder, evil behavior, quarrels and fights.[2] Before a family can face external enemies, it must resist the mutiny in its own ranks. Each family faces an unholy trinity—the world, the flesh and the devil—but the flesh is its number one enemy.[3]

One day I ran outside my office to see who was shouting: Lou and his wife Sheri were verbally vilifying each other. Lou had removed the battery from his wife's car to stop her from driving off. As I arrived, Sheri ran off down the street crying, "Leave me alone! Get away from me!" As I talked to Lou, he swore that his wife refused to talk calmly and had hit him. Lou had calmed down, but suddenly, he bolted after Sheri. Knowing his anger and sensing danger, I told my secretary to call the police and went after them. When I found them a block away, Sheri was still crying and Lou stood handcuffed near a highway patrolman who had noticed Lou grabbing Sheri by her clothes and neck. Soon the police arrived and took charge. Sheri refused to file charges, so the police replaced her battery and she left. As I drove him to his friend's apartment, Lou insisted that Sheri was at fault. Like many violent husbands, and like many nonviolent, normal sinners, Lou shifted the blame. We have not come far from the garden. We still point "Adam and Eve fingers," (as one kindergarten teacher I know calls them) at one another. Now, as in Eden, blameshifting to cover our sin doesn't work.[4] How we love to blame God and other family members for our disobedience!

A Heart Divided

Like the prodigal son who came to his senses and admitted his sin against heaven and his father,[5] so too family members must come to their senses, experience reconciliation with God and each other and then recognize, resist and replace their sinful desires.[6] After God gave me a new heart, just prior to getting married, I went to my father and asked to be forgiven for my rebellion and disobedience; I wanted to start my marriage and family with a clean slate. I was startled by the results: he forgave me, we got along better, and above all, he treated me like an adult. Although I was twenty-six, I had not yet acted like a man. I had continually spurned his advice and become the classic fool of Proverbs. Up to that point, I had blamed him, my mom, sister, teachers, referees or any other available scapegoat. Yet, blameshifting and covering up with fake fig leaves never has kept out the cold or the piercing stare of the holy God.

A family, like an individual, cannot get help if it does not cease to shift blame, come to its senses and face up to its sins. Family members must confess sin before they can fellowship with God and each other.[7] Of course, you know this, don't you? Maybe not. Today, most people, and many Christians, think that family problems, like personal problems, are the result of a psychological or sociological sickness. Therefore, a family with problems needs professional help from a psychologist, marriage-family-child therapist or licensed social worker because the family is dysfunctional or co-dependent, not selfish or sinful. (See Appendix 7.)

Sin, Not Sickness

God does not define families as sick but as sinful. Godliness affects health,[8] but God does not guarantee perfect health until the new heavens and earth.[9] Jesus does promise, however, that His blood washes away all sins—now. The presence of the Holy Spirit brings peace and reconciliation between God and man and between man and man—now.[10] God promises progressive holiness to the believer and to the believing family now.

Sin is complicated,[11] but Jesus and His atonement face the complexities of sin.[12] There are at least four major implications of sin in our lives.

*Sin includes the **imputation** of Adam's sin to us.*[13]

Because Adam was the federal or covenant head of the human race, his sin is imparted to all of us. We are under God's wrath because our head rebelled. (We have something of this notion in our representative form of government, in which a congressman votes for his constituency.)

Jesus Christ, the second Adam, lived and died in the place of His people as their federal or covenant head.[14] His work is imputed, or applied to us by God and we receive it through faith. His life perfectly satisfied God's high demands for holiness and His death appeased God's holy anger against sin.[15] Because of

Christ's work, God removes us from the "dysfunctional," cursed family of humanity and adopts us into His own loving, unified family.[16] Christ takes care of the corporate aspects of sin; we have a new head and family.

*Sin has **individual** implications.*

Also, He takes care of the individual aspects of sin. Because of sin, each person inherits a corrupt, morally rotten nature.[17] Man is totally depraved or corrupt in all aspects of his being. While each individual is not as bad as he could be, there exists no one righteous, not even one; moreover, there is no part of any of us that is righteous, unscathed by sin's corruption. At the Father's word, by the Holy Spirit's regenerating, recreative power, we come alive. We repent and believe in the Risen Lord Jesus Christ.[18] With new hearts, new natures, we have new capabilities for pleasing God. Our natural birth bequeaths us with fallen, rebellious natures; our spiritual new birth gives us holy ones. Christ takes care of the problem of human nature because He gives us hearts like His to do the Father's will.

*Inherent to sin is its **habitual** character.*[19]

Paul says that whoever gives himself over to sin becomes its slave. Our risen Lord Jesus Christ, through the Holy Spirit, empowers us to put to death this old personality or character—to take it off, like a dirty shirt. The Holy Spirit enables us to put on a new one.[20] Thus, we are conformed to Jesus, not to our former father, the devil[21].

*Sin includes conscious, willful **choices** to disobey.*[22]

There are times when Christians consciously rebel, yet the Holy Spirit teaches us to delight in love for our Lord and obedience to Him.[23] Jesus teaches us to delight in the Father's will just as He does.

Christians can rejoice greatly. Our Lord and Savior breaks

the power of sin on all of these levels. This brings genuine lasting hope both to individuals and families.[24]

The Christian Family: Armed for Conflict

The resurrected, exalted Jesus Christ gives a family three essential weapons with which to win the battle that rages under its roof.

1. He gives us the sword of the Spirit, His Word.[25]

In His Word, the Bible, God tells us *what* to do (*what* He requires, *what* He blesses, *what* works, *what* brings peace and joy), as well as *how* to do it.

What to Do for Your Family

A young salesman struggling in his family life, Tom was failing as a husband and father. Although a Christian, he was desperate and thought that divorce or death was his only option. Tom's family were pagans and his father had been a drunken, violent man who committed suicide. As we studied Ephesians 5:21–6:4 in the light of Christ's love and suffering for Tom, he came to see that he should lay down his life for his wife and children. The Holy Spirit softened him. He repented of his self-pity, fear and idolatry, received fresh mercy from Jesus, and began to learn how to put God and others first. Near the end of counseling, Tom commented with tears of joy that he had never known what God wanted of him.

How to Do It

Jesus gives us details of *how* to do the *what.* Though we discover these principles in the Word, they are more than "instructions." We do receive detailed instruction and many insights about how to obey them. For example, in His Sermon on the Mount, Jesus tells his disciples how and how not to give alms, pray and fast.[26] But the word also gives us living models.

Jesus lived among normal people in a real village and a historical country. He Himself models perfectly what God expects of us. The apostles he appointed modeled Him (though not perfectly), serving as patterns of how to live a godly life.[27]

Ben was a typical Southern California softball addict. He played two or three nights a week and participated often in weekend tournaments. His wife and children lived like a widow and orphans. When Ben became a Christian, he realized that his poor leadership was causing problems at home. He knew what he should do, but did not know how, so he came to me for help. Today Ben is a godly husband and father; sports serve him, instead of ruling him. What made the change? Godly coaching. Ben studied the gospels, which focus on Christ's sacrifice for His disciples, and submitted to discipleship and accountability under some godly ex-sports-idolaters.

2. *Jesus provides* the lifegiving Holy Spirit.[28]

Our Lord's perfect life, substitutionary death, resurrection and ascension to glory enabled Him to replace us, to represent us before God.[29] The Holy Spirit, called a Counselor in the Bible, gives us *power* to do *what* God requires in the *way* He wants it done. The Holy Spirit is the Spirit of power, love and discipline.[30] Without His work, the instructions, as good as they are, kill us.[31]

Sue was an independent, stubborn child who ran away from her religious family at fourteen, and entered a life of drugs, prostitution and pornography. She used anger, revenge, drinking, abortion and attempted suicide as weapons to control others. She left her life of crime and married, but used the same weapons against her husband. She knew she was wrong, but justified her selfishness. Today, Sue is a Christian, has a Christian husband, a lovely baby and worships and serves the living God. While not perfect, she is a radically new woman, learning to be a godly wife, mother and servant of Jesus. The Holy Spirit took hold of her, washed her in Jesus' blood, set her apart to serve God, declared her innocent and empowered her to change.[32]

3. *Jesus puts His people in a larger family,* the Church, *to encourage us to love and to obey.*[33]

Jesus commissioned the church to make disciples by baptism and teaching.[34] Evangelism and discipleship are both aspects of making disciples that produce Christlike individuals and families.

At Calvary Community Church, I required couples to receive premarital counseling. Several "mixed" marriages existed in the congregation. They were not mixed in the sense of Asian/American or Black/White, but between a believer and a nonbeliever. I cannot convey a portion of the suffering in these families, pain which convinced me never to marry a believer to an unbeliever.[35] Several engaged couples left, offended. They were married by preachers who did not share my scruples; most of them are now divorced. On the other hand, some individuals responded, were converted, baptized and now serve Christ with joy as part of that congregation. Evangelism blesses families.

My wife is a gentle, godly woman. While I was in the pastorate, several women asked her for help with their lives and families. In her weekly meetings with them, they studied prayer, prayed and set up structured homework to gain control of their lives by the Holy Spirit's power. Others heard and wanted help, so the elders decided to have a Sunday School quarter given to this program. The response was so great, they did it again the next quarter. The program was called Women in the Spirit's Control, or WISC, which led us all to call them "wiskers." Biblical discipleship blesses families.[36]

As people rely on the Lord Jesus, He deals with their sin in its fourfold manifestation by equipping them with this battery of three weapons: the Word, the Spirit, and the church. But you may query: "Does it work, really? After all, the Bible is honest about how ugly the battle in the family can be." Yes, you are correct, God does not pull punches. Ugly things exist, but so do cameos of His grace. Consider the realism and hope the Word of God gives.[37]

As discussed in chapters 6 and 7, marriage conflicts arise in:

- the definition of marriage
- the components of companionship
- the components of cooperative dominion[38]

Marriage can be painful and ugly: Samson died because of his scheming wife; drunken Nabal doubtless mistreated Abigail; wimpy Ahab refused to stand up to the godless tyrant, Jezebel; Ananias and Sapphira schemed together to look like generous philanthropists in the eyes of God's people. Even the best marriages have conflict: Abram and Sarai both laughed in God's face when he promised too much; Isaac never got rid of his inherited lying habits, which brought the worst out of Rebekah. Yet there can be a beauty in marriage that reflects the glory of Christ and His wife the Church: Salmon and Rahab; Boaz and Ruth; Zacharias and Elizabeth; Joseph and Mary; Aquila and Priscilla.

Parents and children have conflicts. Parents sin against their children: the Canaanites sacrificed their children to Molech; Moses failed to circumcise his son and God was going to kill him; Jepthah's oath hurt his daughter; Eli's, Samuel's and David's failure as fathers helped ruin their sons. Even the best families have conflict: Paul's admonitions to the Ephesians and Colossians are proof. But God's grace can make a family a beautiful reflection of the Father's love for His adopted sons: Abraham and Isaac; David and Solomon; Zacharias and John; Joseph, Mary and Jesus; Lois, Eunice and Timothy.

Parents can be the target of retaliatory hatred on the part of children. The famous California twins of the late twentieth century who murdered their parents were not the first to hate their parents. Esau married pagans to provoke his parents; Absalom tried to usurp his father's throne and destroy David's place in God's kingdom; the Pharisees stole from their parents to enrich their self-righteous self-esteem. Paul prohibits such neglect of the family in 1 Timothy 5. On the other hand, the Bible abounds with examples of children who loved and honored their parents, thus reflecting the love and honor that believers have for their Father in heaven: Isaac so trusted Abraham that he obeyed him even though it seemed it would cost him his life; Joseph longed to see his father, Jacob; Ruth was ready to leave all she knew to stay with her mother-in-law, Naomi; Jesus loved His mother enough to go to the cross, in spite of the emotional pain that it caused her.

In each of these areas of family life, Jesus is the answer to your family's sins. His gracious work provides you with the weapons without which victory is impossible. Ultimately, no other instructions, no other spirit, and no other examples can help you —only the new covenant blessings furnished by the living, triune God.[39] There is no other name under heaven by which you and your family must be saved. Your family needs God's love and presence to survive and thrive. Systems that claim to offer love and personal satisfaction without Christ, His cross, His throne, and His second coming have nothing at all to offer. Without Christ's love and power to show it, the best moral systems can only produce a legalistic Pharisaism that locks families into pride and self-centered destruction. Without Christ's law and the power to keep it, religions produce gutless, sentimental, liberal existentialism that cannot distinguish holiness from hellish Marxism or any other heathen alternative to Christianity. Yes, only through the triune God will you and your family win the battle for your souls. Then you will be ready to wage war on all the enemies that encircle you and win the battle for the family.

Notes:

Chapter 11

1. Matt 12:25-29.
2. Jam 3:13 - 4:12.
3. 1 John 2:1-17.
4. Gen 3:11-13.
5. Luke 15:17-21.
6. Mal 4:5-6; Eph 4:17-24.
7. 1 John 1:9; 3:4; 5:17.
8. Deut 28; 1 Thess 5:23; Jam 5:14-16; 3 John 2.

9. The word-of-faith movement that claims believers have inherent rights to health, wealth and prosperity destroys individuals and families. For a theological critique, see D. R. McConnell, *A Different Gospel: A Historical and Biblical Analysis of the Modern Faith Movement* (Peabody: Hendrickson, 1988). For general trends behind this and other heresies, see M. S. Horton, *The Agony of Deceit: What Some TV Preachers are Really Teaching* (Chicago: Moody, 1990); *Made in America: The Shaping of Modern American Evangelicalism* (Grand Rapids: Baker, 1991). These are in the tradition of F. Schaeffer and H. Schlossberg. Present healing is possible, but certain healing occurs only when Jesus will wipe away every tear (Rev 21:3-4).

10. Eph 2; Jam 3:13 - 4:12.

11. *The Westminster Confession of Faith*, Chaps. VI, VII, IX and *The Westminster Larger Catechism*, 21-29, are orthodox statements on the nature and results of sin.

12. Not to believe this is to deny the sufficiency of Christ and His work and is a functional form of heresy based on man's pride which leads to auto-soterism or the works-righteousness that the Protestant Reformation condemned and countered.

13. Rom 5:12-21; 1 Cor 15:20-49. See John Murray, *The Imputation of Adam's Sin* (Grand Rapids: Eerdmans, 1959).

14. Idem.

15. 1 John 2:2.

16. John 1:12-13; Rom 8:12-17.

17. Rom 2:28-29; 3:9-23; Eph 2:1-3; Titus 1:3. See J. I. Packer, *Evangelism and the Sovereignty of God* (Downers Grove: Inter Varsity, 1961).

18. John 1:12-13; 3:5-8; Rom 2:28-29; Eph 2:4-7; Titus 3:4-7; 1 Pet 1:22-25; 1 John 3:9; 5-4.

19. Rom 6. See Adams, *A Theology of Christian Counseling* (Grand Rapids: Zondervan, 1979), chapters 9-11, 14.

20. Eph 4:1-24.

21. John 8:31-47; 2 Cor 3:17-18.

22. Rom 1:21, 32.

23. John 15:10; Gal 5:22-24.

24. Jay Adams, *The War Within: A Biblical Strategy for Spiritual Warfare* (Eugene: Harvest House, 1989) is an excellent treatment of the war against sin within the Christian.

25. 2 Tim 3:15-17; Heb 4:12-13; 5:11-14.

26. Matt 6:1-34.

27. John 14:8-14; 1 Cor 4:16; 11:1; Phil 3:17; 4:9; 1 Thess 1:6; 2 Thess 3:9; Heb 13:7.

28. John 7:37-39; Acts 2:33; Gal 3:14.

29. John 14:16-18; 15:26; 16:7; 1 John 2:1; Rom 8:26.

30. 2 Tim 1:7.

31. Rom 2:28-29; Rom 7.

32. 1 Cor 6:11.

33. Eph 2:19-22; 4:7-16; Heb 10:19-25.

34. Matt 28:16-20.

35. The biblical basis for this is explained in chapter 5 and Appendix 3.

36. Titus 2:3-5.

37. Rom 4:23-24; 15:4-6; 1 Cor 10:6, 11.

38. Jay Adams, *Solving Marriage Problems: Biblical Solutions for Christian Counseling* (Grand Rapids: Zondervan, 1983). His systematic overview of problems and how to solve them is excellent. He organizes the problems around three foci: erroneous concepts, sinful attitudes, sinful practices.

39. Acts 2:14-42; 4:5-12. Note the exclusive nature of salvation. It is appalling that many evangelicals are following liberal, unitarian-universalist teaching that people can be saved apart from Jesus Christ (Appendix 2). Applied biblical principles will bring general blessings, but the Pharisees prove that principles applied by unregenerate people bring death. Christ's presence and power through the Holy Spirit are absolutely necessary if an individual or family is to be saved, to please God and to grow in holiness.

CHAPTER 12

The Family's External Battle

Many people recognize the importance of the family to society.[1] Some laud it; others lampoon it. Is there really a battle over the family, or am I fishing for an alarmist title? There is abundant evidence of battle;[2] time will tell who wins.

The Battle Is On

In Section One, we saw what is at stake; in Section Two, we noted how seldom our families conform to God's standards; in Section Three, we studied the history of the family; in Appendix 3, we will look at Satan's attack on the family and the tragic results. Modern attacks upon the family are well-documented: France in the eighteenth and nineteenth centuries; Russia and China in the twentieth century. The testimony of history is clear: the individual, the clan and the state vie for control of the family and its future. Since the 1930s, Zimmerman and others have pointed to this battle and have tried to define it.

Scholar Russell Kirk pointed to the enfeebled American family:

> After what has been done to it in China, Russia, and lesser lands, the family now knows that it is not impregnable to assault. Thus awakened to peril, the American family may devise means for the recovery of its vigor.[3]

Sociologist Gary Smith, after assessing the arguments for and against the decline of the family, says:

> To a large extent, whether one views the family to be declining or not depends upon one's evaluation of the proper structure, purposes, and duties of this institution. Those who believe that God has designed the family to propagate

> the race, regulate sex, promote human happiness and ensure the proper moral nurture of children have much reason for concern. Judged by this standard, recent developments pertaining to the incidence of divorce, "alternative living" arrangements, abuse and neglect of children, and cases of extreme poverty all significantly hurt family life. Perhaps alarmists romanticized the families of early periods of American history and exaggerate the extent to which the contemporary family has disintegrated. Nevertheless, current trends are very troublesome. Families need strengthening.[4]

The Combatants

Indeed, the battle is real. But who are the combatants? Though God's real enemy is Satan, the battle is played out (as it was for Job) on the playing field of history, in the lives of real human beings and in the four walls of our own homes. Like a lion, the devil wants to devour you and your family. Even though Jesus defeated and defanged him at the cross (proven by the resurrection and ascension), he will try to gum you and the rest of God's heroes to death, just to prove that Jesus is not the true victor. Satan uses brass knuckles in some cultures, as he did through Pharaoh in Egypt and Herod at Bethlehem. In the USA and in other Western nations he has, at least until now, taken the *Screwtape Letters* approach: he tries to lie and finesse his way to victory. What tactics does he use?

Satan uses ***individuals.***

The self-centeredness of Americans is epidemic. A woman appears on the Donahue Show who has abandoned her husband and children for a quest to find herself and is applauded as a folk heroine. With an infantry full of such foot soldiers, Satan can do great damage to the family. How does he recruit such people? Of course none of us needs much encouragement in claiming our own rights and needs. However, we always feel more comfortable if we have a moral excuse. In our day, Satan has successfully used our love of self and psychology to soothe our consciences. Paul Vitz's title says it all: *Psychology As Religion: The Cult of Self-Worship.*[5]

*Satan uses **the family**.*

The atomistic family, predominant in our society, rarely destroys its members. However, sometimes that does happen here (as it does in Islamic and Eastern families). Recently we have seen a spate of cases in which a parent has knowingly killed children. We remember the mother who drove her children into a lake to drown them.

Families can also destroy their members relationally. I counseled a Christian couple about marriage. When they announced their engagement, the woman's mother threatened to disown her if she married her fiance. All attempts by the couple, their pastor and me to find out her concerns failed and her threats kept all the woman's relatives from attending the wedding. For two years, the mother refused contact and reconciliation.

Another Christian couple had continual marital problems: the husband lacked lovingkindness; a passive wife manipulated through bitter submission. Finally, she left her husband, taking the children with her, and filed for divorce on non-biblical grounds. She stayed with her Christian parents, who offered her vast amounts of money not to return to her husband. The demons dance for joy when the family self-destructs.

*Satan uses **the Church**.*

Liberal churches think and act like the world. Their relativism, pragmatism and worldly standards teach families to make poor decisions—to condone homosexual ministers and priests, marital affairs, premarital sex, and abortion. Conservative churches are of two general types. Some evangelical churches think and act more like liberal churches. (We noted some of this thinking in chapter 2 and Appendix 2). Another type is the conservative church that holds to the inerrancy and sufficiency of Scripture, but undercuts the family's centrality in its daily behavior. These churches don't stop to think about the effects of their heavy schedule, which demands many nights away from home; or of the Sunday School, children's church and youth group, which always chop the family into age or grade slices. Naive compliance to the culture's view of the individual, of maturity and of the atomistic family kills generational cohesiveness. Church leaders also can undercut the family: youth pastors encourage teens to trust them and to communicate their desires to them, rather than to parents; pastors make passes at parishioners. I know of an evangelical church where the youth pastor ran a seminar on sex that would give values clarification a run for its money. Well-known evangelical pastors model infidelity and loose living. When Satan can find willing help within the church, why should he look elsewhere?

*Satan uses **governmental powers.***[6]

In the USA, several areas of governmental power burden the family:

Legislation and the Court System

Allen C. Carlson's *Family Questions: Reflections on the American Social Crisis*[7] is a powerful presentation of political problems surrounding the family, and is a gold mine of information on how governmental legislation has hurt the family. He covers the areas of gender, population, sexuality, economics, community, age and the state's involvement in aiding or replacing the family unit. The court system tends to support these governmental trends or even becomes a threat in its own right.

The Public Educational System

We have already noted its roots and its purpose, the replacement of family-controlled and biblically-based education.[8] Economist Thomas Sowell has analyzed the prospects of Western civilization. After arguing that Western civilization is the noblest and best, he elucidates the threats that menace it, both external and internal:

> The external military danger is only one of the threats to the survival of Western civilization. Signs of internal degeneration are both numerous and threatening—declining educational standards, the disintegration of families, drug addiction and violent crimes are just some of the more obvious signs. Will such things alone destroy a society and a civilization? Perhaps not. But the internal and external threats are not wholly separate today, any more than they were in the days of the decline and fall of the Roman Empire.[9]

He goes on to say:

> Much more active agents of demoralization are the intelligentsia, including the media, school teachers, and academics. Despite some welcome exceptions, these classes of people tend generally to take an adversary view of Western civilization. Sins and tragedies common to the human race around the world are discussed by them as if they were peculiarities of Western civilization.[10]

Later he says:

> Why intellectuals have so often repudiated their own country and civilization in the West is a large question on which there are many theories. Perhaps it is precisely the freedom of the common man in the West, including his ability to ignore intellectuals and live his life as he pleases, that has made intellectuals look so favorably on so many foreign despotisms that impose a massive blueprint from the top down. These despotisms to which many leading Western intellectuals give praise, have included both Imperial Russia and China and Communist Russia and China. They have included despots from Robespierre to Stalin to Castro, all of whom have been romanticized by intellectuals.[11]

The political agenda of politically correct thinking[12] and the social agenda of social planners as taught through sex education[13] are only two examples of unbiblical thinking which puts pressure on the family structure. We feel in the nineties the effects of a social revolution which took place in the sixties. In high school in the 1960s, my wife was taught to mistrust all authority, and especially her parents, who were conservative Mennonites in Pennsylvania Dutch country; her teacher was educated by and taught in the state system.

Governmental Licensing and Bureaucracy[14]

Heavy-handed government interference usurps the family's authority and independent initiative. Again, examples abound: counseling is taken from family members and the church and handed to state-licensed pagan practitioners and state-funded institutions;[15] family mercy and Christian diaconal work are taken over by the social welfare departments, headed and staffed by state-licensed social workers;[16] discipline for family sin in child abuse is taken from the family and church and placed in the hands of the Child Protective Services.[17]

A Christian man, a well-respected junior high principal of a public school, had the C.P.S. take his children. Why? His children were loved and loved him in return, but someone found out that he spanked them. Anonymous calls awakened the sleeping giant; the bureaucracy took the children, even though they had no desire to go. Only court action returned them to their parents. This kind of statist intrusion is not limited to the United States.[18]

My wife and I once served as foster parents to twins. While in the training classes, I tried to find out why we were permitted to spank our own children but not the foster children. The state licensed instructor, who was the placement supervisor for our county, agreed that this divided the discipline in the home but her solution was to stop spanking our five. During our rather lively talk, she informed me of the following principles: spanking *is* child abuse; qualified homosexual couples *should be allowed* to be foster parents (they were some of the finest she knew); some people do not know when to stop having children; fundamentalist types like me are the worst abusers in the county;

she could (and she implied that she *would*) prevent foster children from being placed in our home. So much for benign neutrality; justice is no longer blindfolded, just blind.

Satan uses:

- *popular culture*[19], *such as the media*[20]

My wife is very active in the pro-life movement and has directed the Center for Unplanned Pregnancy. Several times, she appeared on the evening news, which you can imagine our family watched keenly. All biblical references were edited out; more often than not, the editing distorted what she said. She has refused to give interviews because of this distortion and several interviewers have promised not to distort her words only to break their word; few have proven trustworthy.

Parents magazine commissioned a public opinion poll to find out if parents think that society is morally bankrupt.[21] Eighty percent said yes; seventy-five percent said that things are getting worse. Yet the author of the article says that right versus wrong is rarely black-and-white and quotes ethicist Christina Hoff Sommers, Associate Professor of Philosophy at Clark University: "I would have expected everybody to have done something unethical; we're human after all; we're not saints." The message from the media comes through loud and clear: families can fudge on fidelity to truth.

- *entertainment and economic interests*

Companies want to make money. Fine. However, they often exploit the family. Little children watch the Smurfs with the soft occultism and are inundated with manipulative commercials geared to create lust for toys. Teens are solicited to sensuality and sex by Jordache commercials.[22] Burger King teaches that it is O.K. to break the rules. Parents are urged to lust after material things; men to desire women other than their wives. I won't take time to deal with movies.[23] Rock groups openly attack parental wisdom and authority. You parents could fill pages with examples.

♦ *private industry*

In Southern California, there is a proliferation of in-house treatment centers geared to help troubled families. New facilities or empty wings of hospitals are utilized for "Christian" treatment centers. At one of these centers, run by nationally known evangelicals, a young lady in her early twenties whose parents I had helped, was treated for anorexic behavior by Christian therapists who encouraged her to digress to her early childhood and to throw food and temper tantrums. Even more startling was the staff's permission and encouragement to her to blameshift: she hated her parents, blamed them for her woes, and did not want to talk with them. Yet, Dad and Mom were picking up the tab for her month of therapy— $20,000, not including the gratuity! Such "cures" destroy the health, unity and financial stability of families.

♦ *voluntary groups*

Even well-meaning organizations set up to help families can end up unintentionally hurting them when structured non-biblically. Our son has played soccer with AYSO,[24] a volunteer organization structured around families. I coached and refereed and have seen families frazzled as they try to get three children to different fields for their games. Although the organization emphasizes family time, large families do not always reap the benefits.

A magazine correctly had "Attack on the Family" emblazoned on its cover.[25] You cannot imagine the amount of effort and ink spent on the family. Every reformer in the history of Western civilization has known that the family is the basic cultural building block, which makes it the primary target in any cultural battle. You and I must engage the enemy: God's glory and your good depend on it. Chapters 2-4 are correct; the stakes are high. Satan is your foe and wants to destroy you, your family, your church, your country and your cultural heritage, and has all the above tools at his disposal.

How Are We to Win?

Jesus Christ is our Commander, the Lord of hosts. As He once stood outside of Jericho with Joshua, so He now stands with us,[26] and therefore, we must be courageous.[27] As David perceived so clearly and shouted to Goliath, "The battle is the Lord's."[28] King Jesus will give us the strategy and the strength, as He did for Joshua and David.[29] Our great Captain will lead us to victory because He conquered death and destruction at His resurrection and has ascended to sit on the throne, from which he will return on the clouds in glory. Until then, we need to pray, to develop a battle plan, to put on the armor of God and to go out to war.

Notes:

Chapter 12

1. See William J. Bennett, "The Importance of the Family to Society," given when he was the United States Secretary of Education to the Fourth Annual meeting of Networking Community Based Services, Washington, D.C., June 10, 1986. Reprinted by Family Research Council, 801 G Street NW, Washington, D.C. 20001.

2. See O. R. Johnston's analysis in *Who Needs the Family*? (Downer's Grove: InterVarsity, 1979), chap. 5 "Family Decay—Roots and Reconstruction." Also, B. and P. L. Berger, *The War Over the Family* (New York: Doubleday, 1984).

3. R. Kirk, "The Enfeebled American Family," *Special Report* #13, June 1981 (Public Policy Education Fund, Inc., Box 123, Grove City, Pa. 16127), 4.

4. G. R. Smith, "The Decline of the Family: Myth or Reality?" *Special Report* #33, March 1986, (Public Policy Education Fund, Inc., Box 123, Grove City, Pa., 16127).

5. P. C. Vitz, *Psychology as Religion: The Cult of Self* (Grand Rapids: Eerdmans, 1977). See also Jay Adams, *The Biblical View of Self-Esteem, Self-Love, Self-Image* (Eugene: Harvest, 1986). See also excellent works that read like C. S. Lewis: W. K. Kilpatrick, *Psychological Seduction: The Failure of Modern Psychology* (Nashville: Nelson, 1983); *The Emperor's New Clothes: The Naked Truth about the New Psychology* (Westchester: Crossway, 1985).

6. Satanic attempts to control the family were mentioned in chapter 9 in connection with Zimmerman's work. For Christian consideration of this vital issue see: R. R. Sutton, *Who Owns the Family? God or the State?* (Ft. Worth: Dominion Press, 1986); Blair Adams, *Who Owns the Children? Public Compulsion, Private Responsibility and the Dilemma of Ultimate Authority* (Waco: Truth Forum, 1991) 5th ed. (Truth Forum's orthodoxy is questionable); G. Grant, M. Horne, *Legislating Immorality* (Chicago: Moody/ Legacy, 1993); J. W. Whitehead, *State vs. Parents: Threats to Raising Your Children* (Chicago: Moody, 1995). The best is George Grant, *The Family Under Seige: What the New Social Engineers Have in Mind for You and Your Children* (Minneapolis: Bethany House Pub., 1994).

7. Allen C. Carlson, *Family Questions: Reflections on the American Social Crisis* (New Brunswick: Transaction, 1988). Carlson's crisp critiques are clear and precise. Although, his overall approach is very helpful it is flawed: he states, XVI:

> To begin with, the author believes that a central purpose of human existence—perhaps *the* central purpose—is the reproduction of the species. This belief derives from

> readings of the natural law and the disciplines of sociology, psychology, anthropology, genetics, and biology. The family serves as the source, protector, and incubator of these human children. All other institutions, be they economic, educational, social, or political, exist to support, preserve, or defend that primary social form.

God and His Word are missing. Carson reads like a young Bloom, and thinks like a young Zimmerman. I only wish such brilliance would call upon God and His wisdom. Man's wisdom, no matter how wise and moral, cannot save the family.

8. See chapter 7, notes 82-84.

9. T. Sowell, "Western Civilization: Prospects and Dangers" *Special Report* #55, December 1989 (Public Policy Education Fund, Inc., Box 123, Grove City, Pa., 16127). This is a speech delivered by Dr. Sowell to faculty and students at Grove City College in Pennsylvania.

10. Idem.

11. Ibid., 4-5. The two Humanist Manifestos prove the anti-family and anti-Christian bias of most of the intelligentsia in the Western world: *Humanist Manifestos I and II* (Buffalo: Prometheus, 1973). Sowell points to the intellectuals. Some are in the educational system or the media; some are not. Paul Johnson, *Intellectuals* (New York: Harper & Row, 1988), chronicles the moral turbidity and vapidity of these men and women. Many are self-appointed cultural messiahs who are covenantal pariahs. To read of their personal lives is to plunge into a moral cesspool; after surfacing one longs for a fresh application of the cleansing blood of Jesus and the purifying water of the Holy Spirit.

12. See Appendix 6.

13. See J. L. Fletcher, Jr., "Sex Education and the Biblical Christian," *Journal of Biblical Ethics in Medicine*, 4:2 (1990), 21-29. Fletcher, a medical doctor, presents biblical and statistical data that prove public sex education has failed.

14. See Sowell, op. cit., 4, note 9, concerning bureaucracy. The state is a threat to freedom when it tries to control the family, the church, or functions of these two God-ordained institutions. State licensing accomplishes this control. This danger is portrayed by the Apostle John in Revelation. To grasp this danger, see B. Adams, op. cit. in note 6, "Licensing and Authority", 70-74; "The Church and the State", 172-200; "Limits to State Authority", 201-214.

For some of the economic effects of licensing, see Simon Rottenberg, "Occupational Licensing," Special Report #18, May 1982 (Public Policy Education Fund, Box 123, Grove City, PA 16127); G. Grant, *The Quick and the Dead: RU - 486 and the New Chemical Warfare Against Your Family* (Wheaton: Crossway, 1991).

15. See Appendix 7. Also, G. Grant, *Grand Illusions: The Legacy of Planned Parenthood* (Franklin: Adroit, 1988, 1992); *Trial and Error: The American Civil Liberty Union and Its Impact on Your Family* (Franklin: Adroit, 1989, 1993).

16. Yale historian Catherine J. Ross says that the liberal welfare state replaced religious charities with a professional, therapeutic model that is often paternalistic. "The Lessons of the Past: Defining and Controlling Child Abuse in the United States," in *Child Abuse: An Agenda for Action*, ed. G. Gerbner, C. J. Ross, E. Ziegler (N.Y.: Oxford U., 1980). For a Christian perspective, see John Sparks, "The American Tradition of Voluntary Charity—A Model to be Imitated" (Special Report #22, June 1983. Public Policy Education Fund, Inc.); George Grant, *Bringing in the Sheaves* (Brentwood: Wolgemuth and Hyatt, 1988).

17. For documentation of this danger, see M. Pride, *The Child Abuse Industry: Outrageous Facts About Child Abuse and Everyday Rebellions Against a System that Threatens Every North American Family* (Westchester: Crossway, 1986); J. W. Whitehead, *Parents' Rights* (Westchester: Crossway, 1985). I do not want to imply that the state should *never* be involved. However, the state cannot bring people to repentance and should not step in unless the family and the church have failed, because all the state can properly do is punish (Rom 13:1-6). When the state tries to take over the job of the family and the church, it senses its own inability and turns to state licensed counselors who label sin as sickness; it replaces ordained ministers by state licensed medical practitioners—but people do not change without the power of God, so everyone despairs of true grace and holiness.

18. See R. E. Schmidt, "Children's Gulag: Sweden's Welfare State," *Chalcedon Report,* 276 (July 1988).

19. For a helpful definition and treatment, see K. E. Myers, *All God's Children Wear Blue Suede Shoes: Christians and Popular Culture* (Westchester: Crossway, 1989).

20. See M. Olasky, *Prodigal Press: The Anti-Christian Bias of the American News Media* (Westchester: Crossway, 1988). Also see the January 1993 newsletter of *Focus on the Family*. Dr. Dobson highlights the special issue of *Time* in the fall of 1992. He says of the issue:

> The magazine consisted of 93 pages of dreary predictions and analyses of the future. Many of their conclusions dealt with the institution of the family, which *Time* believes is destined for the junk heap. For example, the section dealing with marriage and parenthood bore this headline: "The Nuclear Family Goes Boom!" The article went downhill from there. This, says *Time,* is what we can expect in the 21st century.

The twelve predictions he reports are grim and include the death of the family as we know it, multiple marriages, weakened taboos on incest, childlessness, routine victimization of children, the death of theology and Bible study for children, the triumph of feminism and forced abortions.

21. I. Groller, "Is Society Morally Bankrupt?" *Parents* (June 1989), 35.

22. "'Esprit de Corp' Clothing Ads Promote Sex, Abortion Agenda," *Southern California Christian Times*, vol 10, no 5 (May 1992), 16. Even the *best* secular commercial magazines are problematic, e.g., *San Diego Family Press*. This award winner of Parenting Publications of America is available for free in drug stores, supermarkets, etc. While it has useful information, its articles and ads are devoid of God's value system. Because this magazine helps the family in order to exploit its economic resources, the parent must be discerning while using "San Diego County's Leading Resource for Parents and Educators who Care!" If I question its motives, I might be charged with not caring! This is not value-free advertising.

23. See K. L. Billingsley, *The Seductive Image: A Christian Critique of the World of Film* (Wheaton: Crossway, 1989).

24. American Youth Soccer Organization.

25. *Chalcedon Report*, 276 (July 1988).

26. Josh 5:13-15.

27. Josh 1:1-9.

28. 1 Sam 17:45-47.

29. Josh 6:1-5; 23:16; 2 Sam 5:17-25.

Section 5

~

WHAT'S THE STRATEGY?

~

CHAPTER 13

A Battle Plan

Though the battle over the family rages, it is only a skirmish in the larger war between God and those who rebel against Him. Our society pretends that pacifism is possible,[1] but Satan rages and roars against God and His anointed.[2] Jesus and His kingdom oppose the evil one and his minions; you must choose one side and cannot be neutral.[3] Both armies attack and counterattack and the battle lines ebb and flow.[4] Yet Christians can rejoice because our Captain's righteous life,[5] substitutionary death,[6] resurrection and ascension to the throne[7] have already secured our victory.[8] Ultimately, because the battle is the Lord's,[9] we who are His soldiers[10] must willingly remain faithful and fight for Him according to His commands.[11] To win the battle for the family and the war for His honor and glory, you need to understand three convictions of God's heart:

- God defines the war and how to wage it.
- He has an objective in this war.
- He has a strategy to obtain His objective.

God Defines the War

As the Holy, Sovereign Creator, God is independent of His creatures, while they are totally dependent upon Him.[12] Also, He is absolutely pure morally, in contrast to His creation. In the heavenly realms, Satan and his demons rebelled;[13] on earth, he recruited men who sided with him.[14] God opposes all such rebellion.[15]

As a great warrior-king,[16] God rules over a kingdom of unapproachable light[17] and wars against Satan's kingdom of darkness.[18] In the heavenly realms, God commands many armies of angels[19] who fight with the demonic hosts.[20] Jehovah has appointed His Son, the Angel of the Lord,[21] as their captain to lead them.[22] On the earth, under the old covenant, God elected Israel to be His army[23] and also appointed His Son as their captain to lead them.[24] Under the new covenant, the Church as the new Israel is the army of God led by the incarnate Angel of the Lord, Jesus the Messiah.[25] He who is the eternal Son and leads heaven's hosts becomes the messianic Son, the seed of the woman, the second Adam to crush Satan's head and lead many regenerated soldier-sons to glory just as the first Adam led all to death.[26] One day He will return with both angels and resurrected saints to dispense divine justice and retribution to all His enemies.[27]

God's war is a real, life-and-death struggle: God versus Satan; angels versus demons; Israel versus the nations; David versus Goliath; Jesus versus Satan; the Church versus the world, the flesh and the devil; Christ and His army at the second coming against all others. And yet with the first advent of Jesus Christ a unique phase of redemption began which will end only at His second coming. He came as the Lamb of God and the Good Shepherd to lay down His life for His sheep[28] and refused to fight or retaliate, reserving that for the future.[29] He refused to become king without the cross;[30] He rebuked Peter's use of the sword and healed Malchus's ear;[32] He told Pilate that His kingdom was not of this world order;[32] He submitted willingly to injustice,[33] praying for His persecutors.[34]

The Church, though united with Him in His resurrection and seated with Him in the heavenlies,[35] is also united to Him in His death and while *in its state of humiliation* is to fight sin with the same methods He used in His non-retaliatory state of humiliation and suffering.[36] Therefore, even though Satan can use physical attacks and even death as well as moral or religious tactics,[37] Christians, until Christ returns, can only rely on the spiritual weapons given by God.[38] 2 Corinthians 10:3-6 and Ephesians 6:10-29 define our warfare and weapons in this stage of our humiliation.

In 2 Corinthians 10:3-6, Paul teaches that even though we are in the body we do not depend on our physical body to win the war. Rather our arsenal is full of divine weapons that destroy speculations and proud things that oppose the truth of God. Our objective is to capture *every* thought and make it obedient to Christ. Therefore, the word of God—the Bible—(under ministerial authority and direction) is our weapon, not outward worldly weapons, physical or otherwise. We have the objective of capturing *every* thought one by one.

In Ephesians 6:10-20, Paul teaches that the strength of the Lord comes from God's armor because our ultimate enemies are not humans but spiritual rulers, powers and the forces at work behind the world's powers. Satanic spiritual wickedness in the heavenlies calls for the armor of truth, righteousness, peace, faith, salvation and the Word, provided by Jesus our captain[39] and kept in working order by prayer. The good news of the gospel is our weapon by which we take the fight to our foes.

The church and family must understand the nature of this warfare and the present limitations on our weapons and methods of warfare. Therefore, the synergism of the deistic social gospel and the syncretism of Roman Catholicism's papal political power must be rejected as fleshly weapons. However, separatistic pietism or quietistic monasticism must also be rejected because they reject God's objective in the war.[40]

God's Objective: A Christian World Order

His desire is not to preserve the United States of America or even western culture *per se*, but to conquer His enemies' every thought; this includes all people in every place at all times in the world's history. Western culture, or any other, has value only insofar as it reflects biblical values. (By no means pure, Western civilization is nevertheless the most biblically-influenced culture to date.) Scriptural scholar John Murray succinctly summarizes God's objective in "The Christian World Order."[41] God's desire is that the family and church conquer the world, not that they become like, covenant with or withdraw from the world.

Murray defines this objective:

> By the term, *The Christian World Order*, I take it that what is meant is a world order that in all aspects and spheres is Christian, an order so conformed to the principles of Christianity, and so pervaded by the forces that are operative in Christianity, that the whole of life will be brought into willing captivity to the obedience of Christ.[42]

Murray realizes that this goal cannot be accomplished by human strength nor be perfected on this side of the new heavens and earth.[43] He demonstrates biblically that this is not only God's desired, but His demanded objective.[44] He argues that to ignore this comprehensive goal is a functional denial of the Lord's prayer and Christ's sovereign kingship and messianic kingdom.[45]

He wisely warns against trusting *any* program that ignores the supernatural necessity of the regenerating work of the Holy Spirit or that seeks human progress apart from His hand.[46] He elucidates the impact of a Christian world order on the individual,[47] the family,[48] the church,[49] the state,[50] and beyond.[51]

Murray concludes that although the task is overwhelming, Christ has triumphed over His enemies, is seated at the right hand of the Father and gives us His Spirit and therefore the strength to fight to achieve God's objective.[52]

The necessity of a Christian World Order to impact a culture can be seen in *The Fall of Tyrants*.[53] One individual man, his family and his congregation are the focal point for the overthrow of ecclesiastical and political tyrants. However, as his struggle for freedom continues, it is clear that a total cultural order change (as biblically defined by Murray) is necessary to maintain and advance freedom for individuals, families, and churches whether in Romania or in any other nation.

God's Strategy: A Christian World Order

But if we now know the nature of the war and God's objective, what is His overall strategy? How do we develop battle plans in line with His? We need to examine His strategy to reach His ordained objective.

Most secular groups who want to help the family see the need for an overall strategy.[54] Non-Christians see this,[55] but Christians often focus narrowly on the family, failing to see the broader issues of the family's relationship to the church and the state, as well as the world order and cultural issues.[56] If we are to achieve God's objective in this war (and His objective is necessary to preserve the family), then we need tactics that fit into His divine strategy.[57]

B. H. Liddell Hart, a respected military strategist, offers several salient points Christians need to ponder.[58] In his theory of strategy he defines the nature of and interrelationships between: national policy, higher or grand strategy, and pure or military tactics.[59] He insists that military or field strategy *must* be related to the larger considerations of policy and grand strategy *or* the battle may be lost. Even if it is won, it may not aid in the overall war. Of policy he says:

> In discussing the subject of "the objective" in war it is essential to be clear about, and to keep clear in our minds, the distinction between the political and the military objective. The two are different but not separate. For nations do not wage war for war's sake, but in pursuance of policy. The military objective is only the means to a political end. Hence the military objective should be governed by the political objective, subject to the basic

> condition that policy does not demand what is militarily—that is, practically—impossible.
>
> Thus any study of the problem ought to begin and end with the question of policy.
>
> History shows that gaining military victory is not in itself equivalent to gaining the object of policy. But as most of the thinking about war has been done by men of the military profession there has been a very natural tendency to lose sight of the basic national object, and identify it with the military aim. In consequence, whenever war has broken out, policy has too often been governed by the military aim—and this has been regarded as an end in itself, instead of merely a means to the end.[60]

Before we fight Satan and his forces, we need to know our King, His kingdom, His objectives and His methods of warfare. Fighting for fighting's sake is not useful. In human warfare a related problem arises when the politician and soldier are different people. Each can interfere with the other's legitimate duties.[61] The Christian army avoids this because our Commander-in-Chief or Captain is our King.[62] His victory assures ours.[63] Our obedience to His commands assures that we adhere to His policy.

Hart's observations have implications for the battle for the family. Foremost, the battle for the family cannot be isolated from the larger spiritual warfare of Jesus versus Satan. Christians who try to preserve the family must focus on the King, His kingdom and not merely traditional values, and therefore must avoid improper cooperation with the world. Only Christ can redeem the family, not a mixed multitude of co-belligerents." Additionally, Christ's power comes only from the Holy Spirit's use of the Word. Therefore, biblical definitions and methodologies must be employed if His presence is to aid us. Mere pragmatics as opposed to principled biblical methods will destroy and not defend. These implications are the same as, and therefore confirm, the first main point of this chapter: we must grasp the nature of the war. Also, the objective of saving the biblical view of the family must be seen as a subset of the larger objective of the glory of God in a Christian World Order. A successful but isolated skirmish over the family may bring temporary gains but ultimately will not win the battle for the family or will give a limited measure of freedom for the family but allow the loss of cultural freedom which will eventually double back to harm the family. This implication confirms the second main point of this chapter.

Hart goes on to deal with strategy and distinguishes between strategy and tactics.[64] He divides the concept further into grand strategy and pure strategy. In this chapter we will only consider the parallels between the grand strategy of a military battle and the grand strategy that Christians must understand as they fight the battle against the powers of evil. In the next chapter we will consider the more practical aspects of pure strategy or tactics. Hart further differentiates between grand strategy and tactics.[65] He notes several crucial issues in grand strategy which apply to the Christian battle for the family.[66] Further, he relates grand strategy to victory.[67]

As Christians fight for the family, we must see the battle in its overall context of God's war and His objective: a Christian World Order. The biblical view of history as God-ordained and controlled in contrast to the existential temporal view must control our grand strategy which reiterates what we learned about policy. Soul winning and pietistic cultural monasticism are not sufficient to salvage Western culture and save the family. We fight to obtain the fruits of peace, not for the joy of fighting. Hart is also helpful when considering how to govern after victory. He points to presbyterian or republican government as opposed to democratic or individualistic government.[68]

Christians need to recognize and rejoice in the God-ordained diversity in the body of Christ, both locally and at large,[69] and not force a false unity along the lines of the vague, synergistic, amorphous blandness of the liberal ecumenical movement, or the centralized, syncretistic political power of the papal state. Within confessional orthodoxy, the oneness of the body—based on the oneness of the Spirit, the hope of our calling, the Lord, the faith, baptism, our God and Father—calls us to cooperation, unity and toleration of individual differences. Also diversity and dispersion make our forces less vulnerable to attack.

Hart notes that a coordination of people and resources, not chaos and confusion,[70] leads to successful strategy. Lack of coordinated control increases the danger of "friendly fire."[71] An Army can attack itself.

Western Christianity's cherished individualism and independence must be modified. All advances in the systematization of biblical truth came through unified ecclesiastical cooperation.[72] The family was saved only through coordinated cooperation of the family and the church.[73] Today, a church council of ordained leaders committed to orthodoxy[74] needs to be called and needs to define the biblical view of the family[75] and the Scriptural methodologies of helping it.[76]

Hart clarifies the difference between conquest and conservation and governments that aim at either conquest or conservation.[77] States that conquer run the danger of addiction to force; conservative states run the risk of exhausting their energy in futile defensive battles against rapacious states. Conquest is easier to control than conservation.[78]

Aggressive action based on biblical scholarship is needed, not separatistic mystical monasticism. "Onward Christian Soldiers" is not just a stirring hymn, it is realistic theology because Satan will never surrender until he is thrown into the lake of fire.[79] The early part of the twentieth century in the USA proved that defensive battles against modernity exhaust the church's resources which, in turn, leave the culture insipid.[80] Implacable foes like Satan necessitate a conquest not a conservation modality because he will fight to the death: you fight or lose, he gives no vacations.

Hart hammers away at the need for consistent morality because internal compromise and corruption cause more national defeats than losses on the battlefield.[81] Moral virtue is necessary to win and resist the pull to become like the enemy.[82]

Christian commitment and personal holiness are necessary elements for the forces defending the family. If our army degenerates into using Satanic or worldly methods and develops sinful desires, it is worthless and only fit to be thrown out and trampled underfoot.[83] Therefore, to have God's blessing and victory, we must maintain personal, as well as military methodological purity.[84] The poison of modern liberalism destroyed the church's cultural influence.[85]

I am not wise enough to have answers to all the policy and grand strategy issues involved in trying to save the family. But it is absolutely essential to face them *before* we construct pure strategy and tactics. The church has lots of work to do to assure that our strategy and tactics please God.

Notes:

Chapter 13

1. Eph 6:11-18; 2 Tim 2:3-4. The Bible validates the righteousness and necessity of warfare—both physical and spiritual. See L. Boettner, *The Christian Attitude toward War* (Phillipsburg: Presbyterian and Reformed, 1985); R. A. Morey, *When is it Right to Fight?* (Minneapolis: Bethany House, 1985); R. B. Needham, *The Philosophy of Force in Foreign Policy: A Theory of the Just War* (Monterey: M.A. Thesis in National Security Affairs, the Naval Postgraduate School, 1979).

2. Ps 2; 2 Tim 4:9-18; 1 Pet 5:8-9.

3. Matt 6:24; 12:30; Luke 11:14-26.

4. Mark 4:24-25; Luke 11:14-26.

5. Rom 3:21-24; Phil 3:8-9; Heb 5:7-10; 12:3.

6. Rom 3:25-26; 2 Cor 5:20-21; Phil 3:10; Col 2:8-15; Heb 12:2.

7. Acts 2:22-36; Phil 3:10.

8. Eph 1:19-2:3; 3:8-10.

9. 1 Sam 17:47; 2 Chron 20:15; Ps 24:8; Zech 14:1-8; Jn 17:4; 20:30; Rev 19:11-21.

10. 2 Tim 2:3-4.

11. 1 Tim 1:18-19; 6:11-16; 2 Tim 4:1-8.

12. Gen 1; John 1:1-3; Acts 17:24-28.

13. 2 Pet 2:4; Jude 6; Rev 12:3-4.

14. Gen 3; Rom 3:23; 5:12-14.

15. Rom 1:18-25; 8:18-22.

16. For examples of God as a great warrior-king who wages war see: Ex 14-15; Num 9; 10:34-36; 21:4; Deut 32:21-31, 40-43; Josh 10:8, 11-14; Judg 2:10-3:2; 1 Sam 14:10, 15; 17:37; 2 Sam 5:19, 24; 22:7-16; 1 Kgs 20:13, 28; 2 Kgs 6:8-20; 1 Chr 18:6; 2 Chr 6:24-25; Job 25:3; 40:6-14; Is 3:13-15; Dan 7:9-10; Hos 6:4-11; Joel 3; Amos 4:10; Mic 1:2-7; Zeph 3:8-13; Zech 14:1-8; Mal 4:5; Luke 1:46-55, 68-75; 2:33-35; Rom 16:20; Col 1:19-23; 2 Thess 1:5-10; Rev 19:11-21.

17. Ps 104:2; 1 Tim 6:15-16; 1 John 1:5; Jam 1:17.

18. Col 1:11-14.

19. *Saba'ot* means armies, hosts. God is often referred to as the Lord of hosts (the armies of heaven).

20. 2 Kgs 6; Dan 10:10-17; Eph 1.

21. G. Vos, *Biblical Theology: Old and New Testament* (Grand Rapids: Eerdmans, 1948), 85-89.

22. Josh 5:13 - 6:5.

23. Ex 7:4; 12:17, 41, 51. Numbers records their organization into His army including their camp, maneuvers and battles.

24. Ex. 3:2; 14:19-20; 23:20-23; 32:34; 33:2; Josh 5:13- 6:5; Judg 2:1-5; 6:11-24, etc.

25. Rom 16:20; 1 Cor 15:20-28; Gal 6:16; Eph 1:18-23; 3:10; 1 Pet 2:9-10; Rev 19:11-21.

26. Gen 3:15; Matt 4:1-11; Rom 1:1-4; 5:12-21; 16:20; 1 Cor 15:20-28; 45-49; Eph 1:15-2:10; 4:8-10; Col 1:12-23; 2:8-15; Heb 2:5-18; 2 Pet 1:1-11.

27. Ps 149; Dan 7:13-14; 2 Thess 1:3-10.

28. John 1:29, 36; 10:11-18.

29. 2 Thess 1:3-10; Rev 19:11-21.

30. Matt 4:1:11; John 6:15.

31. Matt 26:52-54; Luke 22:50-51; John 18:10-11.

32. John 18:33 - 19:11.

33. Isa 53:7-8; John 19:10-11; Acts 8:32-37; 2 Cor 5:21; 1 Pet 2:21-25.

34. Luke 23:34.

35. Phil 3:20-21; Col 3:1-4.

36. Rom 8:35-37; 2 Cor 1:5; 4:10; Phil 2:17; 3:10; Col 1:24; 1 Pet 2:21-25.

37. The book of Revelation shows that Satan uses false religion and philosophy to deceive the church. If that fails, he takes out the brass knuckles and tries to destroy the church. See also Luke 22:31-32; 2 Cor 2:11; Eph 4:11; 6:11; 1 Pet 5:8-9.

38. Rom 16:20; 13:12; 2 Cor 6:7; 1 Thess 5:8.

39. Isa 11:5; 59:17; 52:7; 49:2; Hos 6:5; Eph 6:10-20. Cf. D. Powlison, *Power Encounters: Recovering Spiritual Warfare* (Grand Rapids: Baker, 1996). Powlison gives *solid* biblical definitions and direction in this essential area. He avoids the errors of modern rationalism that explain away the supernatural, without falling into the errors and excesses of the deliverance ministry models. Both the Marxist materialism of liberation theologies and mystical magic of the word-faith movement's spiritual warfare model miss the mark, albeit in different ways. Metaphorical treatments like Frank Peretti's novels are gripping, but not biblically or exegetically correct. Without the kind of balance Powlison shows in this area, Christians can ignore biblically valid tools, favoring views and methods that come from a distorted Christian life view.

40. See Appendix 6 for an analysis of these categories.

41. John Murray, "The Christian World Order," *Collected Writings of John Murray: Vol 1, The Claims of Truth* (Carlisle: Banner of Truth, 1976), 356-366. It is of note that when he wrote this he was not a postmillenialist. Perhaps the most difficult government agent to address biblically is the civil government. The Bible says a lot about individuals, families, and the church. But the New Testament presents only a general position about the civil government, teaching that it is God's ordained deacon or servant (Rom 13;

1 Pet 2). Personally, I respect the Puritan view of the civil magistrate. Although I'm not a postmillenialist, I do believe the gospel kingdom will conquer every tongue, tribe and nation. While I'm not exegetically convinced of the postmillenial hope of national transformation in every land, I most certainly desire it. I believe we are obliged to disciple not only individuals, families and churches, but also nations. Murray's article is compelling. See Appendix 8 for a brief overview of the Bible and the civil magistrate, especially as it relates to the family and the church as God's other ordained institutions.

42. Op. cit., 356.

43. Idem. Murray says,

> We shall have to acknowledge frankly that we do not have the right from God's Word to believe that a Christian world order in the purity and completeness of its conception will be realized on this side of that great and momentous event towards which the history of this world is moving, namely, the appearing of the glory of the great God and our Saviour Jesus Christ, the visible glorious advent of the Lord himself.

44. Ibid., 357.

> Our dilemma would seem to be indeed perplexing. If we have to wait for the supernatural forces that Christ's advent will bring in its train before the order of absolute right and holiness will be ushered in, is there any sense in speaking of a Christian world order except as an eschatological hope? Particularly and most practically, is there good sense in working towards the establishment of a Christian order when we know that, in the completeness of its conception, it is not attainable in what we generally call this life?
>
> We must be bold to say that the Christian revelation does not allow us to do anything less than to formulate and work towards a Christian world order in the life that we now live. It is not difficult to demonstrate the validity and even necessity of this thesis.

45. Ibid., 358. As Murray puts it:

> And this is just saying that the ideal and goal imposed upon us by the kingship and kingdom of our Lord and Saviour Jesus Christ is nothing less than Christian world order. To recede from this conception and aim is to abandon what is implied in the prayer Christ taught his disciples to pray, "Thy kingdom come, Thy will be done in earth, as it is in heaven" (Matt. 6:10). And it is to renounce what is overtly expressed in the words of the apostle, "For though we walk

in the flesh, we do not war after the flesh: (for the weapons of our warfare are not carnal, but mighty through God to the pulling down of strongholds;) casting down imaginations, and every high thing that exalteth itself against the knowledge of God, and *bringing into captivity every thought to the obedience of Christ"* (2 Cor. 10:3-5).

46. Ibid., 359. Murray states:

    Any idealism or reconstruction that proceeds upon a program that is congenial to fallen human nature, or that is readily adjustable to the impulses and passions and principles of fallen human nature, has denied the very genius of Christian order.

    There is, therefore, something drastic about the transformation that Christian order affects. This is why we are so reluctant to entertain a Christian program or procedure in some of the most practical spheres, such as those of education and industry. We are so often content to have a few amendments and corrections that give a Christian veneer to certain institutions. Without question these corrections may have, to a certain extent, a salutary influence, but these amendments do not change the basically non-Christian character of the principles and methods by which these institutions or orders operate. The Christian principle as applied to every order is radical and revolutionary in the true sense of these words, radical and revolutionary because it is organically regenerative. It deals not by half-measures nor by indirection, but by honest, thoroughgoing effectiveness, with the reality of human sin and with the all-pervasive corruption it has brought in its train.

47. Ibid., 360.

    In dealing with Christian world order there is no concept with which Christianity has furnished us that is more expressive and comprehensive than that of the kingdom of God, and it was none other than our Lord himself who said, "Except a man be born again, he cannot see the kingdom of God" (John 3:3), "Except a man be born of water and of the Spirit, he cannot enter into the kingdom of God" (John 3:5), "Except ye be converted, and become as little children, ye shall not enter into the kingdom of heaven" (Matt 18:3). The kingdom of God begins its reconstruction with the individual. It never submerges the individual in the social mass. It never suppresses or blurs the needs, the interests, the obligations and the destinies of the individual in his relations to God or to men. Christian world order in its zeal to renovate and reconstruct the orders of society must ensure that the needs of the individual are fully met and his interests fully guarded and promoted.

48. Ibid., 361.

> The history of our generation and the commanding facts of developments in science, economics, and politics and the exigencies arising from the close interdependence of all nations are compelling us to give more attention to the question of world order than ever before in the history of our era. We are all aware of the urgent concern that the leading statesmen of all countries are entertaining with respect to this question. As Christians we are compelled to face the responsibility of Christian world order. Let us not camouflage the issue. Until the family, the basic social institution, the institution through which also the individual as the ultimate unit of society is brought into being and through which he receives the heritage, the nurture and the training that will fit him for every social responsibility and function—until the family is redeemed from its sin, whether it be the sin of coarse immorality or the sin of refined godlessness, and until it is renewed and rehabilitated by the grace of God, it is a moral, psychological and social impossibility for Christian world order to be instituted.

49. Ibid., 362. Of the church he says that "it is to function in the areas of faith, testimony, worship and self-government" and:

> Truly it is not the function of the church to put Christian world order into effect. The church must occupy its own sphere of operation and limit itself severely to that sphere appointed to it by Christ. When the church attempts to become totalitarian then it has violated Christian order. But it is the function of the church to establish and promote Christian order within its own divinely instituted domain, and it *is* the function of the church to *proclaim* the world order to which God's sovereignty and Christ's headship obligate in every sphere.

50. Ibid., 364-365.

> The state is the third basic divine institution. It might be thought that, while the redemptive and regenerative forces of Christianity have an obvious bearing upon the individual,

the family and the church, yet the state cannot be regarded as coming in any direct way under the demands and influences of the Christian revelation. The state has to do with civil order, the preservation and promotion of civil righteousness, liberty and peace. It will be said that the civil magistrate in the discharge of his official functions has no religious obligations and therefore should not and cannot be regulated in the discharge of his office by the Christian revelation; in other words, that the Bible is not the rule of conduct for the civil magistrate as it is for the individual, for the family and for the church.

> This position embraces a strange mixture of truth and error. There is truth in this position insofar as it recognizes the limits of civil authority. Civil authority is not totalitarian. Civil authority must never trespass into the sphere of the family, or of the church, and it must guard the God-given rights and prerogatives of the individual. If the distinction of spheres is once blurred or obliterated, then good order is impossible and Christian principles are negated.

51. Ibid. Murray points out the error of cutting off the civil magistrate from God's Word.

> Since civil government derives its authority from God, it is responsible to God and therefore obligated to conduct its affairs in accordance with God's will. The infallible revelation of His will God has deposited in the Scriptures. It will surely be granted that there is much in the Scriptures that has to do with the conduct of civil government, and this simply means that the Word of God bears upon civil authority with all the stringency that belongs to God's Word.

He also states,

> To recede from this position or to abandon it, either as conception or as goal, is to reject in principle the sovereignty of God and of his Christ. The goal fixed for us by the Christian revelation is nothing less than a Christian state as well as Christian individuals, Christian families and a Christian church. And this just means that the obligation and task arising from Christ's kingship and headship are that civil government, within its own well-defined and restricted sphere, must in its constitution and in its legislative and executive functions recognize and obey the authority of God and of his Christ and thus bring all of its functions and actions into accord with the revealed will of

God as contained in his Word. We thus see how radical and reconstructive is a philosophy of Christian world order, if we are to face that conception frankly and address ourselves to the responsibility it entails.

It is, of course, true that all of life is not exhausted by the family, the church and the state. These however, are the basic divine institutes of society. A Christian world order will embrace every department of life—industry, agriculture, education, recreation. But since these institutions are basic, it is inevitable that the Christianizing of every other department of life will proceed apace with the Christianizing of these basic institutions. He points to the importance and immensity of God's objective.

52. Ps 89:13-14; Eph 1:18-21; Ibid., 366.

53. L. Tokes, D. Porter, *The Fall of Tyrants: The Incredible Story of One Pastor's Witness, The People of Romania and the Overthrow of Ceaucescu* (Wheaton: Crossway, 1990). D. A. Kloosterman, "The Situation of the Hungarian in Transylvania," *Christian Observer*, vol 170, no 5, (March 6, 1992), 33-34; I. Geczy, "Psychological Warfare Against Bishop Tokes," *Christian Observer,* op. cit., 40. Also see Josef Tson, "Understanding the Times: Somebody has to be there to rebuild society!" *Crosswinds.*, vol 1, no 1, 5.

For a compelling account of one man's attempt to be a Christian leader of his country, see the video, *Breaking the Chains*, about President Frederick Chiluba of Zambia (Christian Vision, P.O. Box 3040, West Bromwich, West Midlands, B70 OEL, England). Chiluba's attempts, though biblically crude, are noteworthy. The connection between culture, corruption and the family is clearly seen in Lot's family: Gen 18–19.

54. Because God's three ordained institutions—the Family, the Church, the State—are independent yet interdependent, and because all areas of life are interconnected and affect each other, a unified consistent plan is necessary.

55. Richard Louv, "Reweaving the Family," a special report in *The San Diego Union* (March 31, 1991), D 1-6. Louv highlights the need for a coordinated, cooperative effort to aid the family. He points to the roles of the family, the school, businesses and the community at large. In his "Family Manifesto" he states that the family is part of a larger social ecosystem (D-4). Louv destroys what good he hits upon by insisting that the family be defined "as broadly as possible" and ignores God's views on the subject. This is *politically*, but not *biblically* correct thinking.

56. For example, *Moody Monthly*, vol 92, no 1 (Sept 1991): "The Shape of Today's Family: How Faith Makes a Difference" has many helpful articles on the family. However, because it has no unifying principles, it is a series of disjointed personal experiences, all anecdotal in nature. While this is good

as far as it goes, it does not focus on the direction God's people should follow. Focus on the Family, again for all the good it accomplishes, is a prime example. The realization that political action is necessary improves *Focus*'s pietistic individualistic focus and I thank God, as well as Dr. Dobson, for his courageous involvement in the antipornography battle. But this organization unfortunately adopts worldly methods (mentioned in Appendix 6) which lessen its cultural impact.

57. Since God is orderly (1 Cor 14:33), and Paul led the churches in an orderly fashion (1 Cor 4:17; 7:17; 11:16; 16:1; 2 Cor 8:18-19; 1 Thess 2:14; Titus 1:5), we too must conduct our campaigns in an orderly manner.

58. B. H. Liddell Hart, *Strategy*, 2nd rev. ed. (New York: F. A. Praeger, 1967). Hart, a British officer, was so respected as a strategist that General Patton studied him and Marshal Rommel said, "The British would have been able to prevent the greatest part of their defeats if they had paid attention to the modern theories expounded by Liddell Hart before the war" (quote is from the dust jacket). I want to be careful not to impose a nonbiblical structure on God's Word. What the *Westminster Confession of Faith*, Chapter I, Section VI says about the worship of God and the government of the church holds true for the missionary mandate given in the Great Commission in Matt 28:18-20:

> The whole counsel of God, concerning all things necessary for His own glory, man's salvation, faith, and life, is either expressly set down in Scripture, or by good and necessary consequence may be deduced from Scripture; unto which nothing at any time is to be added, whether by new revelations of the Spirit, or traditions of men. Nevertheless, we acknowledge the inward illumination of the Spirit of God to be necessary for the saving understanding of such things as are revealed in the word; and that there are some circumstances concerning the worship of God, and government of the Church, common to human actions and societies, which are to be ordered by the light of nature and Christian prudence, according to the general rules of the word, which are always to be observed.

Hart's observations are not binding upon us, but do give direction and will help us as long as they conform to the general rules of God's Word.

59. Hart, op. cit., chapter XIX, "The Theory of Strategy"; chapter XX, "The Concentrated Essence of Strategy and Tactics"; chapter XXII, "Grand Strategy."

60. Ibid., 351.

61. Ibid., 333-334. Hart says,

> To break down the distinction between strategy and policy would not matter much if the two functions were normally

combined in the same person, as with a Frederick or a Napoleon. But as such autocratic soldier-rulers have been rare in modern times and became temporarily extinct in the nineteenth century, the effect was insidiously harmful. For it encouraged soldiers to make the preposterous claim that policy should be subservient to their conduct of operations, and, especially in democratic countries, it drew the statesman on to overstep the definite border of his sphere and interfere with his military employees in the actual use of their tools.

62. Ps 68:24.
63. Ps 2; Rom 5:12-21; 1 Cor 15:45-49; Eph 1:19-23; Col 2:8-15.
64. Op. cit., 335. As Hart puts it,

    We can now arrive at a shorter definition of strategy as—"the art of distributing and applying military means to fulfill the ends of policy." For strategy is concerned not merely with the movement of forces—as its role is often defined—but with the effect. When the application of the military instrument merges into actual fighting, the dispositions for and control of such direct action are termed "tactics." The two categories, although convenient for discussion, can never be truly divided into separate compartments because each not only influences but merges into the other.

65. Ibid., 335-336.

    As tactics is an application of strategy on a lower plane, so strategy is an application on a lower plane of "grand strategy." While practically synonymous with the policy which guides the conduct of war, as distinct from the more fundamental policy which should govern its object, the term "grand strategy" serves to bring out the sense of "policy in execution." For the role of grand strategy—higher strategy—is to coordinate and direct all the resources of a nation, or band of nations, towards the attainment of the political object of the war—the goal defined by fundamental policy.

66. Ibid., chapter XXII, "Grand Strategy," 366-372.
67. Ibid., 366. As Hart puts it,

    The object in war is to attain a better peace—even if only from your own point of view. Hence it is essential to conduct war with constant regard to the peace you desire. This is the truth underlying Clausewitz's definition of war as a "continuation of policy by other means"—the prolongation of that policy through the war into the

> subsequent peace must always be borne in mind. A State which expends its strength to the point of exhaustion bankrupts its own policy, and future.

68. Ibid., 367. Hart argues that cooperation of diverse groups works better than forced conformity or unity:

> Moreover, regrettable as it may seem to the idealist, the experience of history provides little warrant for the belief that real progress, and the freedom that makes progress possible, lies in unification. For where unification has been able to establish unity of ideas it has usually ended in uniformity, paralysing the growth of new ideas. And where the unification has merely brought about an artificial or imposed unity, its irksomeness has led through discord to disruption.
>
> Vitality springs from diversity—which makes for real progress so long as there is mutual toleration, based on the recognition that worse may come from an attempt to suppress differences than from acceptance of them. For this reason, the kind of peace that makes progress possible is best assured by the mutual checks created by a balance of force—like in the sphere of internal politics and of international relations.

These are the political and ecclesiastical equivalents to the biblical family structure. The one and the many or trinitarian nature of God is reflected in the proper structuring of the family, church and state. Also, we must never forget that Christians are called to love their enemies, not annihilate them: Ex 23:4-5; Lev 19:17-18; Prov 25:21-22; Matt 5:43-48; Rom 12:14-21; 1 Pet.

The United States of America's governmental structure is a good example of diversity and cooperation of governmental branches in a political entity. The presbyterian governmental system of a board of elders or session of a local congregation, the elders or presbyters of a local area and the Synod or General Assembly of the whole church is a good example in an ecclesiastical entity.

69. Rom 12:3-8; 1 Cor 12-14; Eph 4:1-16.

70. See footnote 65.

71. The U. S. military has a proclivity for killing its own troops by careless accidents and firing on them: "Casualties in Principle Wars of the U.S.," *The World Almanac and Book of Facts*: 1987 (N.Y.: Scripps Howard, 1987), 337. In fact, in some conflicts friendly fire accounted for more casualties than did enemy fire. Sometimes the U. S. military does not learn its lessons very well. Captain James M. Martin, USNR (Ret.), "We Still Haven't Learned," *Naval Institute Proceedings*, vol 117, no 7, (July 1991),

64-68, reflects on the damage to USN vessels by mines during the Persian Gulf War and why it was avoidable. On the issue of "friendly fire" see Joshua Hammer, "Risking 'Friendly Fire,'" *Newsweek* (March 4, 1991), 33; *The Progressive*, vol 56, no 3 (March 1992), 10. The second editorial shows that a fourth of the US casualties in the Persian Gulf were the results of "friendly fire" which could have been avoided. Also see Charles R. Schrader, "Friendly Fire: The Inevitable Price," *The Wilson Quarterly*, vol XVI, no 4 (Autumn 1992), 11-12.

72. As noted in Appendix 6, doctrinal advances were made in councils and creedal assemblies.

73. See chapter 9 for the two times the combination of the biblical view of the family and Christianity saved Western culture. The church helped to define, shape and undergird the family. In turn the domestic/biblical type of family helped to shape and preserve the culture.

74. Orthodoxy begins with unwavering commitment to historic Christianity and its doctrines: The Trinity; the two natures of Christ in one person; the Reformational understanding of the exclusivity of Scriptures, faith, grace; the inerrancy, infallibility and sufficiency of the Bible. See F. Schaeffer, *The Great Evangelical Disaster* (Westchester: Crossway, 1984); H. O. J. Brown, *Heresies* (Grand Rapids: Baker, 1984); R. L. Ganz, W. J. Edgar, *Sold Out: How the Evangelical Church is Abandoning God for Self-Fulfillment: A Warning* (Ottawa: Onward Press, 1990).

75. Appendices 2 and 4.

76. Appendices 6 and 7.

77. Op. cit., 368. In Hart's words:

> Another conclusion which develops from the study of grand strategy against the background of history is the practical necessity of adapting the general theory of strategy to the nature of a nation's fundamental policy. There is an essential difference of aim, and must be a consequent difference of appropriate method between an "acquisitive" and a "conservative" State.

78. Idem.

79. 1 Pet 5:8; Rev 20:7-10.

80. See Marsden's works (Appendix 6).

81. Op. cit., 369-372.

82. Ibid., 371-372. Hart says:

> ...the less that a nation has regard for moral obligations, the more it tends to respect physical strength—the deterrent power of a force too strong to be challenged with impunity. In the same way, with individuals it is a matter of common experience that the bully-type and the robber-type hesitate to assail anyone who approaches their own strength—and

are far more reluctant to attempt this than a peaceful type of individual is to tackle an assailant bigger than himself.

The experience of history brings ample evidence that the downfall of civilized States tends to come not from the direct assaults of foes but from internal decay, combined with the consequences of exhaustion in war. A state of suspense is trying—it has often led nations as well as individuals to commit suicide because they were unable to bear it. But suspense is better than to reach exhaustion in pursuit of the mirage of victory. Moreover, a truce to actual hostilities enables a recovery and development of strength, while the need for vigilance helps to keep a nation "on its toes."

Peaceful nations are apt, however, to court unnecessary danger; because when once aroused they are more inclined to proceed to extremes than predatory nations. For the latter, making war as a means of gain, are usually more ready to call it off when they find an opponent too strong to be easily overcome. It is the reluctant fighter, impelled by emotion and not by calculation, who tends to press a fight to the bitter end. Thereby he too often defeats his own end, even if he does not produce his own direct defeat. For the spirit of barbarism can be weakened only during a cessation of hostilities; war strengthens it—pouring fuel on the flames.

83. Matt 5:13.

84. Rom 12:17-21, Jay E. Adams, *How to Overcome Evil* (Phillipsburg: Presbyterian and Reformed, 1977); 1 Pet, Jay E. Adams, *Trust and Obey: A Practical Commentary on First Peter* (Phillipsburg: Presbyterian and Reformed, 1978). N.B., the Lord's demand for purity in the camp: Lev 26:1-13; Deut 20; 23:9-14. Israel's military success depended upon the Lord's presence and power. As Commander in Chief, He demanded purity, or He would withdraw His presence and power. This was symbolic but also included pride that could pervert numbering the troops. See 2 Sam 24; 1 Chron 21.

85. J. D. Hunter's work (Appendix 2) verifies this loss of cultural influence.

CHAPTER 14

Reinforcements

I trust you want to defend and advance the biblical view of the family so that not only your own family, church and culture, but others as well, will be blessed. Now that we have considered policy issues (the nature of our warfare, God's objective in the war, God's strategy), as well as grand strategy issues (God's three ordained institutions, their interrelationships, long-range goals, cooperation, coordination, conquest, morality), let's consider some issues of pure strategy.[1] What are our resources and how can they help in the battle for the family?[2]

Individuals Help the Family

An individual can help his family directly by filling his role in a godly way. Godly individuals serve as role models for their own family members as well as for outsiders. They can also sometimes directly aid families of which they are not members.[3] To be godly, they must be regenerated by the Holy Spirit[4] so they can understand[5] and submit to God,[6] and thereby produce much fruit.[7] Such individuals also help the family by serving faithfully in churches and in government (see chapter 3).

Families Help Families

Fathers can covenant with God that their families will serve Him.[8] Fathers can lead their families in *worship* by leading family worship in the home,[9] by joining a local church and participating in its life.[10] Fathers can lead their families in *work* by teaching that the family is the top priority after God and training members in their biblical roles,[11] by overseeing home school or arranging for educational opportunities that do not violate the integrity of the family,[12] and by starting and overseeing a family business or developing their calling in a way that does not destroy the family.[13] Fathers can lead their families in witness by evangelizing through ministries of mercy and direct *witness*. Suppers and family worship are excellent times to witness to other families and shed the gospel light into dark neighborhoods and communities. Elderly, handicapped, abandoned, confused and hurting people can find a haven in a godly home that serves as Christ's spiritual emergency ward. Sundays can serve as a time to disciple others into the image of Jesus.[14]

The Church Helps the Family

The church is a foundation rock of truth and orthodox theology.[15] It must hold to the biblical view of the family and the roles of its members,[16] and should be salt and light to lost families.[17] It serves as a model to families, since it functions as the family of God.[18] Its leaders are examples of godly fathers[19] and its families are examples of godly homes in worship, work and witness.[20] It evangelizes and disciples individuals and families. Church families should be trained to be light in their communities.[21] Sometimes our churches forget that they can develop a family-oriented structure by making the family and not the individual the basic organizational unit of the church. Instead of dividing people by chronological age or school grade, natural family lines can be followed.[22] Churches should be *very* hesitant about starting a Christian day school and should aid parents in their God-given educational mandate.[23] It can maintain a family-friendly schedule by limiting the time it demands of its members to be away from home and scheduling times for families to be together as families.[24] It can offer biblical counseling. Remedial—as well as preventative—teaching should be a regular part of its life.[25] Church discipline should be practiced so that, if possible, the recalcitrant cases do not end up in court.[26] On a larger scale, the local church can connect with its association of churches or its denomination to develop the biblical policy and grand strategy models spoken of in chapter 13.

Government Aids the Family

In order to best help the family, the government needs to limit itself to its biblical role: to protect good people and punish evil ones, and to promote both domestic and international peace.[27] The state should get out of the licensing business and allow families, private industry and the church to exercise authority in their God-ordained spheres.[28] However, the government *should* legislatively protect the family and the church[29] by enforcing just laws, instead of overriding them.[30] It can protect the family executively by appointing pro-family and pro-biblical officials. On a grander scale, government can look to the family and church to promote morality and provide social welfare. Instead of creating entities to replace these two God-ordained institutions, government should creatively support and depend on them.

The Private Sector Aids the Family [31]

Businesses can strengthen the family by encouraging employees to have strong families, by protecting the family from overwork, and by orienting its services and advertising towards family-enhancing not family-destroying goals. Businesses should stop prostituting themselves for increased profits by pandering to and enhancing anti-family and anti-Christian elements in the culture. Popular culture must not ignore or negate biblical morality, which should inform all values promoted in the media, film, music, theater, etc.[32]

All these resources, and others not mentioned, must be brought to the aid of the family. Within each of these spheres of influence, strategies such as those suggested must be formulated and enacted.

There is no neutral territory. Either these areas will help your family, or they will hinder it. With such sanctified strategies in place, you and your family are ready to practice your tactical maneuvers.

Notes:

Chapter 14

1. Hart defines the process of marshaling and coordinating resources before battle as grand strategy and their placement in the battle as pure or military strategy. (See chapter 13.) In chapter 15 we will consider tactical measures for families.

2. My wisdom is finite and tainted by my sin. Therefore, my suggestions, those of one battle-hardened veteran who has pastored and counseled families for over thirty years, serve only as a starting point in your consideration of biblical strategies. Following the general outline of chapter 12, I will suggest patterns that families and churches can consider and expand.

3. We have had several single friends, male and female, who have been a great help to our family both in its life as a family and in its particular role as family of a preacher. Several of our young single men at Bayview Orthodox Presbyterian Church help single parents by tutoring children who need help with school work, etc.

4. John 3:1-16; Titus 3:3-4.

5. 1 Cor 2:6-16.

6. Ezek 36:22-27; Rom 8:5-8.

7. Matt 5:3-16; John 15:7-10; Gal 5:16-24; Phil 1:9-11.

8. Deut 6:1-9; Josh 24:14-15; chapter 15. The father's covenantal responsibilities transfer to a single mother when she becomes the leader of the truncated family unit.

9. See chapter 3, note 11; chapter 6, note 60.

10. Heb 10:23-31; Appendix 5.

11. See chapters 6-8.

12. See chapter 8.

13. Many men sacrifice their families to advance their career. This is particularly true of military personnel, officers in particular. I know of several men who have left the military or refused promotion in private businesses so that they would not destroy their families. Prayerful thought, in consultation with one's elders at church, should precede any change in career.

14. See note 9 above.

15. Appendices 2, 4, 5. This gives the family the proper world and life view from which it can work, 1 Tim 3:15.

16. Churches that hold to a covenantal view of theology and the family have the most help to offer the family because individuals are not viewed as isolated from their family or the covenant family in the church. For example, today most ministers in the United Reformed Church will answer the question, "How many people do you have in your church?" with the number of families and *not* the number of individuals. Viewing church life covenantally, not individualistically, has profound salutary influence on a church's life.

However, churches who do not think covenantally and who cannot, for conscience's sake, give the covenant sign of baptism to their children (thus treating them as part of the church) must at least struggle to raise their children for God in His nurture and counsel. See my comments in "Who Owns the Children of Divorce?" (chapter 3, note 33).

17. Appendices 1, 4, 6, 7. Also, the church can hold seminars and classes for the community as an evangelistic tool. Along with those, diaconal services can be offered (Gal 6:10). For some ideas, albeit not particularly evangelical, see Richard Louv, "Churches Lend Hand to Families," San Diego Union-Tribune (April 18, 1992), D-1, D-12.

18. Eph 2:11-22.

19. 1 Tim 3:1-13; Titus 1:5-9. For the importance of the ordained leadership being male, see Appendix 2.

20. Eph 5:22-6:4.

21. An excellent example of this is the shepherding home concept developed in the pro-life movement. A Christian family is trained to house and help women who have crisis pregnancies.

22. While Sunday schools and youth groups do not *have* to be divisive to family unity, they most often are. The very concepts come out of an idea that children need to be with their *own* age group rather than adults or their family (see chapter 8).

23. The job of the church is worship, witness, works of mercy and discipleship. While discipleship *is* education, it is not vocational training *per se*. Vocational training is an extension of the family's task of dominion given in the cultural mandate. If you run or participate in a parochial school, make sure Christian parents are integral parts of the process of education and not vestigial appendages that merely pay tuition. The constitutional issue in Christian education should be parental and family rights, not the church versus state issue. This is also true of other legitimate pursuits, such as politics. The church should encourage godly participation by its individual members and families but *not* be directly, organizationally involved.

24. Ironically, when I pastored a church we had a family night that divided families up! Everyone met in age or grade defined groups. This separated the family physically and actually took time it could have been spending together.

25. Appendices 6, 7. One desperate need of the modern church in Western civilization is to take its role as a father to its children (a shepherd to its sheep), seriously and not forfeit it to pagan professionals or to Christians whose methods are synergistic or syncretistic. Regular premarital and pre-parental counseling should be available to all and required for members. When things degenerate because of circumstances or sin, redemptive counseling should be available to all and required for members. I can testify that God has used church-based biblical counseling to redeem, restore and

restructure families rocked by physical abuse and incest. Obviously, God can convict, convert and change families with lesser problems. Lay people can be trained as well as pastors. For example, when older women are trained to disciple and counsel younger women in their family life (Titus 2:3-5), they not only utilize their gifts and graces, but they help pastors to avoid sexual temptation, and they improve the quality of life in the families and in the church. For training in biblical counseling, see the organizations in Appendix 7 as well as the Biblical Counseling Foundation (42600 Cook Street, Suite 100, Palm Desert, CA, 92211-5143, Telephone: 760-773-2667).

The church can counsel special needs groups, as well as aiding them through its deacons. For example, single parents who have double responsibilities can be counseled and trained for economic independency. For someone who has experienced a *biblical* divorce or is a new convert, the church acts as extended family and can help single parents find godly spouses and form holy homes, as Paul instructed Timothy and the young widows in 1 Timothy 5:9-16. Of course, this is more than forming singles groups and permitting the same pagan, individualistic dating patterns to prevail. Through patient, gentle church discipline, coordination with groups such as Peacemakers (see note 26 below), and aid to families in trouble with governmental agents, the church can assist the most troubled, sin-racked families.

26. 1 Cor 6:1-11: the work of Peacemaker Ministries is crucial in this regard, since it exists to help Christians follow this passage. For help in your area, contact Peacemaker Ministries (1537 Ave. D., Suite 352, Billings, MT 59102, 406-256-1583). See also Jay Adams, *The Handbook of Church Discipline* (Grand Rapid: Zondervan, 1986).

27. Rom 13:1-7; 1 Pet 2:13-17.

28. The supreme example of this is the state educational system. While the state has an interest in the literacy and capabilities of its citizens, its interest is not compelling enough to override the family's God-given domain. Prussian and Russian state education—the model for ours—helped to produce totalitarian control of society.

29. For a good start on ideas to protect the family, see Allen C. Carlson, *Family Questions* (cited in chapter 12, note 7).

30. For ideas on this issue see Blair Adams, *Who Owns the Children*? (cited in chapter 12, note 6).

31. Since there are so many areas under this heading, only a truncated introductory list is given.

32. Christians must develop *biblical* strategies and tactics based upon *biblical* policy and grand strategy and not on merely traditional or pragmatic principles, which may be conservative, but *are not* biblical. Conservative or traditional strategies will preserve the status quo which is a semi-paganized culture sliding towards total cultural relativity and oblivion. Christ, not

conservatism, will cleanse our culture. Rush Limbaugh may be right, but he's not righteous. Apart from Christ, he has no standing with the God who loaned him his talents. Dr. Laura's leaning on the law or her tough "torah-ism" is better than loose liberalism. But law without Christ's grace can only provoke disobedience and bring down Christ's condemnation. Curt conservatives cannot curtail the cultural slide. Frenetic pharisees will fail in their attempts to salvage western culture.

Section 6

~

CAN MY FAMILY HELP?

~

CHAPTER 15

Your Family and God's Covenant

As we finish our study of the family and of the battle to control it, let's outline a few tactical maneuvers. I want you as an individual, especially if you are the head of a family unit, to make three key tactical moves. Covenant with God to:

- keep His covenant
- keep His priorities
- keep in contact with His fighting forces.

Keep Your Covenant with God

To keep a covenant with God depends first of all on God's grace itself. But through that grace, you can make two commitments.

You must covenant with God as an individual.[1]

As we saw in chapters 11 and 14, you must be born from above by the Holy Spirit to have the power of new life and must be adopted into God's family so you will become like Jesus, the second Adam, and not remain like the first Adam.[2] You must repent of your self-sufficiency and turn from your self-centered perspective to God's, and believe that Jesus' life, death, resurrection, ascension to glory and pouring out of the Holy Spirit on you is the only way you can follow Him and fight under His command. If this has not occurred, then God's wrath is upon you and your family. In mercy, God offers you grace to change allegiances and families.[3] If you *have* covenanted to be His disciple and fight for Him, you need to grow in holiness and become more like Him.[4] Remember, God has always used individuals, especially individual family heads, to bless others.[5] A second necessity follows from covenanting with God.

You must covenant as the head of a family unit that you and your family will serve God.

Like Joshua, you must choose this day whom you will serve, and thus become a challenge to other families to choose between old idols, new idols, or the one true and living God. Like Joshua, spend time meeting with Him,[6] then heed His encouraging call:

> Moses My servant is dead; now therefore arise, cross this Jordan, you and all this people, to the land which I am giving to them, to the sons of Israel. Every place on which the sole of your foot treads, I have given it to you, just as I spoke to Moses. From the wilderness and this Lebanon, even as far as the great river, the river Euphrates, all the land of the Hittites, and as far as the Great Sea toward the setting of the sun, will be your territory. No man will *be able* to stand before you all the days of your life. Just as I have been with Moses, I will be with you; I will not fail you or forsake you. Be strong and courageous, for you shall give this people possession of the land which I swore to their fathers to give them. Only be strong and very courageous, to be careful to do according to all the law which Moses My servant commanded you; do not turn from it to the right or to the left, so that you have success wherever you go. This book of the law shall not depart from your mouth, but you shall meditate on it day and night, so that you may be careful to do according to all that is written in it; for then you will make your way prosperous, and then you will have success. Have I not commanded you? Be strong and courageous! Do not tremble or be dismayed, for the LORD your God is with you wherever you go.[7]

Now make the same commitment as Joshua:

> Now, therefore, fear the Lord and serve Him in sincerity and truth; and put away the gods which your fathers served beyond the River and in Egypt, and serve the LORD. And if it is disagreeable in your sight to serve the LORD, choose for yourselves today whom you will serve: whether the gods which your fathers served which were beyond the River, or the gods of the Amorites in whose land you are living; but as for me and my house, we will serve the LORD.[8]

Keep God's Priorities

Understand how He views His world. In descending order of importance, God's priorities are: your personal relationships with God, spouse, extended family, and the family of faith; your calling in life; your witness to the world; your citizenship; and your other personal pursuits.[9] If you do not make a schedule to reflect these priorities, all your covenant commitments will dissipate like the morning dew.[10] Also make a commitment to work at shaping your family biblically.[11]

Keep in Contact with God's Forces

Accountability to a local body of believers is essential for tactical soundness.[12] If soldiers were never required to report back to their commanding officers, how effective would military strategy and tactics be? Though the church, fortunately, is not run exactly like the military, we do need fellow believers who help us to take our commitments seriously. Pick someone in the body to whom you will be accountable for deciding and keeping your schedule. Start now, don't delay. Don't worry, fear or hesitate—go for it now. Follow Philippians 4:4-9. Pray with thanksgiving, point your mind to proper thinking, and practice, practice, practice what you know of the Christian life and battle. May the God of peace guard your hearts and minds as a sentinel and grant you the peace that surpasses every human understanding.[13]

May our great God and Savior grant to you and your family victory and the grace to participate in the third Great Awakening. Thus may He bless us.

> Now the God of Peace, who brought up from the dead the great Shepherd of the sheep through the blood of the eternal covenant, even Jesus our Lord, equip you in every good thing to do His will, working in us that which is pleasing in

His sight, through Jesus Christ; to whom be the glory forever and ever.[14]

Now to Him who is able to keep you from stumbling and to make you stand in the presence of His glory, blameless with great joy, to the only God our Savior, through Jesus Christ our Lord, be glory, majesty, dominion and authority, before all time and now and forever. Amen. [15]

Notes:

Chapter 15

1. For an explanation of the concept of covenant, see O. Palmer Robertson, *Christ of the Covenant* (cited in chapter 4, note 1).

2. John 3:1-16.

3. John Blanchard, *Right with God* (cited in Introduction, note 18).

4. Helpful works on personal holiness are: J. I. Packer, *Knowing God* (Downers Grove: InterVarsity, 1973); Jerry Bridges, *The Pursuit of Holiness* (Colorado Springs: NavPress, 1978); The *Practice of Godliness* (Colorado Springs: NavPress, 1983); Richard L. Ganz, *You Shall Be Free Indeed: The Statutes of Liberty for Godly Living* (Ottawa: The G S G Group, 1989).

5. See Appendix 3. This chart gives a quick overview of this phenomenon:

Family Head	Covenantal Administration	Covenantal Promise	Covenant Sign
1) Adam	Covenant of life or works	Fellowship with God in the Garden	Tree of Life
2) Adam	Covenant of grace or salvation	Seed of Eve to crush Satan's head	Seed in Adam's image
3) Noah	Covenant of Preservation and Protection	Regularity of God's Providence	Rainbow
4) Abraham	Covenant of Promised Son to Elect Family-Nation	Elect Son to bless the world	Circumcision
5) Children of Israel Moses as Mediator	Covenant of Separation	Angel of the Lord to bless and curse Offer to be second Abraham	Sabbath System
6) David	Covenant of Kingdom	Eternal Rule through Son on His Throne	Temple
7) Jesus Christ	New (last) Covenant	Eternal Kingdom with New Heaven and New Earth	Baptism Lord's Supper Holy Spirit

6. Ex 33:7-11.

7. Josh 1:2-9.

8. Josh 24:14-15.

9. See Jay E. Adams, *Christian Living in the Home* (Phillipsburg: Presbyterian and Reformed, 1972), chapter 7.

10. A higher priority is always considered and entered into the schedule before lower ones, although it may not receive as much time. For example, personal worship gets first preference and the *best* time slot, but does not receive as much time as does work. Only monks could do otherwise! For help on scheduling, see Jay Adams, *The Christian Counselor's Manual* (Grand

Rapids: Zondervan, 1973), 171-216, 281-2. For help understanding priorities, see J. Adams, *Maintaining the Delicate Balance in Christian Living* (Woodruff: Timeless Texts, 1998).

11. I strongly suggest that, as a couple or family unit, you work through one of the helpful manuals mentioned in Appendix 9: *Christian Living in the Home*, *Preparing for Marriage God's Way*, *Strengthening Your Marriage*, or *Your Family God's Way*.

12. Heb 10:19-31. See Appendix 5.

13. Phil 4:4-9.

14. Heb 13:20-21.

15. Jude 24-25.

APPENDICES

APPENDIX 1

Biblical Texts that Deal with the Family

This is an index of texts that touch on the family and related matters. Those in bold type are major texts that have major formative influence in a doctrine of the family.

GENESIS

1:26-31; **2:7**, **18-24**; **3**; **4**; **5:1-5**, 6-32; **6:1-9:19**; 9:20-29; 10; 11; **12:1-3**, 8, 10-20; 13:1-13; 14-16; **17**; 18; 19:8; 20; 21; **22:1-19**, 20-24; 23; **24**; 25; **26**; **27:42-28:9**; 28:10-22; 29; 30:25-43; 31-36; **37**; 38; 39; 41:50-52; 42-45; **46:1-7**, 8-27; 48; **49**; **50**.

EXODUS

1:1-7; 2:16-22; 4:18-26; 6:14-27; 9:24; **10:1-2**, **8-10**; **11**; **12**; **13:1-16**; 17:1-7; 18; **19**; 20:12, 14, 17; **21:1-11**, **15**, **17**; **22:16-17**, 21-24, 28-30; **23:17**, 31-33; 28:1; 29:8-9; 30:30; **31:12-17**; 32:1-14; 33:7-11; 34:10-28.

LEVITICUS

10:1-3, 19-20; **12**; **15:16-33**; **18**; **19:**1-4, **19-22**, 29; **20:1-5**, **9**, **10-16**, **17-21**; **21:1-15**; **22:10-16**; **25:10**, **25**; 26:29-30; **27:1-8**.

NUMBERS

1; 2:32-34; 3:1; 4:1-2; **5:**6-10, **11-31**; 6:7; 8:5-19; 10:11-28, 29-32; 11:10-35; **12:1-15**; 13:2; 14; **16**; 17; 18:8-20; **20:2-12**, **24**; **26**; **27:1-14**; **30**; 31:1-20; 32; 34:16-29; **35**; **36**.

DEUTERONOMY

1:9-18, 23, 31, 37-40; 2; 3:6, 18-20; **4:9-10**, **25-26**; **5:1-5**, **9-10**; **6**; **7**; 10:15-22; **11:18-21**; 12:12, 18, 31; 13:6-11; **14:1-2**, 22-27; **15**; **17:14-20**; **19:6**, **12**, **18-21**; **20:5-7**; **21:10-21**; **22:1-4**, **13-30**; 23:2, 17, 19; **24:1-5**, **16**; **25:5-12**; **27:16**, **20**, **22**, **23**; **28:4**, **11**, **30**, **32**, **50**, **53-59**; **29:29**; 30; 31:9-13; 32.

JOSHUA

2:18-19; 4:1-9; 6:22-23; 7; 13-22; **23:1**, **12-13**; 24.

JUDGES

1:10-15, 22-36; 2:1-5, 10; **3:6-7**; 4:8-10; 5:9; 6:15-16; 8:22-23, 27; 9; 11:1-3, 28-40; 12:8-15; 13; 14; 16:1, 4, 16-17, 31; 17-21.

RUTH

1 SAMUEL

1:1-11, **19-20**; **2:5**, **12-36**; **8**; 9:21; 10:20-21; 14:49-51; **16:5-13**; 17:12-15, 28-29; **18**; **25**; 30:1-20.

2 SAMUEL

2:26-27; 3; 5:1-2, 13-16; 6; 7; 8:18; 9; 11-19; 21:1-4; **23:3-5**.

1 KINGS

1; **2**; **3:1-3**, 16-28; 8; 9:24; **11:1-13**; 13:22; 14:1-18, 21; 15:1-3, 9-11, 24-26, 33-34; 16:6, 8-13, 25-34; 17:7-24; 20:14; **21**.

2 KINGS

3:1-3, 26-27; 4:1-37; 5:13, 27; 8:1-7, 16-19, 24-27; 9:7-8, 28; 10:11, 17, 30-31, 35; 11:1-3; 12:1-3, 21; 13:1-3, 9-11; 14:1-2, 5-6, 16, 20, 23-24, 29; 15:1-4, 7-9, 17-18, 23-24, 27-28, 32-35, 38; 16:1-4, 20; 17:1-2, 40-41; 18:1-4; 19:37; 20:21; 21:1-6, 18-22; 22:1-2, 20; 23:1-3, 31-32, 36-37; 24:3-4, 6, 8-9, 18-20; 25:7.

1 CHRONICLES

1-9; 11:1-3; 14:1-7; 15:29; 16:15, 28-30, 43; **17**; 21:16; 22:6-13; 24-27; **28:1-3**; 29:6.

2 CHRONICLES

1:1-3; 5:2-3; **6:4-11**; **7:17-22**; 8:11; 9:31; 11:4, 18-21, 23; 12:16; 13:1-2, 21; 14:1, 2-6; 15:12, 16-18; 16:13-14; 18:1-2; 19:1-3; 20:13, 35-37; 21:1-6, 12-17; 22; 24:1-3, 20-22; 25:1-4, 28; 26:1-5, 23; 27:1-4, 9; 28:1-4, 27; **29:1-2**, **6-11**; 30:1-9; 32:20-22, 33; 33:6, 20-23; 34:1-2, 28; 35:3-4, 12, 24; 36:15-21.

EZRA

1:5; 2; 7:1-5; 8:1-19; **9-10**.

NEHEMIAH

1:5-7; 2:1-5, 16; 3; 4:14; 5:7; 7; 9:3-38; 10:1-31; **13:4**; **23-31**.

ESTHER

1; 2:5-7, 15; 3:6, 8; 4:13-17; 9:28-32; 10.

JOB

1:1-5, 6, 20-22; 2:1, 9-10; 5:3-4, 24-26; 8:4, 8-10; 16:7; 17:13-16; 18:13; **19:13-22**; 20:10; 21:7-16; 22:6; 24:9, 20-21; 27:13-23; 29; 30:1-14, 29; **31:1-4**, **9-12**, 16-23; 32:1-12; 39:13-17; 41:5; **42:10-17**.

PSALMS

2; 8:2, 4-5; **9:12**; 10:14, 18; **16:5-6**, 17:14; 18:50; 19:5; 21:9-10; 22:9-10, 22-23, 27-28; 23:6; 25:12-15; 27:9-10; **28:9**; 29:1; **34:11**; 35:14; 37:25-26, 37-38; 38:1; 44:1-2; **45**; 48:6; 49:5-20; 50:20; 58:3; 68:5-6; **69:5-12**, 34-36; 71; **72**; 73:15, 74:2; **78:1-8**, 9-72; 79:13; **80**; **87:5-6**; 89:1-4, 19-37; 90:13-17; 91:9-16; 92:12-15; 94:5-7; 96:7; 98:3; 102:18-28; 103:17-18; 105:6; 106:4-5, 34-39; 109:6-15; 112:1-6; 113:5-9; 115:14-15; **122:6-9**; **127**; **128**; **131**; 132:11-12; 135:5-8; 137:7-9; 139:13-16; 144:3, 12; 145:4-7, 12; 146:5-9; 148:11-12.

PROVERBS

1-9; 10:1, 5, 7, 17; 11:29; 12:1, 4, 15; 13:1, 10, 13-14, 18, 22, 24; 14:1, 11, 26, 28; 15:5, 17, 20, 25, 27; 16:31; 17:1, 2, 6, 13, 17, 21, 25; 18:19, 22; 19:7, 13, 14, 18, 26, 27; 20:7, 11, 20, 21, 29; 21:9, 19; 22:6, 14, 15, 17-21; 23:13-16, 19-21; 23:22-27; 24:3-4; 25:24; 27:8, 10, 11; 27:15-16, 23-27; 28:7, 24; 29:3, 15, 17; 30:1-6, 11-17, 20-23; **31**.

ECCLESIASTES

2:7-8, 18-26; **4:7-12**; 5:13-14; 6:1-3; **9:7-10**; 11:9-10; 12:1.

SONG OF SONGS

ISAIAH

1:2-9; **3:4-7, 12**; **4:1-2**; 5:1; **7:10-17**; **8:1-4, 18**; **9:6-7, 17**; 10:1-4; **11:1-4**; 13:15-16, 18; 14:20-22; 23:4; 26:16-18; 28:9-10; **30:1-5, 8-26**; 31:6; 32:9-13; 37:22; 38:18-19; 39:5-8; 42:14; 43:1-7; 27; 44:1-8; 45:9-12; 46:3-4; 47:1, 8-9; **48:1-19**; **49:1, 5, 14-16**; **50:1**; **51:1-2**, 18-20; 54:1-8; 56:4-5; 57:3-4; 60:4-9, 14-16, 21-22; 61:8-9; 62:4-5; **63:15-19**; **64:8-9**; **65:12-25**; **66:7-14**.

JEREMIAH

1:4-8; **2**; **3**; **4:1-4**, 22, 30-31; 5:3, 7-9, 17; 6:10-12; **7:16-20, 30-34**; 8:10, 19; 9:4-9, 20-21; 12:6-13; 13:20-27; 14:16; 15:7-9; 16:1-9; **18:19-23**, 19:8-9; 20:13-18; 22:15-17, 23; **23**; 25:10; 29:4-7; 30:20; 31:1, 9, 15-20, 28-34; **33:14-22**; **35**; **44:7-10, 15-19**, 47:3; 49:1-6; 50:37, 43.

LAMENTATIONS

1:1-3

EZEKIEL

5:10, 17; 8:3, 6; 9:5-6; **14:12-20**; 16; 18; 20:21-38; **22:1-12**; **23**; 24:15-27; 36:13; 46:16-18; 47; 48.

DANIEL

1:3-7; 6:24; 9:4-20.

HOSEA

1-3; 4:1-2, 10-19; 5:3, 6-7; 6:10; 7:4; 9:11-17; 10:14-15; **11:1-11**; 13:12-13; 14:3.

JOEL

1:3, 8; 2:12-17, 28-29.

AMOS

2:7; 3:1-2; 4:1-3; 5:2; 7:17; 8:13.

OBADIAH

18

MICAH

2:2, 9; 4:8-13; 5:3; 6:6-8; 7:1-13.

ZEPHANIAH

1:13; 3.

ZECHARIAH

1:4-6; 2:7, 10; 8:1-5; 9:9; 10:7; **12:10-14**; **13:1-3**; 14:16-21.

MALACHI

1:6; **2:10-12**, **13-16**; 3:3, 5, 7; **4**.

MATTHEW

1; 2:4; **3:9**, **16-17**; **6:1**, **4**, **6**, **8**, **9**, **15**, **18**, **32-33**; **7:9-11**, **21-23**; 9:18-26; **10:32-39**; **11:**11, **25-27**; **12:46-49**; 14:6-12; **15:1-9**, 21-28; 17:14-21; **18:1-10**, **35**; **19:1-15**, **27-30**; 20:20-28; **21:**14-17, **33-46**; **22:1-14**, **23-33**, **41-45**; 23:8-11.

LUKE

1:5-25, **26-80**; **2:21-52**; **3:23-38**; **4:14-30**; 7:11-17; **8:19-21**, 38-56; **9:32-36**, 37-42; **46-48**, **57-62**; **10:21-22**, 38-42; **11:1-13**, **27-28**; **12:13-15**; 13:34-35; **14:25-27**; **15:11-32**; **16:18**, 19-31; 17:1-10; **18:15-17**, **38**; 19:9; **20:9-19**, **27-39**, **41-44**; 22.

JOHN

1:9-18, **34**; 2; **3:3**, **5-8**, 16-21, **27-36**; 4:16-19, 23-24, 43-45; 6:32-71; 7:1-10; 8:17-18, 23, 31-59; **9:1-5**, 35; 10:1, 6; 11; **12:**12-19, **20-36**, **42-50**; **13:1-2**, **12-20**; **14-17**; **19:25-27**; **20:17-18**.

ACTS

1:15-16; 2:38-39; 5:1-11; **6:1-6**; 10:22-23; **11:1**; 13:15, 23, 26; 14:2; 15:1, 7, 23, 32; **16:31-34**; **17:14**; 18:1-2, 24-28; 21:4-6, 20; 23:16-22; 28:17.

ROMANS

1:1-4, 9, **26-27**, **30**, 32; **2:28-29**; **4:16-17**; **5:12-19**; 6:1-14; **7:1-6**; **8:12-17**; **9:6-9**; 16:13.

1 CORINTHIANS

1:9, 16, 26; **4:**6, **14-17**; **5**; **6:1-11**, 12-20; **7:1-40**; 8:11-13; **9:5**; 10:15-17; **11:2-16**, 27-34; 13:11-12; **14:**20, **33-37**; **15:20-28**, **42-49**.

2 CORINTHIANS

1:3; **6:**11-13, **14-18**; **11:1-3**; **12:14-15**; **13:10-11**.

GALATIANS

3:7, 15-16, 19, 23-29; **4:1-7**, **21-31**; **6:10**, **16**.

EPHESIANS

1:13-14; **2:11-18**; **3:14-15**; **5:22-33**; **6:1-4**.

PHILIPPIANS

2:12-16, 19-30; 3:1-17; 4:1.

COLOSSIANS

1:1-2, 13-20, **28-29**; 2:8-12; **3:18-25**; **4:1**, 7, 9.

1 THESSALONIANS

1:3; **2:6-8**, **11-12**, 19-20; **4:1-8**, 9-18.

2 THESSALONIANS

3:6-15

1 TIMOTHY

1:1-2; **2:8-15**; **3:1-13**; 4:3-5; **5:1-2**, **3-16**.

2 TIMOTHY

1:1-2; **3-5**; 2:1, 8, 22; **3:2-7**, **14-17**.

TITUS

1:5-12; **2:1-10**.

PHILEMON

1-2, 10, 16, 20.

HEBREWS

1:1-9; **2:8-18**; **3:**1, **5-6**; **5:5-10**; 7:3, 28; **11:24-26**; **12:1-13, 23**; **13:**1, **4**.

JAMES

1:9-10, **18-19**, 27; 2:14; 4:1-6; 5:7.

1 PETER

1:2-3, 13-25; **2:18-25**; **3:1-7**; 4:17; 5:13.

2 PETER

1:10, **17-18**; 3:15.

1 JOHN

1:1-4; 2:1, 12-15, 22-25, 28; 3:1, 7-24; 4:4, 7; 5:1-4, 21.

2 JOHN

1, 2, 13.

3 JOHN

4

JUDE

REVELATION

2:12-29; 3:19; **12:1-10;** 14:1-2; 17:14-15; **19:7-9**; 21:22; 22:16, 17, 21.

APPENDIX 2

The Family and Theology

The "culture war" has replaced star wars. On AM radio station KFI Los Angeles you can listen to conservative Rush Limbaugh in the morning and to liberal Larry King in the evening. This battle for control of Western civilization in the USA is documented both by Christians and non-Christians.[1] And now, Dr. Laura Schlessinger has added her program and books to the culture clash.

Why does this war rage? In the beginning, Christianity heavily influenced our country. Now liberals and conservatives battle for power while Christians are often ignored. Believe it or not, theological conflicts helped to create this war. From our vigorous start based on the Protestant Reformation, English Puritanism and later the Great Awakening, we slid into pietism and cultural isolation.[2]

In the twentieth century, the modernist-fundamentalist battle was joined. Christianity's vestigial cultural influence began to die in the teens, '20s and '30s as modernity marched methodically on. From the '60s through the '80s the influence of fundamentalism continued to decrease with the early defection of its child, evangelicalism. By and large, the church lost the battle to be salt and light. Nonbiblical ideas not only prevailed in the university, but in the seminary as well. Secular ideas ruled in the pew as well as in the classroom. Since the church is salt and light, if it becomes unsavory and dim, the gospel call dulls and fades. As the church goes, so goes the culture around it. F. Schaeffer's *The Great Evangelical Disaster*[3] and H.O.J. Brown's *Heresies* [4] chronicle this debacle within the household of faith. Recently, Christian sociologist J. D. Hunter traced this process with care and precision.[5] Hunter's data force the conclusion that the church's theological scholarship is a mixture of secular and sacred ideas, more bogus than biblical, more psychological than prophetic. The church has lost its influence over the world.

This erosion is seen in the theological thinking of well-known evangelical scholars. For example, Clark Pinnock's *A Defense of Biblical Infallibility*[6] is one of the finest defenses of this doctrine ever written. Yet, he has since changed his views in radical ways. By 1986, he held a position akin to process theology which teaches that God is limited in knowledge; God is neither omniscient nor infinite.[7] By 1988, he had come to believe that people can be saved apart from the person and work of Jesus Christ; personal regeneration and sanctification by the Holy Spirit are not necessary.[8] By 1990, he held that both liberalism and fundamentalism are wrong and that his kind of evangelicalism will save theology. However, many of his views are indistinguishable from old liberalism! More astounding is his rejection of the infallibility of Scripture; he said that it contains errors.[9] Cult researcher and theologian R. A. Morey exposes the seriousness of his slide.[10] Needless to say, the gospel has been flung to the winds in such a headlong plunge.

But, you say, what does this have to do with the family? The family and theological issues related to it are at the center of this process. To combat certain "family-related" sin, twentieth-century Christians employed feminism and other egalitarian forms of liberation theology, which increased the cultural slide by making the church more like the world rather than encouraging it to influence the world, as Jesus asked it to do, in its role of salt and light. Thus, theologians changed cultural norms for ill.[11] In fact, it was primarily the issue of the woman's role in the family that helped to open this theological Pandora's box.

Two evangelical scholars demonstrate that a change in the views of the family and its structure will inevitably necessitate changing the structure of theology. Paul Jewett's *Man as Male and Female*[12] is the most scholarly defense of the evangelical feminist position. He holds to egalitarianism in marriage, but his argument is marred by a denigration of Scripture: the Old Testament contains errors;[13] these errors led to the oppression of women;[14] the Apostle Paul made mistakes in his letters;[15] Genesis

1–2 are not real history as we understand literal history;[16] the humanity of the biblical writers necessitates errors in their writing;[17] Christ, like Paul, was so influenced by his culture that he held erroneous ideas.[18]

By 1991, his position had evolved radically.[19] Throughout his more recent book, Jewett uses the feminine pronoun for theologians. While a minor point, it is an irritant. His style is lucid and enjoyable, and some of what he says is helpful. Therefore, this usage of "she" is meant to be a burr under the reader's saddle. Jewett describes his theology as neo-evangelical because he "has the Bible in one hand and the newspaper in the other."[20] He claims he resists "the canons of modernity"; one wonders if the paper isn't more authoritative than the Bible. Jewett evaluates protest or liberation theologies positively (though he does not endorse them unequivocally), and he equates them too facilely with the Protestant Reformation.[21] Jewett claims that the analogical nature of biblical language allows us to use its analogies in new ways. For example, since God is personal, it is not necessarily wrong to refer to God as "She."[22] Jewett belittles hierarchicalism for hiding behind the Trinity and claims that the submission of Christ to the Father, to obtain our salvation, says nothing to women in particular, only to people in general.[23] Jewett says that the Trinity should still be referred to as the "Father-Son-Spirit," since Jesus was a man. However, it would be orthodox to call God "Mother-Daughter-Spirit."[24] His position on the Trinity is inadequate. Jewett refers to God as "She." He says that Hosea learned the love of God and then gave it to Gomer, which parallels God's love. Jewett says of God that "her" love for Israel, caused "her" anger to burn at Israel. One wonders how God could be Israel's husband and "she." Is God now a lesbian?

The strongest theme in Jewett's work is his disdain for the biblical doctrine of inerrancy and those who hold to it. He believes there is no inerrant Church or Bible.[25] He condescendingly states that the Chicago Statement of the *Council on Biblical Inerrancy* is not worthy of his time and that therefore, he does not answer it.[26] Biblical criticism is to be accepted, while scholars such as B. B. Warfield are not.[27] Even though he admits that fundamentalism is closer to the truth than liberalism, he castigates any attempts to harmonize the Bible.[28] And of course Genesis 1–11 is not time and space history, even though it is not myth.[29]

If Jewett does not convince us that there is an organic unity between one's view of family structure and one's theology, then surely Virginia Mollenkott does. Dr. Mollenkott is a committed feminist egalitarian who wrote the foreword to Jewett's *Man as Male and Female*. Since then she has written books defending this position.[30] In 1978, with L. Scanzoni, she wrote *Is the Homosexual my Neighbor*?[31] and concludes that homosexuality is not condemned by the Bible, although violent homosexual rape and promiscuity are. Later, she argues that the pro-choice abortion position is biblically correct; a pro-life stance is not.[32] Not surprisingly, she has admitted she is a lesbian.[33] In her book, *Sensuous Spirituality: Out from Fundamentalism,* she says:

> When I was young, I memorized a lot of Scripture, all from the venerable King James Version of 1611. One of the passages I memorized was Jeremiah 17:9: "The heart is deceitful above all things, and desperately wicked: who can know it?" I now understand passages like that to be talking about the human ego-nature that imagines itself separate from God and separate from all other creatures, as opposed to the eternal and holy Self that is the human essence. In other words, I now understand that such passages refer to what the apostle Paul called "flesh," *sarx*: "the state of illusion in which the natural, fallen [human being] found [herself] believing that [she] had [her] life at [her] own disposal, that [she] could live out of [her] own resources, that [she] was not utterly and wholly dependent upon God" (Cole, 95). Paul contrasted "flesh" with "spirit," the sense of connectedness with God that is at the human core. But that is not what I was taught during my early years. Instead, I was given to understand that passages about the ego or "flesh" were descriptions of my deepest, most essential being, the very core of my personhood, which

could be redeemed and controlled only by the installation of a totally-other Christ-nature (a pacemaker of the soul).

Consequently, I was suspicious of any psychologists or theologians who spoke of the goodness and beauty of the human core, "the dearest freshness deep down things" that Jesuit poet Gerard Manley Hopkins rejoiced in. No matter how much distortion has been produced in the personality because of its response to threats and traumas, several psychologists pointed out, underneath all the damage lies hidden a beautiful Self. I desperately wanted to believe them, but I was blocked by the interpretation of the Bible that I had been taught. And of course, at the time, I was confusing a human interpretation with the absolute truth of what the Bible teaches.

So how does a fundamentalist who believes she is essentially and totally depraved become transformed into a person who knows she is an innocent spiritual being who is temporarily having human experiences? The answer is: through a long and gradual process involving the study of hermeneutics; a great deal of dreaming and learning to interpret those dreams; extensive journaling; psychological use of the *I Ching* and the *Tarot* to learn something about the movement of my unconscious mind; agonizing struggles with *A Course in Miracles*; studying the works of Paul Norman Tuttle; reading up on the hermetic tradition and on spiritual healing; much pondering of great theological poets like John Milton and Emily Dickinson; listening to and reading outstanding thinkers among my contemporaries; learning how to love and be loved; the experience of my mother's death and thereafter our continued closeness; here and there, some psychotherapy; and some mildly mystical experiences.

Inasmuch as I still sometimes revert to the judgmentalism and divisiveness of a human ego that is on its own in a hostile world, the process continues. But there was for me one distinct "holy instant" when my basic perception of myself flipped into a different mode. Prior to that "holy instant" I had inched my way from believing myself totally depraved (although redeemed by God's grace) to believing myself a basically decent human being who was having some lovely spiritual experiences. But one day while I was meditating, I experienced a reality that was even better

> than that: like my Elder Brother, Jesus, I am a sinless Self travelling through eternity and temporarily having human experiences in a body known as Virginia Ramey Mollenkott.[34]

She goes on to affirm among other things: the value of occult mysticism and spiritguides;[35] the fallacious character of Christian doctrine and the true Aramaic doctrine that amounts to the ancient enemy of Christianity, Gnosticism;[36] the nonliteral but allegorical nature of biblical revelation;[37] the necessity of subverting conventional churches so they will accept egalitarianism and lesbianism;[38] the truth of pantheism;[39] the erotophobia of conventional churches.[40]

Progressively, her positions deviate more and more from the Scriptures. Each perversely attacks the family structure that God requires.[41] Jewett and Mollenkott show how basic family issues can be involved in theological decline. Change the biblical doctrine of the family and you will change your view of God, the Bible, etc. Which is the chicken and which the egg is hard to determine, but most likely the family issue pushed them into adjusting other doctrines that eventually led to liberalism, which is not Christianity.[42] Paganism is not far off.[43]

How shall we respond to this familial and theological decline?

Steven B. Clark calls the Jewett-Mollenkott approach to the Bible, "Christian Liberationist Exegesis" and ably and irenically exposes its fallacies.[44] William Oddie also deals with this mentality in *What Will Happen to God? Feminism and the Reconstruction of Christian Belief.*[45] Oddie focuses on the extent of the corruption of various aspects of Christian theology by a consistent feminist position. Harold Harrington proves the same things,[46] and Robert Letham delineates the effects of feminist theology as clearly as any other writer, proving that an orthodox doctrine of the Trinity is impossible on a feminist reading of Scripture.[47] Letham's contention is underscored by Jewett's confusion on the Trinity.

The journey of several Christian feminists adds evidence to the theory. They have often moved on from acceptance of homosexuality and abortion to nature worship and the adulation of female deities; they are only being consistent. If you change your view of the family and its structure, your God must change or you will change gods. Peter Jones, professor of New Testament at Westminster Theological Seminary in California, demonstrates the integral connection between ancient Gnosticism, new age thinking and feminism and their hostility to biblical Christianity and its God-created norms of male-female relationships.[48] He shows the inevitable direction of feminist thinking and the conflict between pagan and godly thinking as it affects many aspects of our life and theology in *Spirit Wars: Pagan Revival in Christian America.* He points out that this is pure paganism in his handy summary book, *Gospel Truth, Pagan Lies: Can You Tell the Difference?*[49] Charles Colson deals with the practical implications of unisex thinking,[50] while Donald G. Bloesch demonstrates that feminism has acutely embarrassing parallels to the German Christian movement.[51] (Perhaps Rush Limbaugh's term "Femi-Nazis" is not that far off.)

On the issue of men and women and their roles in the family and church, see the footnote for a list of helpful references.[52] Ecclesiastical battle lines over the role of women have formed, including two evangelical groups. Both advertise nationally and send out purpose statements and literature. The literature demonstrates the intricate relationship between the family and theology.[53] And, of course, denominations are affected as well.[54]

Notes:

Appendix 2

1. J. Burnham, *Suicide of the West: An Essay on the Meaning and Destiny of Liberalism* (New York: John Day 1964); A. Bloom, *The Closing of the American Mind* (New York: Simon and Schuster, 1987); F. Schaeffer, *Whatever Happened to the Human Race*? (Grand Rapids: Revell, 1979); H. Schlossberg, *Idols for Destruction* (Nashville: Nelson, 1983); W. Dannemeyer, "The Cultural War in America," *Crosswinds*, vol 1, no 1 (Winter 1992), 17-19; W. J. Bennett, *The Devaluing of America: The Fight for Our Culture and Our Children* (New York: Summit Books, 1992); Peter Jones, *Spirit Wars: Pagan Revival in Christian America* (Mukilteo, WA: Winepress, 1997, reprinted under a new title by Regal, 2001).

2. For the most comprehensive, clear analysis of the causes, religious nature, parameters and significance of the culture wars, see J. D. Hunter, *Culture Wars: The Struggle to Define America* (Basic Books, 1991).

3. Wheaton: Crossway Books, 1993.

4. Grand Rapids: Baker, 1984.

5. *American Evangelicalism: Conservative Religion and the Quandary of Modernity* (Rutgers University, 1984); *Evangelicalism: The Coming Generation* (University of Chicago, 1987).

6. Phillipsburg: Presbyterian and Reformed, 1967.

7. Cf. D. & R. Basinter, eds., *Predestination and Free Will: Four Views of Divine Sovereignty and Human Freedom* (Wheaton: InterVarsity Press, 1986).

8. See M. A. Noll and D. F. Wells, eds., *Christian Faith and Practice in Modern World Theology: Theology from an Evangelical Point of View* (Grand Rapids: Eerdmans, out of print).

9. *Touching the Maze: Finding our Way through Modern Theology from an Evangelical Perspective* (New York: Harper & Row; 1990).

10. "Alarming Mega-Shifts in Evangelicalism," *The Researcher*, vol 1, No 2 (March/April 1992), 1-2.

11. See note 22, chapter 2.

12. Grand Rapids: Eerdmans, 1975.

13. Jewett, op.cit., 88-90.

14. Ibid., 112.

15. Ibid., 116, 118, 127, 138.

16. Ibid., 120-1.

17. Ibid., 135.

18. Ibid., 136-7.

19. See *God, Creation and Revelation: a Neo-Evangelical Theology* (Grand Rapids: Eerdmans, 1991).

20. Ibid., xvi.

21. Ibid., 13-4.

22. Ibid., 44-48.

23. Ibid., 322-3.

24. Ibid., 324-5.

25. Ibid., 143.

26. Ibid., 129-30, footnote 40.

27. Ibid., 134.

28. Ibid., 140.

29. Ibid., 470-9.

30. See, for example, *Godding: Human Responsibility and the Bible;* and *The Divine Feminine: The Biblical Imagery of God As Female* (Nashville: Crossroad/Continuum Books, out of print).

31. New York: Harper and Row, 1978.

32. "Reproductive Choice: Basic to Justice for Women," *Christian Scholar's Review* (March 12, 1988), 286-293.

33. "Heterosexism: A Challenge to Ecumenical Solidarity," *Women and Church: The Challenge of Ecumenical Solidarity in an Age of Alienation*, eds. M. A. May; M. K. Hellwig (Grand Rapids: Eerdmans, 1991), 38-42.

34. Virginia Ramey Mollenkott, *Sensuous Spirituality: Out from Fundamentalism* (Nashville: Crossroad, 1992), 15-6.

35. Ibid., 19.

36. Ibid., 26.

37. Ibid., 41.

38. Ibid., 47.

39. Ibid., 92-3.

40. Ibid., 96.

41. For a detailed history of Mollenkott's theological journey, see Mary A. Kassian, *The Feminist Gospel: The Movement to Unite Feminism with the Church* (Wheaton: Crossway, 1992), 237-239.

42. See J. G. Machen, *Christianity and Liberalism* (1923, Reprint, Grand Rapids: Eerdmans, 2001).

43. For proof see *Womenspirit Rising: A Feminist Reader in Religion*, eds. C. P. Christ; J. Plastow (San Francisco: Harper Collins, 1992 ed.). Especially chilling is Starhawk's "Witchcraft and Woman's Culture," 259-268.

44. *Man and Woman in Christ: An Examination of the Roles of Men and Women in the Light of Scripture and the Social Sciences* (Servant, 1988, out of print), 221-31. Though out of print, this volume can be accessed electronically at http://www.cbmw.org. Go to the bookshelf section, and you can download Clark's book.

45. London: SPK, 1984, 97-99.

46. "Feminism's Fatal Assumption," *The Christian Statesman*, vol CXXXV, No 4 (July–August 1992), 41-43.

47. "The Man-Woman Debate: Theological Comment" *Westminster Theological Journal*, 52 (2/1991) 65-78.

48. *The Gnostic Empire Strikes Back: An Old Heresy for the New Age* (Phillipsburg: Presbyterian and Reformed, 1992).

49. *Spirit Wars* (see note 1); *Gospel Truth, Pagan Lies: Can You Tell the Difference?* (Mukilteo, WA: Winepress, 1999).

50. "What Can Gender Blending Render?" *Jubilee* (Jan 1991).

51. *The Battle for the Trinity: The Debate over Inclusive God-Language* (Ann Arbor: Servant, 1985).

52. S. T. Foh, *Women and the Word of God: A Response to Biblical Feminism* (Phillipsburg: Presbyterian and Reformed, 1979). S. B. Clark, *Man and Woman in Christ.* (See note 44). Very comprehensive. Except for a too-naive acceptance of scientific data and an occasional Roman Catholic bias, this is an excellent work. J. B. Hurley, *Man and Woman in Biblical Perspective* (Grand Rapids: Zondervan, 1981). W. Neuer; trans G. J. Wenham, *Man and Woman in Christian Perspective* (Wheaton: Crossway, 1991). This is the best quick overview; many of his observations are clear, critical and challenging. Except for his repeated implication that the Old Testament oppressed women and therefore contradicts the New Testament, Neuer is helpful. J. Piper, W. Grudem, eds. *Recovering Biblical Manhood and Womanhood: A Response to Evangelical Feminism* (Wheaton: Crossway, 1991). If you must get one book on the subject, this is it. Twenty-six individual essays—many are excellent, exegetical studies—answer all your questions, the objections of evangelical feminists, and some questions you never thought of. See also their website: http://www.cbmw.org. M. A. Kassian, *The Feminist Gospel.* This is a must-read to understand the nature and history of secular, religious and biblical feminism. Kassian's biblical wisdom and irenic style speak to this topic from the heart of a committed Christian woman who loves both God's Word and other women.

53. Christians for Biblical Equality (122 W. Franklin Ave., Ste. 218, Minneapolis, MN 55404) best represents the position of "egalitarianism," and Council for Biblical Manhood and Womanhood (2825 Lexington Rd., Box 926, Louisville, KY 40280) best represents what is known as "complementarity."

54. For a study on how this issue has affected the Christian Reformed Church, see the May 1992 issue of *The Outlook*, "The Family of Man and the Family of God: Parallels and Principles." It has recently caused great controversy in the Southern Baptist denomination, and even in the conservative Presbyterian Church in America the issue of the use of women's gifts in the church is the subject of heated debate (see http://www.pcanet.org).

APPENDIX 3

The Family in Biblical History

Those who fail to remember history are doomed to repeat it.[1]

True, yet today perhaps most people ignore history.[2] Even worse, most people ignore biblical history.[3] Professional historians who study the family ignore it.[4] Ignoring history may have grave consequences; ignoring biblical history has eternal consequences. Just remember these examples are for us at the end of the age (1 Cor 10:11-14).

Biblical history is the story of God's mercy, grace, and salvation. God Himself emphasizes the importance of the history of His redeeming His people, of remembering that history, of recounting that history to coming generations, and of acting differently in the light of that history.[5] Remembering is at the heart of our worship as we remember Him and His sacrifice until He returns.[6] Paul emphatically states that if the resurrection is not a real, historical, time and space event, then we are still in our sins, still under God's wrath, and are to be pitied more than any other group of people.[7] All attempts, whether ancient or modern, to divorce Christianity from history fail, because Christianity is welded to history. The Bible, including Genesis 1–11, is not myths invented by men to give meaning to life, but truth revealed by God to dispel pagan myths. God knows we need this history to unlock the meaning of all other history.

In order to appreciate the systematic theology of the family in chapters 5–8, we need to understand how the family fits into, and plays a significant part in, biblical history. The Bible starts with God and moves through creation, the fall, ancient history before and after the flood, the patriarchal period, national Israel, New Testament times and finally on into eternity. From these key periods of history, God wants us to glean key concepts. There is no room to be exhaustive, but I will highlight points critical to the history of the family. Read the key passages first.

The Pre-Fall Period (Genesis 1–2)

The main lesson: God outlines His perfect plan in creation.

Genesis 1:26-31

Two things critical to family issues stand out. First, man is the image of God and not an animal. As noted previously, individual and corporate aspects of man image God, and, therefore, men and women marry and do not merely mate. While physical or formal similarities between animals (especially mammals) and man exist, human sexuality differs from theirs. Second, marriage is a God-ordained institution and man is not given the freedom to define, redefine, or ignore marriage.[8] Remember the attitudes of Jesus and Paul: this is not only true history, it is normative for today.[9]

Genesis 2:18-24

First, the *purpose* of marriage is given: it is not good for Adam to remain alone. He needs a companion in his task of dominion, someone to fill his lonely void, a partner to produce offspring and to complete and complement him. Second, the *plan* of marriage is given: leave, cleave, and weave (become one flesh or one personality). Third, the *purity* and *pleasure* of marriage are noted. Adam was excited to have Eve, and both were naked and not ashamed.[10]

The major thrust of this historic account is to reveal God's intentions for marriage and family life. God's redemption moves us toward perfection. Without this model, man meanders about, muddling from one mistaken idea of marriage to the next. It cannot be stated too strongly just how important this true, God-revealed norm is: you will construct an idolatrous view of marriage and the family unless these texts are taken seriously.

The Post-Fall, Antediluvian Period (Genesis 3:1–6:13)

The main lesson: sin perverts the perfect created order of family life.

Four texts are central:

Genesis 3:1-24:

This text is the historic account of the fall into sin. Satan subverts the God-ordained authority structure circumventing Adam and approaching Eve, a standard revolutionary tactic. This sin results in blame-shifting: Adam blames Eve and God; Eve blames Satan; family strife begins. Adam shirks his responsibility, fails to lead, and accuses Eve. Therefore, God curses appropriate spheres for Adam and Eve: work and childbearing, the major foci of their God-given roles. Yet, He gives hope for the family that will arise out of the family: the seed of the woman means grace and victory; where sin abounds, grace and hope much more abound.

Genesis 4:1-26

Here we find the account of the first family and the effects of the Fall on family life. Children are not naturalistic occurrences, but gifts from God (1, 2, 25). Sibling rivalry starts immediately and leads to jealousy, hatred and murder (2–8). Blame-shifting and denial of the responsibility to care for other family members begins (9). Yet, the family is the source of governmental justice (10–16). Also, sin leads to bigamy, pride, arrogance and violence (19–24); note the connection between pride, sexual lust and violence. In the midst of this, formal worship starts in the family (26). The curse devastates family life but worship, i.e. calling on God, develops in the family.

Genesis 5:1-31

This passage recounts the story of Adam's line. Children, as well as parents, are the image of God (1–3), and can trace their heritage back to Adam and then God, in whose image Adam was made. Therefore, children do not *become*, but *are* humans. God does not specially create the image in each new child; each is the image at conception. Note that family lines are important. Adam's godly seed receives the inheritance of God's covenant through the firstborn son. Cain's line is recorded, but is the seed of the serpent. Seth's line is the godly pure seed, not physically but covenantally, as evidenced by the next text: godliness can be a generation by generation occurrence in a family.

Genesis 6:1-13

Here we discover the cause of God's judgment in the flood: violence which develops from the corruption of intermarriage (1, 2, 12). The seed of the woman marries the seed of the serpent; the line of Seth marries the line of Cain.[11] This intermarriage is religious and covenantal, not racial, since there is only one race at the time.[12] God records what happens when children of godly parents marry unbelievers. One of Satan's chief tactics in destroying God's creation is the intermarriage of the sons of God and the daughters of men. In defiance of God's desires they marry whomever they want. Men are the chief offenders, although women can and do sin in this way. Such sensual, self-centered ignoring of God corrupts Seth's line (2), as the sons of God pick up the violent lifestyle of Cain (13). Few modern authors highlight this satanic scheme or its tragic results: strong, infamous covenant breakers (4). Fame and a family name do not ensure godliness.

Sin limits generational joy. God limits the life of man to one hundred twenty years, so enjoying many generations, as did Adam, Seth, etc., is no longer possible and knowing one's roots becomes harder. Also, parental sin, especially violence, destroys children. The children of the world are born in sin and taste judgment even though they have not yet sinned as their violent parents have: both are swept away in God's wrath.

These texts highlight the perversion of pre-Fall perfection. The family and its problems today started immediately after the

Fall with God's curse. If we do not take this history seriously, we will not turn to the risen, exalted Jesus Christ who is the true seed of the woman who saves us from God's wrath and who alone can fix our families.

Noah and the Development of Nations (Genesis 6:9–11:32 and Job)

The main lesson: language groups and nations develop from family lines.

God continues His covenant of redemption through a man and his family line but fresh rebellion arises and God confuses and scatters families. Man's sin cannot thwart God's covenant nor His plan to fill the earth; He always wins. Five key passages stand out.

Genesis 6:8-10, 22–7:3

One righteous man can bless his whole family (6:8-9; 7:1). One righteous family can bless the whole human race. Righteous families can be caretakers over creation, be blessed by God and really count (6:3).

Genesis 8:20 –9:17

Note, worship is in a family which becomes the womb of the church (8:20). Also, mankind is depraved (8:21). All need God's grace, even children, a fact that has vast implications for family life. Yet, God covenants with all living creatures for the sake of men (8:22). Again, God reissues the cultural mandate of the original covenant and renews the family as the chief caretaker over creation and as the womb of society and culture (9:1). Sin and redemption do not negate the cultural mandate to be fruitful, multiply and rule. Graciously, God provides providential protection (9:2), political provision (9:3-4) and political punishment (9:5-6), to enable Noah and his family to do the job. By implication, that protection grows out of the family or clan.

Symbolically, God gives the rainbow as a sign of His gracious promise never again to wipe out the whole race by water. God's grace flows out of the family.

Genesis 9:18-28

The curses and blessings of family life, just as in the post-Fall, antediluvian period, stand out. Parental sin affects children who cannot help but be hurt by it (20–23). Moreover, the blessings or curses of parents do have an effect on the inheritance of future generations (24–27).[13] Also, as children grow up and become parents, their faithfulness or sin become new parental patterns that, in turn, affect their children. Respect for parents is a significant obligation; God curses familial rebellion.

Genesis 10

Genesis 9:18-19 states that all people come from the lines of three families. Note that these are real families. All nations existing in Moses' time had roots in these men and their family lines. The family is the womb of nations and governments as each family-clan moves off to occupy its territory and become a nation unified by a common language (5, 31, 32).[14]

Genesis 11

Verses 1-9 expand the details of how so many families and nations have come to exist from Noah's family. Sin can take on corporate, social forms. Many families band together sinfully to gain more power and fame to resist God's mandate to scatter and fill the earth (4). Then, children and future generations suffer the pain of forced scattering by the curse of confused language (6-9). Communication, already cursed in the garden, becomes even more difficult as God curses man by confusing language so that communication becomes convoluted and corrupt. Moreover, the danger of a centralized, powerful government to both the family and the church screams out. Not until Pentecost, and then only in the church, is there a God-ordained reversal of Babel. Until Christ returns, the power struggle between the family and the state will continue and the church alone can be a just referee between them as post-biblical history proves (see chapters 9 and 10). This period also points to Jesus, the true ark, to save us from the flood of God's wrath. He is the one righteous man who saves his whole family (1 Pet 3:18-22).

The Patriarchal Period (Genesis 12–50)

The main lesson: Israel grows out of one particular family.

God's grace is given to Abraham and his seed after him until the formation of the church-nation Israel. The key texts and lessons highlighting the lives of the patriarchs are many and varied. Abraham is the model of the man of faith. Twelve passages stand out.

Genesis 12:1-9

The call of God is higher than loyalty to family. As a result, his family will be blessed as a family, not just Abraham as an individual. Also, God will bless all the families of the earth through his family. N.B., God's call means the whole family goes with the father or leader, with worship still in a family context.

Genesis 12:10-20; 20:1-18

The authority of the husband is clear. However, Abraham abuses that authority and sets a poor example of a sinful, selfish husband who endangers his wife to protect himself.

Genesis 13:1-13

Abraham works hard to maintain peace within the family. Therefore, he lets Lot choose first and sacrifices to maintain family peace.

Genesis 13:14-18

God honors godly families. While the book of Job teaches

that trouble can come even to godly families, God cares for His covenant-keeping followers.

Genesis 14

Note that governmental functions, including war, are executed by the family. Also, godly families honor God economically by the tithe. Therefore, godly families seek to remain free from obligations to pagan rulers where possible and to be self-sufficient.

Genesis 15

God renews and expands His covenant promises to this elect family. Significantly, faith is the key to a successful household and line. Covenant trust and faithfulness are the conduit of God's blessings.

Genesis 16

Unbelief, especially as it is contrasted with faith in the last chapter, triggers trouble. Note that a culturally accepted form of surrogate motherhood creates family strife that still exists thousands of years later. Hagar's son, Ishmael, causes trouble (Gen 25:12-28), and his descendents still do so today. Yet, God gives general blessings to Hagar because of Abram. Even in sinful situations, a godly family will be a blessing to its members.

Genesis 17

Again, God reassures Abram of His covenant promises, gives him a sign (circumcision) and a new name. Also, God promises Abraham productivity: many nations will come out of him. Incidentally, his numerous progeny is a blessing and should not cause fear of overpopulation. Moreover, the covenant is bigger than an individual and extends to the whole household; all the males are to be circumcised, including those of future generations.

Genesis 18 and 20

The family can be a blessing to relatives. Again Lot is blessed by Abraham, but by intercessory prayer, not armed defense (Gen 18). Also, to harm a godly family, even a sinful imperfect one, is dangerous business (Gen 20). Correspondingly, closed wombs are viewed as a curse; if children are a blessing, lack of them is a grief.

Genesis 22

God comes before family. He is worthy of absolute loyalty and is more important than His gift, children. Thus, being faithful to God and being a good father must be sustained over many years. As is often the case in Scripture, a family, and an incident in its life, becomes a paradigm of the grace of God. God spares Isaac but does not spare His own Son, His only Son, whom He loves (Matt 4:17; 12:18; 17:5), who, instead of the man on the altar, becomes the ram in the thicket (John 1:29, 36), and thereby shows us how much God loves us (1 John 4:9-10, 19).

Genesis 24

Parents must oversee children's marriages, and make a point of getting to know the family of the prospective spouse. Although mature Christian parents will not attempt to "run" their grown-up children's' lives in a dictatorial fashion, parents have a duty to prayerfully persuade their young adults to avoid searching for prospective spouses among pagans (6, 9). In a loving, godly home, young people have an honest and open communication with their parents, allowing for discussion of these important matters, as well as many others. God will surely be involved in and bless these efforts (7). Though our cultural expression of parental involvement may vary from that of an Indian family, or of the Jewish families mentioned in the Old Testament, we cannot dismiss parental involvement as merely culturally irrelevant or archaic. Christian parents who deprive their children of such guidance may block the covenantal blessings that the Bible ties to such action.

Genesis 25:1-6

Material wealth is to be given to children as an inheritance. Also, a special responsibility to the firstborn son exists. Moreover, wisdom is needed to divide wealth among children.

Abraham's life provides many examples—both godly and sinful—that relate to family life as well as to the life of the individual saint. Isaac's life teaches many of the same lessons.[15] Outstanding are the following: conception is from God (25:21); children in the womb are known by God (25:23); a father's sin often repeats itself in his descendants (26:1-11); governmental functions are performed in the family (26:26-31); parental favoritism to children fuels sinful sibling rivalry.

In Jacob's life, we see the effects of his fathers' sins.[16] Jacob experiences: the sibling rivalry and hatred of Esau, the "child" wars of Leah and Rachel, in-law troubles with Laban, the creation of an economic basis for his marriage(s), the family reaction to Dinah's rape, the issues of levirate children and incest in Judah's life, and the prophetic preparation of his sons for his death. God gives us rich models—both positive and negative—in the lives of the patriarchs that are not merely moral models but historical acts of God's redemption in action;[17] these lives teach many lessons, which emphasize two key truths: *sin destroys family life.* Reuben's incest costs him his right as the firstborn son, (35:22, 49:4) and Simeon and Levi's violent overreaction to Dinah's rape is punished by a scattering in Israel (34: 49:5-7). *Saving grace covers sin.* Levi's scattering is turned into a blessing as his family is appointed to a priestly function. Judah sins greatly: he marries a Canaanite woman, has two evil sons who die, breaks his word and withholds his third son from Tamar, his widowed daughter-in-law, as required by the levirate concept.[18] She has a legitimate complaint but sinfully and slyly commits incest with Judah to gain an heir, and bears Zerah and Perez, who is the direct ancestor of Jesus. God is merciful and gracious, and He blesses even such sinful families.

Genesis 37 and 50 show two lessons from Joseph's life that affect the family: parental favoritism, pride and rivalry destroy families and can kill (Gen. 37); God's grace can bring forgiveness, mercy, love and blessings. Joseph's reply to his brothers in

Genesis 50:19-21 is a lesson in grace:

> "Do not be afraid, for am I in God's place? And as for you, you meant evil against me, God meant it for good in order to bring about the present result, to preserve many people alive. So therefore, do not be afraid; I will provide for you and your little ones." So he comforted them and spoke to them.

The patriarchs teach how family life can be both good and bad.

Israel: Formation, Legislation, Prophetic Judges (Exodus 1–1 Samuel 8)

The main lesson: God's law directs the family and family related areas of life.

Also, many God-given models of family life are drawn from the lives of God's people.

Exodus 1–2

Families can resist a repressive government bent on destroying a whole ethnic group. The family unit may be singled out for destruction which is the best way of killing a whole people. The fear of God is more important than the fear of man and it alone can protect the family from literal destruction: the midwives' protection and Moses' parents' defiance of Pharaoh become the foundation of the whole history of Israel as a nation.

Exodus 4:18-26

This passage describes Moses' trip to Egypt. Moses honors his father-in-law and respectfully asks to be released to go back to Egypt (Ex 18; Num 18:29-32). Further, as Moses takes God's staff to do God's work, his family comes with him. Also, God calls Israel His firstborn. The battle for the freedom of the people of God is a family matter. Israel, God's son, blesses all the earth and is the foundation of God's eternal family. Pharaoh has a firstborn son who will sit on his throne to continue his worldly power. As Pharaoh pits himself against God and His son, his own son becomes involved and is killed. Family cannot avoid being dragged into conflict and affected by war. As a result, the godly family must keep its obligations to God. Moses fails to circumcise his son and disobeys like Pharaoh, so God moves to kill Moses, but Moses' quick-thinking wife saves him and the boys by doing the job. Even godly families must humble themselves, follow God's law and do His work in His way or they will have God's opposition (Jam 4:6-10; 1 Pet 5:5).

Exodus 4:29

The elders lead Israel. National leaders emerge from the family and clan structure, honored because they are heads of their fathers' households (6:13-27). God works through leaders who already have shown they are capable leaders in the family and in the broader household of their fathers (Num 11:16-17).

Exodus 12

This text records the institution of the feast of Passover which is to be eaten in households. If an individual household is too small, it combines with another. The very celebration of redemption is a household affair: families, not individuals, gather.

In Exodus, Leviticus, Numbers and Deuteronomy, many laws relate to family life. While the Mosaic law structure is not legislatively in force today, the principles taught in it are abiding and must not be ignored.[19] The laws themselves or the general principles they teach provide a wealth of divine wisdom. Neither modern society nor tribal cultures can afford to ignore these truths. To do so is to substitute man's finite, sinful wisdom for God's infinite, perfect truth. Man's law leads to tyranny, God's to liberty. Some of the specifics of these statutes are in chapters 5–8 of this book, but note that the statutes touch on: marriage, sexual conduct in marriage, divorce, children, inheritance, rebellious children, marriage of children. These laws are unique to Israel and give us new ideas about families, or clarify previously known pre-Mosaic principles.[20]

Numbers 12:1-15

The Bible heroes are not exempt from sibling rivalry in godly families. Miriam incites Aaron to complain. Both Miriam and Aaron are jealous of Moses, speak against his wife and use her Cushite background to criticize their brother. Mercifully, Moses intercedes for Miriam. As a model of mediatorial mercy in a family context (like Joseph), Moses points us to our brother Jesus Christ, who intercedes with the Father on our behalf.

Numbers 27:1-11; 36:1-13

The inheritance plays a vital role in family life. Whether or not you live in a rural, agrarian society where land is passed on from generation to generation, the principle holds true.[21] Parents should give an inheritance to their children, to help them serve God.

Deut 2:32-34; 3:16

Total destruction of Canaanite cities includes the women and children, evidencing a unity among family members. While God's law demands that fathers and sons be punished for their own sins, the federal covenantal unity between generations is real and sin can damage whole families. Achan shows that the sins of fathers can profoundly impact children among God's people as well as in pagan society (Josh 7).

Joshua 2; 6:22-25

Here we read the details of Rahab, her family, and her realignment, conversion and covenant with God and His people. Loyalties can change from idols to the living God, and such changes affect whole families; Joshua spares Rahab, her father's household and all she has (6:25). This graciousness can last for generations. In Rahab's case, her people live among Israel at least until the day the book of Joshua is written (6:25). Family conversion can have eternal significance; Rahab marries Salmon and is Christ's direct ancestor (Matt 1:5).

Joshua 13–21

God's inheritance is divided up by tribe and family. God uses the very structure of the family and extended family to organize His people. You may question the abiding validity of such a structure for today's nations, but cannot miss that God *did* use it and therefore, a nation *can* be organized around families.

Judges

By the end of Joshua, family and public life degenerate. Just as pre-Fall perfection sharply contrasts with post-Fall perversion, so vigorous conquest under Joshua contrasts with vulgar corruption of Israel under the judges. The strength of the family, church and nation all rise and fall together, an intriguing interconnection. The period abounds with negative examples of family life. Families disobey God and intermarry with Canaanites which leads to spiritual apostasy (3:5-7), God's judgment and national slavery (8). Israel cries to God and He delivers. Thus starts the national roller coaster ride, so clearly described in Judges 2:11-23, with ups and downs intimately wed to Israel's families and their love lives. The lives of Jephthah the Gileadite (11); Samson (13–16); and the Levite (19–20), reinforce lessons from previous periods.

The case of Micah and Dan (17–18), shows how moral degeneracy and family problems go hand in hand: everyone does what is right in his own eyes (17:6). Micah makes an idol and hires a Levite as priest to run his family religion. The tribe of Dan steals the idol and the priest, asking him to be a father and priest to them; they say it is better to be a priest over a tribe in Israel than to the house of one man. Here the family and extended family overstep their bounds and try to control the church. In sinful and degenerating times, the family itself can become a source of oppression!

1 Samuel 1–2

Finally, two more negative examples need to be examined carefully because of their historical significance. The first is Eli's family. Polygamy brings strife, especially child wars. God, not chance, gives children, and children can be given back to God for service to Him; Hannah lends Samuel to God for life. However, in contrast to Samuel, Eli's sons are so wicked that God destroys them. Eli does not know what his sons are doing and only hears about their wickedness through others (2:23-24). He has lost control and only verbally rebukes them (2:24; 3:13). Eli sets a bad example for Samuel.

1 Samuel 8:1-18

The second example is Samuel himself. Eli's family pattern (sons who do not follow the father's godly example) leads to Israel's sin. They request a king, and reject the Lord as king over them. The Israelites figure, "The other nations have kings, why don't we? The other nations do not struggle as we do, why not have a central government?" This request results in the monarchy, and God punishes Israel by giving it exactly what it wants.[22] As an outgrowth of the repressive theft under Saul's kingship the family suffers. Sons and daughters will be taken to serve the king; wealth, land, and the means of productivity will be confiscated through taxation. Governments can and do oppress the family.

Ruth

Ruth and Boaz shine as an exquisite example of beauty, love and grace in darkness, and give us a view of the family at its best. The family can be a place of joy and sorrow, as seen in the life of Elimelech, Naomi, Mahlon and Chilion. Marriage can form loyalties as deep as those in birth families. Our fellow citizens, our land and our god are all interrelated. Boaz personifies the principle of the kinsman-redeemer, who saves Ruth by placing her under his name, and purchasing her, bringing her into the family of Israel. Though we hate to "go against the flow" of our society, we Christians must remember that a responsible, redemptive model of marriage works far better than a reckless, romantic view. Wonderfully, after conversion, outsiders can be drawn into a godly family and to the true and living God (Ruth 1:16-18; 4:18-22; Matt 1:5). What a breath of fresh air Boaz is as he does not do what is right in his own eyes, but does what God requires.

National Israel: The Monarchy and the Davidic Covenant (1 Samuel 9–2 Chronicles; Isaiah–Jeremiah; Hosea–Zephaniah; Psalms–Ecclesiastes)

The main lesson: Many of the kings and their sons illustrate the negative influence parents can have, yet God graciously raises up godly kings in spite of their training.

The monarchy shows how one family can influence a whole nation. While government is different in Western culture today, and even countries with kings are not run like the monarchy of Israel, the influence one family can have for good or ill still holds. As with the last historical period, negative examples of family life far outweigh the positive.

1 Samuel

Saul, the first king of Israel, is a wicked rebel whom God judges and rejects (15). The court intrigue that surrounds David's relationships to Saul, to his daughter Michal, and to his son, Jonathan, sheds light on inter-family relationships, showing that a royal family affects a whole kingdom (16–18). These passages reinforce lessons learned from previous biblical data. The intensity of David and Jonathan's commitment to each other shows that godly ties can outweigh ties to evil blood relatives.

David's life, reign, and teaching provide much material for reflection when we study the family. David, as king and man after God's own heart (13:14), serves as a type or model pointing to his greater son, Jesus. The sons of Korah, Levitical songsters who write psalms and lead in praise, lift up the king as a prefigurer of the Messiah (Ps 45).[23] David teaches about worship and the family in his many psalms and he urges the sons of Korah to write psalms, which also teach facts about the family. God's covenant with him shows how one family can bless many (7). His faithfulness to God in the face of family pressure to do otherwise is commendable (Ps 69:5-12). He canonizes the inter-connectedness between families and the worship of God in his poetic Psalm 122.

2 Samuel

Yet, in spite of all this, David's sins loom large. He violates God's law and takes many wives (3:1-5). This penchant for women leads to adultery with Bathsheba and to murder of her husband (a good friend of David's, by the way). This ugly and horrifying rebellion on David's part leads to enormous family problems (12:9-14): Amnon's incestuous rape of Tamar, Absalom's murder of Amnon, and Absalom's rebellion and incestuous contempt for David are the bitter fruit reaped by David in his house (13–15). Like Eli and Samuel, David does not discipline his children. Ammon (1 Sam 13); Absalom (2 Sam 13, 14); and Adonijah (1 Kgs 1:5-6; 2:13-25), are self-centered, arrogant, undisciplined men who create national problems. David is an example for us both to imitate and to shun.

1 Kings; 2 Chronicles; Proverbs; Ecclesiastes; Song of Solomon

Solomon's life and teaching give us much instruction about the family. Proverbs contains crucial instruction on: adultery, child training, respect for parents, etc. The Song of Solomon is a marital love treatise *par excellence*. Ecclesiastes contains limited material on the family. Solomon, like his father David, realizes the connection between the family, the church and the state and writes a Song of Ascent to be sung on the road, as Israelites walk up to worship in Jerusalem (Ps 128). Proverbs is a training manual for young men destined to be leaders in homes and perhaps in the government. Solomon's wisdom, if gained, is a blessing to any parent or child. His prayers requesting wisdom from God (1 Kgs 3), and God's blessing on the newly constructed temple (1 Kgs 8) are model prayers. While we can learn some principles directly from his life, we learn far more from the One he typified—the King of kings who is the temple of God, Solomon's greater Son, Jesus (Matt 12:42).

Unlike Jesus—but like his father, David—Solomon is a sinner. He extends his father's greed for women and even arranges marriage alliances with pagan nations (1 Kgs 3:1; 7:8, 11:1-13; Neh 13:26). Today Christians puzzle over God's strong reactions, yet the lesson is clear: no intermarriage. This is not a *racial* issue, but a *covenantal* one. To pass off God's structures as a requirement solely for Israel in Old Testament times is to miss the point of Israel's uniqueness. God always underscores the religious results of intermarriage, never the physical or racial, as the ground for prohibiting such marriages (Ex 34:16; 1 Kgs 11:2). Make this a racial issue and you despiritualize God's law and God's people. The bottom line is: do not follow Solomon's example of sin, watering down God's covenant by mixing it with pagan customs.

Solomon also fulfills Samuel's prophecy about family life under a king by placing heavy personal and financial burdens on Israel's families (1 Sam 8:10-18; 1 Kgs 5:13-18; 9:20-22; 12:4, 9-11). A large, powerful central government is always costly to the family. The danger and burden of corrupt government on the family is also highlighted in the account of Ahab and Naboth (1 Kgs 21).

The post-Solomon years emphasize that parents are models. Phrases like "walking in the ways of his father" (1 Kgs 15:26), or "he committed all the sins his father had done before him" (1 Kgs 15:3) show that generational modeling is a reality. Consequently, parents profoundly impact the lives of children.

During these tumultuous days in Israel, when a ruler takes over, he often kills whole households, sometimes for personal vengeance, but sometimes as an expression of God's judgment. Jehu kills all of Ahab's house in a political power move as God's instrument of justice (2 Kgs 9:6-10; 10:11). The concept of covenantal unity in a household, as well as the modeling influence of parents, is why the whole household is under the ban, as were those of the Canaanite generations before.[24] Even the Canaanite destruction is tied to generational sins. This interconnectedness of generations is balanced by limitations of punishment (e.g., Amaziah rightly executes his father's assassins but not their children, 2 Kgs 14:1-6).

1 Kings; 2 Chronicles

Finally, the life of Jehoshaphat underscores and adds a new twist to the lesson from Solomon's life: intermarriage to pagans is destructive to family and national life. Though Jehoshaphat is a good king (1 Kgs 22:43), he allies himself with Ahab by marriage (1 Kgs 18:1), and later works with Ahab's son (2 Chr 20:35), both of whom are kings of Israel, *not* pagans. Although outward members of God's people, Ahab is married to the wicked pagan Jezebel, and Ahaziah is wicked like his father. These sinful alliances almost cost Jehoshaphat his life (2 Chr 18), and do cost him much of his wealth (2 Chr 21:25-37); God condemns and curses them (2 Chr 19:1-3; 20:35-37). Because the marriage covenant reflects God's covenant with His people, and because every other human covenant flows out of the marriage covenant, God wants marriage kept pure. Jehoshaphat is not a quick learner.

This period gives us rich data which must not be ignored. Cultural differences between ancient Israel and the United States of America or other Western countries are obvious, but basic truths remain the same. David, Solomon, and others ignore God's desires for the family as revealed in His law, and the history of Israel reveals how seriously God takes this flaunting of His design. Can our society, which prides itself on freedom and justice, arrive at such goals by ignoring God's structure for families? We and our leaders must not follow the ungodly examples that God's Word has shown us.

Isaiah–Jeremiah; Hosea–Zephaniah

The prophets of this period make many references to family life and a few key passages indicate their understanding of the family. Isaiah prophesies that the Lord is going to punish Jerusalem and Judah by removing human and material resources (Isa 3:1-12). As noted before, sin brings God's judgment, part of which is the destruction of families.[25] Also, God's authority structure is reversed: children and women will rule, rather than men. The breakdown of proper authority is the first step in social chaos (Jer 44:15-19). Family and societal failure go hand in hand, because family, church, and state authority structures rise and fall together. Isaiah and others foresee a time when all three God-ordained institutions will prosper.[26] These blessings are received through personal, familial and national repentance (Joel 2:12-17; Mic 7:7-10).

The Rechabites are a positive example of a strong family. God uses their familial loyalty to illustrate what Judah should do for Him (Jer 35), then makes a wonderful promise: Jonadab, the son of Rechab, will never lack a descendant before Him, because they honor their forefather (35:18, 19). God is still interested in individuals and their families in the midst of nations.

As we learned earlier, the family provides an important analogy to the nature of God, government, society and redemption. Isaiah talks of his own children as gifts from God and as signs (Isa 8:1-22). This concept (8:18) is applied to Jesus in Hebrews 2:13. The New Testament quotes portions of Isaiah 8[27] because it ties the work of salvation in Christ to the redemptive analogy of the family: both the father-son relationship[28] and the husband-wife relationship are used.[29] (Should we be surprised that, as the authority of the husband in the family is attacked in our society today, we also see a breakdown in parental authority, and a theological attack on the Father-Son relationship of the Trinity?)

As Christians in today's world, we must hold fast to the good news that our Husband has come to save us, and He can reverse the destruction of the family, church and state. God's fearful judgment fell first on Israel, then on Judah, as they went into captivity, but God brought them back because He never forgets His *people* or breaks His covenant *promises.*

National Israel:
Exile, Restoration, Post-Exilic Decline
(Ezekiel, Daniel, Ezra–Esther, and Haggai–Malachi)

The main lesson: A repeat of the previous period.

Ezekiel; Daniel; Esther

God's wrath and grace rest upon the family in its interconnectedness with the church and the state. God still views the family as He did in the period of the law and the earlier prophets. Daniel shows how sin destroys families but godly training holds: young Judeans in exile prove that godly training can help keep a young person steady during the most horrendous of circumstances. What parent would not be proud of Daniel and his three friends? Esther proves that a disrupted but godly blended family can be the means of salvation for a whole nation. Ezekiel reaffirms truths revealed earlier: the family is a divine analogy; children of believers belong to God (16:20, 21); the husband-wife covenant reflects the covenant between God and His people (16:1-63; 23:1-49); God will treat individuals and families justly according to His law (18:1-32); family sins are a cause of His wrath (27:1-12); God requires loyalty to Himself before loyalty to the family (24:15-24). Ezekiel clarifies these biblical themes as he preaches to God's people exiled in Babylon. Chaos and captivity do not change the truth.

Ezra–Nehemiah

When Israel returns to the land after the exile, one sin looms large: intermarriage. Ezra's prayer, pleas and plan (Ezra 9-19), and Nehemiah's vehemence and prayer (Neh 13:23-31), show the seriousness of this sin. Interestingly, Nehemiah does not forget the lessons learned from Solomon's life because he has experienced the horror of the exile (13:26).

Haggai; Zechariah

During these painful days when nothing of the splendor of Solomon is left, the latter prophets look forward to the Messiah's coming and reign. In a beautiful passage, God promises to protect Jerusalem and Judah and destroy its enemies (Zech 12:1–3:9). In the days of Zechariah's promise, God would pour out the Spirit of grace and supplication who would cause God's people to weep over a pierced Messiah. Individual, church and national repentance are all expressed in familial terms. Each family of each clan or extended family weeps, apart from others. Divine, personal cleansing transpires in the family. What are the results of the Holy Spirit's movement? Primarily, sin is washed away from individuals and religious leaders. As a result, idolatry ends. Consequently, loyalty to God exceeds loyalty to family and friends, as it should. As the Shepherd is struck, the sheep scatter, but will be regathered, refined, and brought together again as families, as God's people (Matt 26:31). Praise God, Jesus the pierced Good Shepherd, has done it![30]

Malachi

Malachi brings God's lawsuit against a faithless, declining, post-exilic Judah, whose sins include many family-related sins. Among the foremost is intermarriage with non-covenantal people (2:10-12). God's covenant is profaned by an unlawful marriage covenant. Malachi reaffirms the consistent Old Testament view that two marriage covenants, the divine-human and the human-human, are inextricably bound together. The foreign woman is the daughter of a foreign god and belongs to her father, thus tainting true worship.

Following close behind intermarriage is unlawful divorce.

The wife is a companion by covenant and people who have the Holy Spirit should not wickedly break covenant. This treachery is equal to covering one's wife with violence, a practice which God hates. Also, it keeps Him from gaining His godly seed, i.e., children.[31] God guards the family with divine jealousy because He knows if you break one covenant, you'll break the other. This is violence against God and spouse.

Intriguingly, the Old Testament ends with its focus on the family. God says that those who sin will have no descendants, but those who fear the Lord and His messianic Son will be victorious over enemies (4:1-3). Malachi exhorts us to remember and obey the law (4:4). In the future, Elijah will return as forerunner of the Messiah (4:5-6) and sinful splits in families will be reversed. The family, land, or people who do not turn to the Lord will be put under the ban. How solemn, but what hope, what promises! Remember, we are reviewing biblical history not just to collect facts, but for God's Spirit to touch us and purify our families. A nation without redeemed, Spirit-filled, Christ-adoring families is under a curse. God grant us grace to love Him and each other in our families so that He may not strike us with a curse, but touch us gently in blessing.

The Kingdom of God: Pre-Resurrection (Matthew–John)

The main lesson: Jesus reinforces the Old Testament view of the family, but now places it in the reality of His Kingdom.

More clearly than ever before, the people of God are identified as the children of God, sons of the heavenly Father.

This period centers on Jesus Christ. Several major emphases stand out. Of note, Jesus' family line is Davidic, the right line for the Savior, the messianic King (Matt 1; Luke 3). Significantly, Jesus is the eternal Son who becomes the messianic Son and reveals the nature of God (cf. John). God's character is a model for our family life and the Old Testament ideas of God as Father and Husband are filled in, expanded, fulfilled and exemplified by Jesus. Moreover, Jesus teaches that the kingdom of God functions as a family (Matt 6:9-15). Family is the major metaphor used to describe the people of God. God's adopted family needs to model its relationships after those of the divine family of the Father, Son and Spirit. As Jesus talks and acts like the Father, so the church talks and acts like Him. In addition, Jesus' human family and His dealings with His parents and siblings are the perfect model for us.[32] Also, Jesus teaches about marriage, divorce and singleness, reinforcing the Old Testament, but placing their authoritative teachings in the present reality of His kingdom (Matt 5:27-32; 19:1-14). Further, Jesus reissues the Old Testament principle that God and His family demand a loyalty above that of the physical family (Matt 10:34-39). Nevertheless, family obligations are not abrogated by the kingdom, but are still binding (Matt 15:1-9). Finally, some things change. For example, Passover becomes the Lord's Supper and is moved from the family into the church, the family of God. Jesus' character and teaching are normative, exemplary patterns for us until he returns.[33]

The Kingdom of God: Post-Resurrection (Acts–Revelation)

The main lesson: the teaching of Jesus is expanded.

The family remains a model of the Savior, the church and salvation.[34] Further, the apostles teach about the family.[35] In addition, there are specific teachings on the relationship of the family as it interacts with the church, church discipline,[36] the place of women in the worship and service of the church,[37] and physical care of relatives and widows.[38] This material is unique in that it is the final revelation of God on the family and because we live in the same time period (i.e., post-resurrection).

The Kingdom of God: The New Heavens and New Earth (Matthew 22:23-33; Mark 12:18-27; Luke 20:27-40; Revelation 21-22)

The main lesson: A radical difference will come in the new creation.

God's children will not die. N.B., we will not give and take in marriage, but be like angels. Also, God's family is the ultimate family that will last forever. Finally, history has a consummation point and will not go on forever nor will it end in some evolutionary omega point. God is in control and no matter what happens, there is hope for the family because the Son, our Savior and our Husband, who calls us to the eternal wedding feast of the Lamb, sits on the throne at the Father's right hand (Ps 2; Acts 2).

This overview of the family in biblical history is, to my knowledge, unique. To ignore history in general, or the history many have called "His-story" in particular, is to fall into a deadly trap. Without God's teaching on the family and His models of godly families, man's reason, experience and experiments will always stray from His desired pattern. Salvation in any area, including the family, comes only from God.

Notes:

Appendix 3

1. This is usually attributed to George Santayana (1863-1952), philosopher and man of letters.

2. Today, in general, there seems to be two opposite responses to history. One is a Hegelian type of idealism: history is right because it is the only reality. The other is an existential type of withdrawal: history is irrelevant; only individual choices count. For the best, concise, biblical view of history see C. Gregg Singer, *Christian Approaches: To Philosophy; To History* (Craig Press, 1978).

3. Even among professing Christians, a strong tendency exists to view the Bible in mythological terms. The Bible, if viewed as true at all, is certainly not real time and space history. It is true in essence, but definitely not in accurate, historical details. Rather it is viewed as a religious edition of Aesop's Fables: it gets its points across, but through spiritual fairy tales. This is not the place to argue for the validity of and historicity of the biblical text: this is assumed. Again, I would point you to F. Schaeffer's *Genesis in Space and Time* (Downers Grove: Intervarsity, 1972).

4. In my research, not one historian, anthropologist, sociologist or other academic mentions *historical* data from the Bible. Even those few Christians who do work in the social sciences and take the Bible to be God's word ignore the historical data of Scripture. Only J.D. Hunter mentions it in passing.

5. The theme of remembering God's mighty acts as well as His commands echoes and re-echoes through the Bible. Ex 13:3; 20:8; Num 15:39, 40; Deut 5:15; 8:2, 18; 9:7; 15:15; 16:3; 12; 24:9, 18, 22; 25:17; 32:7; Ps 77; 105; 106, are but a few texts in the Old Testament. Rom 4:23, 24; 15:4; 1 Cor 9:10; 10:1-13, in the New Testament show how important God's actions and the biblical accounts of them are to Christianity.

6. 1 Cor 11:25, 26.

7. 1 Cor 15:12-19.

8. James Casey, *The History of the Family* (Oxford: Basil Blackwell, 1989) makes this common mistake. While he has many useful insights, he fails to understand the God-ordained nature of marriage and the family and thereby distorts his data and his conclusions. In his conclusion he states:

> I shall not attempt to summarize here the arguments of this book. To do so, I fear, would create a misleading impression that the history of the family had more of a unity of theme than it does in fact possess. Rather, my aim has been to suggest the complexity, but at the same time the fascination, of a subject which touches on so many areas of human experience. Like a torchlight or a litmus paper, the family is perhaps less interesting in its own right than for what it

can tell us about social relationships generally.

> The problem ultimately for the student of the family is that of remembering that he is dealing with a concept, a creation of men's minds and of their culture, rather than a material thing. As a way of understanding social structure it can be as helpful or as problematical as its sometime rival, class. To pretend that the family is something else, a biological relationship or a household, is to risk impoverishing the investigation. It is natural that we should want to know a little more about where our Western family, centered round the conjugal couple and its offspring, came from. But to take the categories which are familiar to us - the household, the husband-wife and parent-child relationship - and order the data of the past round them may be to pre-empt the terms of the inquiry. To understand the past demands more of an effort on our part to understand it on its own terms.

9. See chapter 1, notes 1 and 2, in this book.

10. *Bos* means (1) to be ashamed, to feel shame; (2) to be disappointed in hope or expectation, including blushing; (3) to be confused, perplexed, troubled, frustrated. There was no mixture of shame, confusion, disharmony, or displeasure before the Fall. Everything, including sexuality, was good and holy, ruined only by rebellion.

11. Obviously, this cannot be angels having sex with humans since angels do not have physical bodies or sexual gender. Oddly, F. Schaeffer mentions this view but does not reject it (op. cit., 125-127). Jesus taught that the angels do not have sexuality, Matt 22:29, 30. Someone might say that they have free sexuality instead of any formal marriage and free sex is what we will have in heaven. But that runs against the fifth commandment. To speculate that God will change His mind is not sound, nor necessary, since the "godly line" explanation makes sense. Remember the old saying that a text without a context is a pretext. The context of Gen 1–6 does not mention angels, but does mention two lines: Seth's, one of covenant keepers; Cain's, one of covenant breakers. For excellent discussions of this key issue, see C.F. Keil, F. Delitzsch, *The Pentateuch*, vol 1 (Grand Rapids: Eerdmans, 1986) 127-135; H.C. Leupold, *Exposition of Genesis*, vol 1 (Grand Rapids: Baker, 1942), 249-254.

12. The race had only one language and was still united in other ways. The only important division was between those who called upon the living and true God and those who rebelled and followed Cain's example.

13. For the significance of Canaan being cursed and *not* Ham see Keil and Delitzsch, op. cit., 156-160, and Leupold, op. cit., 348-353.

14. The people separated: *parad* means to separate or divide; here to scatter. The separation, as we will be told in chapter 11, is by language, each

man according to his *lason*, "tongue" or "language." They moved into their own *eres*, "earth," "ground," "land," "region" or "territory." Families grow into *mispahah*: "family," "clan" or "tribe." Each clan has its own language and territory. Further growth, generation by generation, leads to the expansion of the clan: *toledot*, "generations," "descendants," "families" or "family history"; in turn it develops into *goy:* "people" or "nation." Family, language and territory seem to be the elements needed to develop these nations.

15. Gen 25:21-28; 26:1-6, 7-11, 12-33; 27.

16. Gen 25:29-34; 27:1-45; 29; 32; 34; 36; 37; 38; 46; 49.

17. Rom 4:23-4; 15:4-5; 1 Cor 10:6; 71; 2 Tim 3:16-7. See E. P. Clowney, *Preaching and Biblical Theology* (Grand Rapids: Eerdmans, 1961).

18. For a later, God-ordained version of this concept, see Deut 25:5-10.

19. The question of the law in the Old Testament is one that has perplexed Christians for centuries. Some ignore it because we are under grace, not law. However, Paul's use of the law, e.g., 1 Cor 9:8, 9, makes this antinomian position invalid. On the other hand, to keep the law as is and to ignore the historic developments in the coming of Jesus Christ and the Holy Spirit was condemned by the council of Jerusalem, Acts 15. A good summary of the law and how you should relate to it is found in the *Westminster Confession of Faith*, chapter 19, "The Law of God." Today's individualistic, existential, lawless age ignores law. The Law, whether actual enforcement of specific laws—"do not commit adultery"—or the application of the principles of the general equity of a law—"Do not cook a kid in its mother's milk," i.e., do not participate in pagan practices of worship or import them into the worship of the true and living God—is the only concrete, God-revealed guide to living that we have. Are man's reason, experience, experiments, and intuition on the same level as God's revealed word? God forbid. As useful as these sin-tainted tools are, they are not on a par with Him or His word. While not bound by the law as a way of salvation, we must not become lawless or substitute man's law for God's.

20. N.B., some of the jurists in the American colonies quoted Old Testament case laws as precedent for their decisions. The Massachusetts Body of Liberties, a code of laws written by Nathaniel Ward (see Section 94, "Capital Laws"), had Scripture proof texts attached. John Cotton previously had submitted a draft entitled, "A Model of Moses and His Judicials." See Morgan, *Puritan Political Ideas* (New York: Bobbs-Merrill, 1964), 177-202.

21. Even in those days the Levites had no land holdings. Their inheritance was a specialized ministry for God. Therefore, the principle holds even if land is not the content of the inheritance. Today, land is still important, though less so.

22. Individuals, families, churches, schools, businesses and governments must be very cautious about prayer. One of the worst things that can happen, Jam 4:1-3, is to ask with wrong motives and get "no" as your answer. Even

worse, God may give you the desire of your sinful cravings, Num 11:1-35! The Israelites wanted meat and God gave so much it came out of their noses and became loathsome. They were struck down while the meat was still in their mouths because of their carping rejection of God.

23. H.C. Leupold, *Exposition of the Psalms* (Grand Rapids: Baker, 1949), 351-353, rightly contends that the typological nature of the psalm was known even from its earliest days.

24. A study of these generational relationships would be both interesting and profitable for family studies.

25. Jer 31:15-17; Matt 2:18; Hos 9:11-17; Amos 3:1; 2; 7:17; Obad 18; Mic 7:1-7.

26. Isa 60:4-9; 65:17-25; Jer 31:15-17; Mic 7:11-20.

27. Isa 8:8, 10 is quoted in Matt 1:23; Isa 8:12-13 in 1 Pet 3:14-15; Isa 8:14 in Luke 2:34, Rom 9:32 and 1 Pet 2:8; Isa 8:17-18 in Heb 2:13; Isa 8:22 in Rev 16:10.

28. Isa 30:1-5; 10, 12, 15, 18; Jer 2:26, 27.

29. Isa 50:1-3; 62:4, 5; Jer 2:1-3; 3:1-10; Hos 1:2-9; 2:1-23; 3:1-5; Zeph 3:14-17.

30. For a sound exposition of this beautiful passage see H.C. Leupold, *Exposition of Zechariah* (Grand Rapids: Baker, 1965), 223-257.

31. See my article, "Who Owns the Children of Divorce?", *Journal of Pastoral Practice*, vol 8, no 3 (1986), 46-47.

32. Matt 2: 12:46-50; Luke 2; 11:27-28; John 2:1-11; 7:1-13; 19:25-27.

33. Matt 5:48; 11:28; 1 Cor 11:1; Eph 5:1; 1 Pet 2:20-21.

34. 1 Cor 4; Eph 3:14-21; 5:22; 1 Tim 5:1-2; Heb 2:13; 12:1-13; 1 John.

35. 1 Cor 6:12 - 7:40; 2 Cor 6:14 - 7:1; Eph 5:22 - 6:4; Col 3:18 - 4:1; 1 Thess 4:1-8; 1 Tim 2:11-15; 6:1-2; Titus 2:1-15; Heb 13:4; 1 Pet 3:1-7.

36. 1 Cor 5:1-13.

37. 1 Cor 11:1-16; 14:33-35; 1 Tim 2:11-15; Titus 2:3-5.

38. 1 Tim 5:3-16.

APPENDIX 4

The Family and Gender Roles

As the natural sciences developed in the nineteenth and twentieth centuries, they tended to view gender roles as biologically dictated necessities.[1] Since man is an advanced animal, his sexuality and mating are biologically determined, as are male aggression and war. Biblically, even though man's body is made of the same substances as the bodies of animals, he has the breath of life from God (Gen 2:7), and is the image of God (Gen 1:26, 27). Therefore man's sexuality and gender roles cannot be explained in mere bio-physical terms.

Within academic circles, sociology and cultural anthropology often took a different approach. Frank Boaz, Margaret Mead, Margaret Sanger and others insisted that sex roles are culturally determined, and sexual differences, other than physiological, are learned; therefore roles are malleable along feminist revisionist lines. Cultural determinism is the causal explanation of sexual roles. Margaret Mead's expression[2] is the classic statement of cultural determinism which has helped to spawn the neo-feminism of the twentieth century. Biological differences are downplayed, if not totally ignored, which is an exercise in idolatrous cognitive rebellion (Rom 1:18-27).

Sometimes you get a mixture of these two deterministic approaches. One collection of essays includes sociobiological approaches, appeals to stoic or neo-platonic thought, denigration of Christian ethics as historically insignificant, the cultural acceptability of homosexuality, the total cultural relativity of values, and the movement from Freud's psychoanalysis to Kinsey's mechanical sexology.[3] Clearly, one thing is excluded: Christianity. M. Foucault writes about the editor of this collection, P. Aries, and himself, "We both think that the prevailing notion of Christian ethics badly needs revision."[4]

Amidst all the biological and cultural determinists, a few traditionalists cry out for traditional values and sex roles, and base their appeals on the reasonableness of the roles and the assumption that natural laws and their pragmatic outworkings which underlie these roles are clear to the willing observer. The best academic example of this approach is C. C. Zimmerman's and L. F. Cervantes' text on marriage and the family.[5] G. Gilder's *Men and Marriage*[6] is a popular work in this tradition. Gilder observes many problems with the relativistic attacks on traditional values and presents his points with powerful polemical punches, yet gives no authoritative basis for monogamy and traditional roles. The closest he comes to reasons for his position are neo-Freudian allusions, pragmatic appeals, and semi-evolutionary concepts. As engagingly as he writes, he gives nothing close to a "thus saith the Lord."[7] Most traditionalists combine biological and cultural factors in their approach to sexual roles and thus avoid the oversimplification in the first two approaches but have no definitive proof for their chosen sex roles in marriage. (See Appendix 6.)

Christian responses to these cultural trends are varied.[8] Liberal Christians most often parrot the world, insisting that hierarchical sexual role models *cause* domestic abuse and violence.[9] One author who treats the issues of abuse is M. Fortune. In 1987 Fortune was an ordained minister in the United Church of Christ and director of the Center for Prevention of Sexual and Domestic Violence in Seattle. She follows a liberationist approach to biblical texts and comes to dubious conclusions such as her theory that Jesus on the cross took upon Himself our *undeserved* suffering so we would not have to suffer injustice.[10] Whatever happened to God's wrath against sin? She also implies that hierarchical structures automatically lead to abuse. Sadly, a leading evangelical feminist, Letha Scanzoni, gives a favorable evaluation on the back cover.

Conservatives or fundamentalists like Dobson hold to traditional values and roles. It is hard to determine whether they believe the roles are valid because of God's creative design or because of tradition and pragmatism. W. P. Blitchington writes from this perspective.[11] His book on sex roles and the Christian family is a fine piece of work and much of what he says has validity. However, his dependence on incorrect ideas in the social sciences taints his work. The fact that he sees genetic tendencies as responsible for homosexuality,[12] and understands sexual drives in Freudian terms[13] causes a discerning reader some moments of doubt. However, he does a masterful job of relating Zimmerman's findings and in exposing the fallacious use of social science data by evangelical feminists, especially Mollenkott.[14] I only wish that Blitchington had exposed Freud or done without him and that he had given more biblical exegesis. Also from this conservative perspective, G. A. Rekers writes some good material.[15] However, he depends even more heavily than Blitchington on the social science literature, and his work demonstrates an utter dearth of exegetical data. More satisfying is his work with M. Brown. The epilogue to their book is especially crisp and helpful because of the biblical data that strengthen the arguments.[16]

Evangelicals like Jewett, Mollenkott and Scanzoni, mentioned in Appendix 2, hold to a secularized, social-science cultural relativism. Their approach is hardly distinguishable from that of secular feminism. In fact, their views are worse, since they are like a chocolate-covered banana: a secular core is covered with a thin layer of melted down, badly exegeted texts. In this case, the covering is liberationist exegesis of the Bible. Sound works on this subject that argue from Scripture are difficult to come by. By far the best exegetical works are those of Foh, Clark, Hurley, and Piper and Grudem. (See Appendix 2.)

The male-female relationship issue is very important because "sexuality in man is symbolic of *ethical and covenantal* realities in God."[17] For a book that ties together the issues in Appendices 2, 4 and 6, see Noel Weeks, *The Sufficiency of Scripture.*[18] His chapters about sexual roles are chapter 18, "Women in Teaching/

Ruling Offices in the Church"; chapter 21, "The Scriptures and 'Advances' in Psychology"; and chapter 22, "Rabbinic Exegesis in the New Testament." However, the entire book is must-reading.

Notes:

Appendix 4

1. D. Morris, *The Naked Ape: A Zoologist's Study of the Human Animal* (New York: Dell, 1969).

2. Margaret Mead, *Coming of Age in Samoa: A Psychological Study of Primitive Youth for Western Civilization* (New York: Dell, 1961).

3. *Western Sexuality: Practice and Precept in Past and Present Times*, ed. P. Aries and A. Bejin; trans A. Forster (Oxford: Blackwell, 1985).

4. Ibid., 14.

5. C. C. Zimmerman and L. F. Cervantes, *Marriage and the Family: A Text for Moderns* (Chicago: Regnery, 1956).

6. Gretna: Pelican, 1986.

7. For other popularly written traditional works see G. Lentz, *The Embattled Parent* (Westport: Arlington, 1980); H. M. Voth, *Families: The Future of America* (Chicago: Regnery, 1984).

8. Richard Brookhiser, "Of Church Pews and Bedrooms," *Time* (August 26, 1991), 70.

9. See R. L. Clarke, *Pastoral Care of Battered Women* (Phila.: Westminster, 1986) and M. M. Fortune, *Keeping the Faith: Questions and Answers for the Abused Woman* (San Francisco: Harper & Row, 1987).

10. Fortune, ibid., 21.

11. *Sex Roles and the Christian Family* (Wheaton: Tyndale, 1980).

12. Ibid., 145, 149.

13. Ibid., 147, 151.

14. Ibid., chapter 7, "Psychology, Sex Roles and Scripture."

15. *Shaping Your Child's Sexual Identity* (Grand Rapids: Baker, 1982).

16. M. Brown and G. A. Rekers, *The Christian in an Age of Sexual Eclipse* (Wheaton: Tyndale, 1981). See especially the Epilogue, "A Defense without Apology."

17. R. R. Sutton, "A Covenantal View of Male/Female Roles," *Covenant Review*, 4:4 (April 1990), 1.

18. Edinburgh: Banner of Truth, 1988.

APPENDIX 5

The Family and the Local Church

In the Old Testament, the privileges of God's people were limited to those who were properly enrolled in Israel.[1] The rights of worship and citizenship were contingent upon this legal status. In the New Testament, having your name written in the Lamb's book of life is a life and death matter.[2] This enrollment depends not on outward actions, but on the working of the Holy Spirit in the heart.[3] However, the fact that salvation is a heart matter does not imply the insignificance of outward forms. God was angry at Moses for his failure to circumcise his sons, and Stephen felt it important to baptize the Ethiopian eunuch after he had understood the gospel in his heart. True circumcision or baptism is a heart matter, but this does not negate the obligation and importance of employing outward God-mandated sacraments and procedures.

In the New Testament, as soon as a person confessed Christ he was immediately made a part of the covenant community.[4] Baptism was the sign and seal of adoption into the church, God's family. Once baptized, a believer came under the teaching and authority of the apostles,[5] was joined or united with God's people, and identified as one of them.[6] As a member of God's people, the believer participated in communion, the feast of the family of God.[7] *Kollao* means "to join closely together, unite; to bind closely, or unite something with something else; to cling to something; to associate with or attach to."[8] Inevitably, such membership implied being under the authority of the elders or united to the church.

No independent Christians, no divine orphans roamed the streets of Jerusalem. God's plan for the apostolic church is the same as it is for His church today. You and your family need to be part of a local church. If you or your family runs into trouble, you need the church's help because, after the family, it is the next institution to have jurisdiction over people. P. Leithart gives a clear, concise presentation of the biblical position about church membership.[9] Also, S. Pribble has a helpful pamphlet on this subject.[10]

How do you pick a church? The reformers in the sixteenth century said a true church had three marks.[11] The first is the true preaching of the Word. Today you need to screen church leaders for two key concepts and their commitment to them: the inerrancy and infallibility of the Bible and the sufficiency of the Bible. You might give them *The Chicago Statement on Inerrancy* or Noel Weeks's book, *The Sufficiency of Scripture* and see if they can agree to it without mental reservation. The second mark of a true church is the right administration of the sacraments. Make sure you understand the proper number and nature of the sacraments.[12] Today many fail to understand these means of grace. The third mark is the faithful exercise of church discipline. For the best treatment of this divine mark, see J. Adams's work on church discipline.[13] The neglect of church discipline is one of the greatest deficiencies in the modern church.

These three are as necessary today as they were in Calvin's times, or in the apostles' age. When you choose a church for your family, ask for a copy of the church's statement of faith; study it and compare it with the Scriptures. See if these three areas are included. You may add other marks as you deem them to be critical. Their statement of faith should adhere to the historic creeds and formulas of the church (e.g., The Apostles' Creed, The Nicene Creed, The Formula of Chalcedon and a confession of faith grounded in the Protestant Reformation such as the *Westminster Confession of Faith).* Also, ask to interview the pastor and leaders of the congregation to see what they believe and practice. Discuss their view of the family and how they adjust their ministries and schedules for the sake of families.[14] If it is a denominational church, you need to include the denomination and its stances on these issues.

Resist the temptation of isolation. Resist the temptation to stop going to or joining a true church. Resist the temptation to "excommunicate" the organized church and to start your own by "ordaining" yourself and pastoring your own family in a house church. You will not help your family by a modern reenactment of the parable of the Good Samaritan. Do not "rob" the church, beating it and leaving it to die, or "passing it by" as did the priest and Levite. Christ died to save, sanctify and give structure to His church. Don't despise His beloved, or expect her to entertain you. Go for His glory and her good, and then you will be blessed, and so will your brothers and sisters, who need you as you need them.

Notes:

Appendix 5

1. Deut 7:61-65; 9:1-3; 13:1-3; 23:1-8.
2. Rev 3:5; 13:8; 17:8; 20:12, 15; 21:27.
3. Rom 2:28-29.
4. Acts 2:41, 47; 4:4; 5:14; 6:1, 7; 9:31, 35, 42; 10:47, 48; 11:21, 24; 14:1, 21; 16:5, 31-34; 17:12.
5. Acts 2:42; 5:1-16.
6. Acts 5:13.
7. Acts 2:46-47; 1 Cor 5:6-8; 11:14-22.
8. Acts 5:13.
9. "Why Should I Join a Church?" *Biblical Horizons*, no 12, April 1990, 1 (P.O. Box 1096, Niceville, FL 32588).
10. *Is Church Membership Optional?* (distributed by Faith Presbyterian Church, 2540 South Main St., Akron, Ohio 44319).
11. See Berkhof, *Systematic Theology* (Grand Rapids: Eerdmans, 1941), 576-578 for a concise discussion of these three marks.
12. See J. Calvin, *The Institutes of the Christian Religion*, Library of Christian Classics, vol. XX, trans. F. L. Battles (Phila: Westminster Press), Book Four, chapters 14-19 and L. Berkhof, op. cit., 616-658.
13. Jay Adams, *Handbook of Church Discipline* (Grand Rapid: Zondervan, 1986).
14. For some thoughts, see chapter 14.

APPENDIX 6

The Family and the Social Sciences

Today, more than ever, Christians need discernment.[1] One particular area of concern for Christians in general and families in particular is the social sciences, which have taken over the job of advising individuals, families, nations and cultures on how to order their lives and prosper—a job once held by philosophy and religion in pagan cultures, the Law and the Prophets in Israel and the Old and New Testaments in the church and Western civilization.

The family and church have always needed discernment because Satan and pagan culture—Egyptian, Canaanite, Assyrian, Babylonian, Medo-Persian, Greek, Roman and barbarian—have always been their enemies, and pagan wisdom and power have always threatened to destroy God's people.[2] God's strategy for His people has always been to make them holy, to bring them out from the world and be separated unto Him. However, a further problem arose with the gospel age: the church—the Israel of God—is multi-ethnic salt and light dispersed throughout the world, not localized in one place, or one nation. Because secular paganism is never neutral, but slavishly committed to Satan, it always tries to swallow the church. Whether by deception or murder, Satan employs pagans to destroy the woman and her Seed, as John's Revelation shows us.

God's family is His conquering army and fights under His banner. This battle calls for His divine strategy, command, tactics and weapons.[3] Most often Christian soldiers respond to pagan attacks in one of four ways. Many are captured by the enemy and become carbon copies of their captors. They are *secularized, synergistic heretics* like the early Gnostics: Jerusalem becomes Athens. Others try to capture the enemy by accommodating the message and methods of Christianity and amalgamating them with the "best" of pagan thought under the banner of "common grace." They are *syncretistic integrationists* like Justin Martyr, Origen and the Alexandrian school of thought: Jerusalem is built on and integrates with Athens. Still others recoil from the wickedness of the world, withdraw and try to live a separate spatial existence, like Old Testament Israel. They are *separatistic, monastic mystics* like Tertullian and the desert monastics: Jerusalem has nothing to do with Athens. Finally, there are those rare men who understand the two cities—the city of man and the city of God—and who faithfully exegete and study the whole counsel of God in the Bible in order to apply it to all areas of life, so that God's covenant people rule through the City of God, which is set upon a hill as light and salt to the nations. They are *scriptural scholars* like Athanasius and Augustine: Jerusalem conquers and converts Athens.[4]

What are the historical results of these pagan attacks? In the ancient world, they provoked several groups: secularized heretics, syncretistic Aristotelians (who eventually produced Thomas Aquinas and medieval Catholicism), and separatistic monastics. Yet a counterattack by a few scriptural scholars produced a solid foundation for the church: the ecumenical councils such as Nicea and Chalcedon, scriptural clarification of the triune nature of God and the two natures of Christ in His one incarnate person, the Augustinian view of man's nature and human history, and the biblical and intellectual foundations of modern Western European civilization.[5]

At the end of the Middle Ages and the beginning of modern Europe, paganism regrouped and attacked in the Renaissance, producing liberal secular humanism that spawned the Enlightenment and its revolutions (e.g., the French and the Russian). Christianity responded with a liberalized brand of cultural Christianity, the syncretistic scholasticism of the Counter-Reformation and Protestant scholasticism, and with the separatistic pietism of the Radical Reformation. But a counterattack by scriptural scholars like Calvin, Knox, Luther and others produced the Reformation and its confessions of faith;

its biblical clarification of the doctrines of justification, faith, grace, and salvation; its understanding of the foundational nature of the Scriptures; parliamentary constitutionalism in politics; and the economic cultural prosperity inherent in the Protestant views of science and work ethic.[6]

Beginning in the nineteenth century, modern neo-paganism —in the forms of rationalistic materialism, scientific positivism and modern totalitarian statism (often empowered by occult pantheistic mysticism)—has attacked Christianity and its view of man, family, society and history with a demonic vengeance.[7] Christian responses have included the continued secular synergism of liberal traditions, both Protestant and Catholic; the continued syncretism of scholasticism, both Catholic and Protestant; and the anti-intellectual separatism of some sectors of fundamentalism. But again, a small counterattack by a handful of scriptural scholars like B. B. Warfield, J. Gresham Machen, Cornelius Van Til, John Murray and Jay Adams produced the Scriptural clarification of the inerrancy and infallibility of Scripture and its application to all areas of life. We are in the middle of this attack and counterattack with the major doctrinal issue being the sufficiency of Scripture in all areas of truth including philosophy, science, sanctification, and counseling and ministerial methodologies.[8] The battle ebbs and flows with no small amount of defectors from Bible-believing, evangelical circles to liberal synergism (Appendix 2) and to the syncretistic scholasticism of Roman Catholicism. I know several converts from Evangelicalism to Catholicism.

This history explains *why* you should be profoundly concerned with science in general and the social sciences in particular. When you read a book on the family—secular or religious, academic or popular—you must know which presuppositions and perspectives shape the author's presentation and position because they will mold and color his data, conclusions and advice. While no one fits perfectly into airtight categories, analysis and labels help us to discern and judge. Does the author hold a position similar to secular paganism (whether rationalistic, empiricist, intuitive or a combination of them), to synergistic liberal religion, to syncretistic scholasticism, to a natural law perspective, to separatistic pietism or to sound scriptural scholarship?[9] David Powlison and others show that science in general and the social sciences in particular are not neutral presuppositionless disciplines.[10]

For now, let's concentrate on modern sociology and its impact on the family and sexuality by building on Appendix 4. Considering the history of sociology and its treatment of sexuality and gender roles, let us examine how these issues impact the culture.

The history of human society is fascinating.[11] Hayek documents the history and ideology of mainstream sociology from original sources. He contends that Saint-Simeon builds on Hegel and Rousseau and that he desires to define and control society and its processes through social engineers empowered by the state to achieve the goal of socialism. Comte, a student of Saint-Simeon and the founding father of modern sociology, tries to form a scientific religion—positivism—to carry out these goals.[12] Mainstream sociology has consistently believed in the evolutionary, positive, unbroken progress of society in the past, and it opts for future control of this process by the Platonic ideal of an elite oligarchy of scientist-philosophers.[13] This sociology has produced the school of cultural determinism in cultural anthropology. Margaret Mead is the champion of this position in gender roles.[14]

Against mainstream sociology stood a handful of traditionalists. Fredrick LePlay passionately opposed Comte's post-revolutionary attempts to reshape French society and looked for continuity with the pre-revolutionary past to ensure stability in the future.[15] Later, Pitirim Alexandrovich Sorokin challenged this mainstream approach at its core. Sorokin was a former Bolshevik, imprisoned three times by Czarist troops. After the 1917 blood bath, he became an antirevolutionary professor and was imprisoned by the Communists. After coming to the United States, he taught at both the University of Minnesota and Harvard, and drew the antagonism of the left-leaning academic world.[16] He taught the idea of nonevolutionary cycles in society's movements and that the natural sciences were not the model for the social sciences. C. C. Zimmerman built on LePlay and Sorokin and gathered massive data on the history of the family.[17] These traditionalists are all but ignored by mainstream writers as if they never lived, wrote or taught; although LePlay is praised by critics, his work is often "damned by faint praise."[18] Evidently, an ideological battle exists in sociology with neutrality an impossibility. What has this conflict produced in the area of our concern—human sexuality and gender roles?

Mainstream sociology produced M. Mead's *Coming of Age in Samoa*, the showpiece of evolutionary cultural relativism that opened the door to the role reversals of modern feminism. It also led to the research of Alfred C. Kinsey that opened the floodgates of perversity—pornography, bisexuality, homosexuality, bestiality, etc. It also influenced the philosophy of Planned Parenthood, whose founder and leading light, Margaret Sanger, openly hated Christianity, blaming it for all our cultural ills:

> The Roman Catholic hierarchy, of course; but along with them all the forces of reaction, the hopeless dogmatists of the ages; the conformists, the reactionaries—call them Lutherans or Puritans or Fundamentalists or Pharisees.[19]

Combine cultural relativism and this view of sexuality and you get the trendy, politically-correct approach to education at universities such as Stanford, where freshmen courses on non-Western thought, sex roles and ethnic diversity are required to stamp out racism, sexism, ethnocentrism and homophobia.[20] No wonder Stanford students have been heard shouting, "Hey, hey, ho, ho, Western Civilization has got to go."[21]

Traditionalists have made major critiques of prurient intellectual exhibitionism[22] and their strength is in exposing the destructiveness of the purported scientific or empirical data behind Mead and similar approaches.[23] Patrick J. Buchanan says in "Sex, Lies—and Dr. Kinsey" *(San Diego Union*, Oct. 20, 1990):

> For four decades, Alfred C. Kinsey has been hailed as a pioneer of human sexuality, the "Patron Saint of Sex," the "giant on whose shoulders all sex researchers since his time have stood."
>
> Comes now a book that makes Dr. Kinsey out to be a Cardiff Giant, a fraud, the great scientific charlatan of the 20th century.
>
> *Kinsey, Sex and Fraud: The Indoctrination of a People* suggests that Kinsey's famous works, *Sexual Behavior in the Human Male* and *Sexual Behavior in the Human Female*, are the "most egregious example of scientific deception in this century."
>
> Authored by Dr, Judith Reisman and Edward W. Eichel, edited by Drs. John H. Court and J. Gordon Muir, *Kinsey Sex and Fraud* stakes the reputations of all four researchers on the truth of that charge. Kinsey had an impact on our society as great as the genuine geniuses to whom he is often compared: Newton, Galileo, Einstein. His findings have shaped our attitudes about sexuality, especially homosexuality and the sexuality of children. They are the basis of what is taught in sex education. Yet, his work, the authors allege, was sexual and moral propaganda masquerading as science; and Al Kinsey was himself a deceitful and unethical mountebank.

Buchanan closes by asking,

> How could Kinsey get away with scientific fraud for 40 years? First, a vast industry has been erected on his "research" that will defend to the death its founding father.
>
> Second, most scientific frauds come to light when similar or identical research is done; but no researcher can repeat Kinsey's experiments on children without facing indictment and a prison sentence for sexual abuse.
>
> A mountain of research and detail, this book should lead to final demolition of the dreadful Dr. Kinsey. About time. For today, America is living with the terrible social

> consequences, from AIDS to family collapse of the "sexual revolution" he launched. It is past time we took a hard look at the character of the man we yet hail as a great revolutionary.

Not only must the buyer beware, but the individual, family, church, state and culture seeking truth must also beware!

But in the face of these mainstream attacks on our cultural past, are the counterattacks by traditionalists enough? Will they give us God's wisdom about your family and how to impact the culture for Christ? No, you and I will need more—God's advice. Let's summarize the different approaches, both secular and Christian, to see how they view society and sexuality, and to understand how they propose securing influence over culture. Then I will give some criteria for working in the area of the family and the social sciences so that you, your family, and your church may conform to God's design and desires in the culture in which we live.

One approach is secular paganism's mainstream sociology. *Theoretically*, society is viewed as an unbroken evolutionary progression from primitivism to positive maturity. *Sexuality* is viewed in the supposedly academic terms of Mead and Kinsey and produces deceptively distorted pieces of academic work, such as Margaret DiCanio's *The Encyclopedia of Marriage, Divorce and the Family*.[24] Typical feminist positions and rhetoric are given as "facts on file" (e.g., in the introduction, the articles on marriage contract, and on the marriage of convenience). *Changing society* is viewed through Hegelian statism and Saint-Simeon's desire to shape society through the political power to control legislation and judicial enforcement and to monopolize educational institutions. Today's politically correct thinking was nurtured in this womb.[25] This statist mentality is totally antithetical to biblical Christianity and most of the writing from this perspective is demonically, diametrically opposed to Christ and His Word. It is thoroughly damaging to your family.

Another approach is secular humanism's traditional or counterrevolutionary sociology. *Theoretically*, men like LePlay, Sorokin and Zimmerman have good critiques of mainstream ideas, but they are committed to a natural law philosophy that rises no higher than a deistic or rationalistic view of society. The problems of the Aristotelian nature/grace dichotomy of Aquinas or Kant are clearly delineated by F. Schaeffer.[26] *Sexuality* is seen in terms of traditional roles based on natural laws inherent in the cosmos. Often these laws and roles are proven by the same kind of faulty social science data that is used to support the mainstream position.[27] To *change society* this school uses an inconsistent mixture of conservative or libertarian defenses of the freedom of individuals in academic and political matters, but also the rather antithetical defense of heavy dependency upon the state and its academic institutions. They declare academic freedom and have formed the National Association of Scholars.[28] My *alma mater,* Westminster Theological Seminary in Philadelphia, is defended when its academic accreditation is threatened over the women's issue.[29] For a shocking tale of politically correct bullying, see Joseph S. Salemi's story of two professors fired at Dallas Baptist University.[30] Avery Dulles gives a Roman Catholic perspective.[31] Notwithstanding the many courageous writers exposing such tactics, traditionalists are well entrenched in the world's system, and look to academic elites protected by the state to change society.[32] The arm of the flesh is still the arm of flesh, even if it is conservative.[33]

Another approach is Christianity's synergistic liberalism. *Theoretically*, society is seen through mainstream sociology's eyeglasses. For years, theological liberals have been sociological liberals, but now many evangelicals have become neo-liberals.[34] There are some particularly blatant examples of a bad marriage between theology and sociology.[35] R.S. Anderson and D.B. Guernsey are authors who have both taught at Fuller Theological Seminary. In their work, they naively replace psychology with sociology, leaning heavily on neo-orthodox theology. In a peculiar argument, they imply that there is a higher order than creation and that therefore holding to a particular historical cultural manifestation is idolatrous. This argument means that cultural relativism is correct. They also imply that holding to God's law is legalistic, that sin is ontological and not ethical, and that the Bible cannot be equated with the word of God. While the authors claim to hold to the Scriptures, they functionally reject them and swallow neo-orthodox theology and secular sociology almost *en toto*. *Sexuality* and family life are viewed through secular egalitarian glasses. A husband and wife team, the Balswicks, evidence the influence of this bad theology on sociological thinking about the family.[36] In a telephone conversation on January 15, 1990, Dr. Jack Balswick assured me that he held to a high view of Scripture and not Jewett's extreme position and that he was influenced by Ray Anderson. The Balswicks hold to egalitarianism as the biblical view of marriage. Also, they fail to mention spanking as biblical discipline. Although Dr. Balswick assured me that it is not wrong, he sees it as a last resort that proves one's failure as a parent. Not even a hint of this soft position enters the book! Dr. Balswick also assured me that a biblical systematic theology of the family is needed. Biblical theology could have kept this sincere couple from being influenced by neo-orthodox theology and secular sociology. Bad theological companions corrupt good sociological and family thinking! For authors such as these, *societal change* is viewed from a liberal or quasi-liberal perspective.[37]

A different approach is Christianity's traditional syncretistic scholasticism. *Theoretically*, society is viewed through Thomistic lenses created by classic Roman Catholic theology.[38] However, conservative evangelicals are being drawn to such an approach. L. N. Geisler gives a "ringing defense" of Aquinas's theology.[39] The Christian Research Institute (CRI), the well-known apologetic ministry started by Walter Martin, has defended the church of Rome.[40] Several acquaintances have converted to Roman Catholicism. *Catholic Answers* is a San Diego-based Roman

Catholic evangelistic/apologetic organization which often aims at evangelicals. Protestants, as well as Catholics, give too much credence to faulty secular social science.[41] *Sexuality* is viewed from the traditionalist position, although committed Christians do include scriptural proof.[42] *Changing society* is viewed pragmatically and often advocates traditional conservative methodologies. For all the good Focus on the Family does, it shoots itself in the foot by depending on private practitioners who are academically trained and state-licensed instead of Christian disciplers or teachers who are biblically trained, ordained and overseen by the church.

Yet another approach is the separatistic pietism of the remnants of fundamentalism. *Theoretically*, the Bible is sufficient and there is no need for study to supplement the Bible. *Sexuality* is viewed in traditional terms. *Changing society* remains unnecessary or falls into a general conservatism of the previous variety. The danger of mere traditional conservatism without the power of the gospel is illustrated by a man named Terry who called in to the Rush Limbaugh show on December 14, 1990. Terry said that his fundamentalist church was escaping its separatistic past and getting more involved and that they were being heavily influenced by Rush. While Terry's church is doing well to become involved in legitimate areas of concern, they must be careful not to throw out the gospel along with their false separatistic monasticism. A danger for syncretism and separationism is Pharisaism: the law without God's grace to pull it off produces conservative moralists who have an outward form of godliness, but no inner power to be holy.

The proper approach is scriptural scholarship, historically found in the Bible, Augustine, Calvin, Machen, Murray and Adams. *Theoretically*, scriptural social science has started with men like C. Gregg Singer, Jay Adams, David Powlison and others who are attempting to think biblically about society.[43] Let me suggest that scriptural social science must develop our understanding of three key issues. First, we must realize that the noetic effect of the fall (the corruption of man's ability to think) affects science by distorting man's observations and conclusions.[44] If we are to think straight, we need biblical categories.[45] Second, the Bible's content focuses primarily on God and man. Therefore, the Scriptures will be more directly involved in forming the content of the social sciences than the natural sciences. The combination of the first and second points means there will be greater distortion of truth in the secular social sciences than in secular physical sciences. Third, the development of scriptural social science will only grow under the Holy Spirit's hand.[46] A biblical approach to social science will follow these seven criteria:

1. Reality must be understood through biblical revelation so that reason and research submit to it.

2. Science must be exegetically based before experience is examined.

3. Social science is a moral activity, not a neutral mechanical or medical activity.

4. Science must be centered in Christ and His kingdom, not around man and Babel-like utopias.

5. Social science depends upon godly wisdom (Prov), knowledge of the Word of God, and the work of the Holy Spirit, not merely upon some general skills given by God's common goodness, although such skills may help.

6. Social scientists need biblical pastoral oversight to aid this process.

7. Social research and planning should not be done by academic and government agents apart from the church's exegetical and moral guidance.[47]

Sexuality and gender roles must be defined and developed exegetically and covenantally, as well as creationally, under the above criterion.[48] Changing society must begin by having a biblical view of society.[49] Scriptural sociology must have a biblical theoretical base (as described in the seven points listed above), and must aim at a comprehensive, unified plan that takes into consideration the biblically defined relationship between family, church and state.[50] The Coalition on Revival is a California-based organization that attempts to develop a biblical view of society and to implement desirable changes in many areas of life, both private and public. It has produced extensive statements regarding seventeen areas of cultural activity.[51]

To fail to construct such a scriptural social science is to open up the individual, the family, the church and the society at large to gross demonic manipulation, such as that written about by C. S. Lewis in the *Screwtape Letters*.[52] The church must not capitulate to the power of mainstream sociology. Traditional "natural law" theology and sociology will not do the job, for they are most often barren of the Spirit's power through the Word. You and I need discernment lest we bring such "scientific" paganism into our families, Christian education, churches and counseling, and thereby participate in society's politically correct gender confusion with all of its horrific consequences. Instead of being PC, let's be BC (biblically correct), with a biblical world and life view and scripturally-based social sciences.

Notes:

Appendix 6

1. J. Adams, *A Call to Discernment: Distinguishing Truth from Error in Today's Church* (Eugene: Harvest House, 1987).

2. Gen 3; Deut 7:1-11; Ps 1; 2 Cor 2; 6:14-18.

3. 2 Cor 10; chapters 13-15 of this book.

4. G. Gregg Singer, *Christian Approaches: To Philosophy; To History* (Craig Press, 1978).

5. J. R. Rushdoony, *The Foundations of Social Order: Studies in the Creeds and Councils of the Early Church* (Phillipsburg: Presbyterian and Reformed, 1972).

6. See chapter 9 of this book, as well as M. Weber, *Protestant Ethics and the Spirit of Capitalism* (New York: Scribner's, 1958); Gary North, "Max Weber: Rationalism, Irrationalism, and the Bureaucratic Cage," in *Foundations of Christian Scholarship: Essays in the Van Til Perspective*, Gary North, ed. (Vallecito: Ross House, 1976).

7. See *Humanist Manifesto,* vols 1, 2 (Buffalo: Prometheus Books, 1973).

8. Gary North ed., op. cit.

9. D. Powlison has defined the issue: "Which Presuppositions? Secular Psychology and the Categories of Biblical Thought," *Journal of Psychology and Theology*, 1984, vol 12, no 4, 270-278. See also J. R. McQuilken, "The Behavioral Science under the Authority of Scripture," *CAPS Bulletin* (1977), 431-43 and W. L. Isley, "What is Truth? A Biblical Perspective," *Journal of Biblical Ethics in Medicine*, vol 5, no 4, 65-66.

10. See also secularist T. Kuhn's work: *The Structure of Scientific Revolutions* (Chicago: U of Chicago, 1970); *The Essential Tension* (Chicago: U of Chicago, 1977).

11. See F. A. Hayek, *The Counter-Revolution of Science: Studies on the Abuse of Reason* (Indianapolis: Liberty, 1979) 2nd ed.; Zimmerman and Frampton, *Family and Society: A Study in the Sociology of Reconstruction* (London: Williams and Norgate, 1936); Archibald B. Roosevelt and Zygmund Dobbs, *The Great Deceit: Social Pseudo-Sciences* (West Sayville: Veritas Foundation, 1964).

12. Note the religious nature of sociology and its god-like attempts to control men, families and societies through science, education and political power.

13. B. F. Skinner, *Walden Two* (New York: MacMillan, 1948).

14. M. Mead, *Coming of Age in Samoa: A Psychological Study of Primitive Youth for Western Civilization* (New York: Dell, 1928, 1955, 1961).

15. Zimmerman and Frampton, op.cit., 82-84.

16. Zimmerman, *The World's Greatest Sociologist: His Life and Ideas on Social Time and Change* (Saskatoon: U. of Saskatchewan, 1968).

17. See chapter 9 of this book.

18. J. Casey, *The History of the Family* (Oxford: Blackwell, 1989).

19. Quoted in Zimmerman and Cervantes, *Marriage and the Family: A Text for Moderns* (Chicago: Regnery, 1956).

20. "New Courses in ethnic diversity, sex roles—to be required at Stanford," *San Diego Union*, Dec. 13, 1990, A-3.

21. *Journal* (Summit Ministries, P.O. Box 3207, Manitou Springs, CO 80829), May 1991, 8.

22. Zimmerman and Cervantes, op. cit.; Hayek, op. cit.

23. D. Freedman, *Margaret Mead and Samoa: The Making and Unmaking of an Anthropological Myth* (Cambridge: Harvard, 1983); B. Gullihorn-Hole, *Anthropology on Trial* (Boston: WGBH Educational Foundation, 1983), aired on television.

24. New York: Facts on File, 1989.

25. "Taking Offense," "Learning to Love the P.C. Canon," "He Wants to Pull the Plug on the P.C.," "A View from the Front," *Newsweek* (Dec 24, 1990) 48-55; "Upside Down in the Groves of Academe," "Academics in Opposition," *Time* (Apr 1, 1991), 66-69.

26. *Escape from Reason* (Downers Grove: InterVarsity, 1968). See the evaluation of Zimmerman in chapter 10, and Gary North's essay on Max Weber, op. cit.

27. Cervantes' contributions in *Marriage and Family* and George Gilder's *Men and Marriage*. (See description in Appendix 4.)

28. "He Wants to Pull the Plug on the PC," op. cit.; "Academics in Opposition," op. cit.

29. C. Iannone and S. T. Logan, "God, Man, and Middle States," *Academic Questions: A Publication of the National Association of Scholars*, vol 4, no 4 (Fall 1991), 49-61. Similar criticisms about women and ethnic diversity have been leveled by the Western Association of Colleges and Schools against Westminster Theological Seminary in California, where I am an adjunct professor. I could add several personal episodes where PC thinking has attacked me, my family and friends, costing academic appointments.

30. "Political Correctness at Dallas Baptist University: The Firing of David Ayers and John Jeffrey," *Measure*, no 108 (Aug-Sept 1992), 1-13.

31. "The Teaching Mission of the Church and Academic Freedom," *America*, vol 162, no 15 (Apr 21, 1990), 397-402.

32. Zimmerman, *The Family of Tomorrow: The Cultural Crisis* (New York: Harper and Brothers, 1949).

33. Jer 17:1-10.

34. See Appendix 2. For information on Fuller Seminary where Jewett taught for years, see George M. Marsden, *Fundamentalism and American Culture: The Shaping of 20th Century Evangelicalism, 1870-1925*

(Oxford U., 1980); *Reforming Fundamentalism* (Grand Rapids: Eerdmans, 1987); J. D. Hunter, *American Evangelicalism* (New Brunswick: Rutgers U., 1983); *Evangelicalism: The Coming Generation* (Chicago: University of Chicago, 1987).

35. R. S. Anderson, D. B. Guernsey, *On Being Family: A Social Theology of the Family* (Grand Rapids: Eerdmans, 1985).

36. J. O. Balswick and J. K. Balswick, *The Family: A Christian Perspective on the Contemporary Home* (Grand Rapids: Baker, 1989).

37. J. O. Balswick, J. K. Morland, *Social Problems: A Christian Understanding and Response* (Grand Rapids: Baker, 1990).

38. See the problems with this approach under my section on secular humanism.

39. According to the *Baker Book House Academic Book Release Catalogue 1991-92*, commenting on *Thomas Aquinas: An Evangelical Appraisal* (Grand Rapids: Baker, 1991).

40. "What Think Ye of C.R.I.'s Defense of Rome?" *The Researcher*, vol 2, no 4, 1-4. (Sept-Oct, 1993).

41. M. and D. Bobgans, *Psychoheresy: The Psychological Seduction of Christianity* (Santa Barbara: Eastgate, 1987) exposes this tendency.

42. See Appendix 4, concerning Blitchington and Rekers.

43. North, ed., op. cit.

44. Rom 1:18-3:31.

45. Heb 4:12-13.

46. Heb 5:11-14.

47. For a fuller explanation of the relationship of the Scriptures to social science, see my article, "Eeny, Meeny, Miny, Mo: Is Biblical Counseling It or No?," *Journal of Pastoral Practice*, vol 9, no 4 (1989), 44-57.

48. For the best works, see Appendix 2.

49. J. Murray, "The Christian World Order," *Collected Works of John Murray*, vol 1 (Carlisle: Banner of Truth, 1976).

50. See chapters 13-14 of this book.

51. The Coalition on Revival, P. O. Box 1139, Murphys, CA 95247.

52. Nashville: Broadman & Holman, 1999.

APPENDIX 7

The Family and Counseling

If you or your family get into trouble, "Who ya gonna call?" Probably not ghost-busters, but a psychiatrist or psychologist. Families—even Christian families—have problems. Most people think their family is dysfunctional and needs a mental health professional. God thinks families are made up of sinners who suffer accordingly and need His Son and Spirit. Two big questions loom large: what kind of help do families need? And who should give this help?

Appendix 6 shows that definitions are important. Today, the problems are problematic! People do not even know what goes wrong with individuals and families. What can go wrong in people: physical; physical and spiritual; or physical, spiritual and mental (or emotional) areas? The bible of psychiatry and psychology, *The Diagnostic and Statistic Manual of Mental Disorders*[1] has been under fire for some time. In an article that puts into question the classifications of the psychiatric world, Erica Goode quotes Dr. Allen Frances, Professor of Psychology at Columbia University and Chairman of the Task Force of DSM IV: "The DSM IV must be taken with an educated grain of salt", and Dr. Bryan Siegel, Professor of Psychology at University of California in San Francisco: "People need to realize that these categories are not given by God."[2]

Amen! These categories make the discerning reader wonder if DSM stands for Denying Sin Manual! More people are questioning the very legitimacy of the concept of mental illness itself. Renowned Professor of Psychiatry Thomas Szasz points to the political pressure of gay therapists who got homosexuality removed from DSM III as an example of how categories are arbitrarily chosen and concludes that the DSM approach confuses diagnoses with real diseases: "Diagnoses are not diseases."[3]

Why is there this confusion? Remember the history of social sciences, discussed in Appendix 6. Dr. Franklin E. Payne Jr. points to the reduction of moral-spiritual issues to medical-physical entities.[4] William L. Playfair, also a medical doctor, exposes how this model allows the doctor to reap great financial gains and the patient to escape moral responsibility for his action.[5]

Although the definition of problems is confused, the method and system to treat them has been chosen as if there is no confusion. Conventional cultural wisdom dictates a medical-mechanical model; therefore, treatment is by professionally trained, state-licensed medical or professional personnel in a medical insurance-supported private practice or state-run and funded institution. Treatment is never to be by a theologically trained, ordained pastor or supervised layman in a church-based or charitably-supported ministry. The culture war, Appendix 2, crops up in counseling as clearly as in any other area of social interaction. Bad theology (Appendix 2) and wrong gender roles (Appendix 4) that arise from fallacious social science (Appendix 6) combine to cut out the family and the local church (Appendix 5), and dump bad advice on hurting families. Mechanical methods that treat family members as programmed machines[6] ignore the fact that man is the image-bearer of God.[7] Yes, whom are you going to call? What help is there for your family? What are the problems? Who does God say should give you answers and help?

Secular psychology does not have the answers, because it has at least 250 discernible approaches.[8] In addition to these usual approaches, one must consider the unusual ones.[9] Psychotherapy is a mess. Academic journals offer nothing distinctive from the other 250 approaches.[10] You can have any therapy you want at Alice's Restaurant and Therapy Emporium. Nor does psychotherapy work.[11] In short, psychotherapy is a fraud and not even all pagans buy into this fictitious model. Thomas Szasz has challenged it for years.[12]

Psalm 1 should be sufficient warning to keep us from this ungodly mess. However, Christians are slow learners (Appendix 6). *Synergistic* Christian thinkers ape the world in content and method. Whether old line liberals,[13] newer neo-orthodox thinkers,[14] or neo-evangelicals drifting left,[15] these synergists are hard to distinguish from pagans in their approaches to counseling. For example, Osterhaus mimes a family systems approach and all but ignores biblical categories and data; he has no scripture index because he does not need one. He forcibly interjects false ideas into biblical terms which are then converted into pagan social science concepts, such as the right brain/left brain fallacy.[16] He interprets Joseph Alleine and Jonathan Edwards *through* William James.[17] He concurs with Michael Scanlan's view of inner healing.[18]

Syncretistic Christian thinkers see some of the problems of this practical paganism and raise a warning. Some Roman Catholics see the religious nature of counseling and make some devastating critiques of secularism.[19] One psychologist, Bill Coulson, formerly Carl Rogers's right-hand man, has rejected his mentor's humanism and returned to Roman Catholic roots. However, the centrality of Christ and His grace, the word of God and the Holy Spirit are all missing in Coulson's and other Catholics' systems. They can construct no distinctive substitute for the world's wisdom.

Protestant syncretism is not much better. While personal faith is seen as essential, all too often the content of counseling is unregenerate man's worldly wisdom coupled with personal mystical experiences that individually or in tandem negate the centrality of Christ and His sufficiency.[20] Whether it is Alpha Counseling, Minirth and Meier Clinics, New Life Treatment Centers, Rapha Counseling or a host of other alternatives, the content *and* methodology are not biblically-based, but eclectically syncretistic at best. Even Focus on the Family—for all the good it does—falls into this trap. Focus's content is a mixture of biblical ideas and secular psychology with the emphasis on the latter so that the counsel is more psychological than biblical and exegetical.[21] An article in Focus's own magazine was entitled "Who We Are and What We Stand For."[22] The statement contains many biblical ideas mixed with Arminian theology and secular psychological ideas. For example, just as the world is questioning and jettisoning self-esteem,[23] Focus tenaciously clings to this turn-of-the century German liberal theological anachronism.[24]

Focus's model of ministry is the medical, state-licensed practitioner. I was rejected for their referral list because I refuse to be state-licensed, in spite of the following facts: at the time, I had three graduate degrees, including an M.A. in Psychology, I was teaching pastoral counseling on a graduate level, I was ordained, I had pastored for eight years and I had proven spiritual gifts to teach and disciple. Materials and counseling will help you and your family only to the extent that they are filled with biblical content. Most syncretists' counsel contains more heresy than help. However, some have more biblical content.[25] Use discernment in reading Christian counseling advice.

Separatistic pietists who deal with the family are rare but still exist. One example sticks in my mind. I marked an entrance exam for the National Association of Nouthetic Counselors, an agency that accredits and supervises biblical counselors. This candidate was well-educated and held many degrees, but believed that anything beyond reading appropriate passages of Scripture and prayer with the counselee would be an attempt to preempt the Holy Spirit's work. This exam was given to me in the late 1980s, not in 1580! Need I say he failed?

Scriptural scholarship has developed biblical counseling over the last thirty years.[26] Adams and others started a foundation in 1968 to develop biblical counseling theory, practice and training. The Christian Counseling & Educational Foundation has training programs for lay people and pastors, as well as graduate programs at seminaries.[27] Adams has shown that counseling must be constructed from the all-sufficient Scriptures; *everything* that is *not* physiological can be handled by biblical counseling done through the church. Your family does not need the counsel of the ungodly. Is this radical? Yes. Is it biblical? Yes.

C.C.E.F. founded the now-independent National Association of Nouthetic Counselors,[28] which accredits and supervises biblical counselors. I started a branch of C.C.E.F. in California in 1982. Later, this became a separate entity, operating as a specialized ministry of Bayview Orthodox Presbyterian Church, of which I am an associate pastor. The name was changed to the Institute for Biblical Counseling and Discipleship.[29]

These organizations can refer you to the nearest trained biblical counselor. Whom *are* you going to call? Call the psych-busters. If you are a disciple of Jesus Christ and want to be like Him and want your family to reflect His glory, then I pray you'll call your pastor or a consistent biblical counselor. May you and I and our families be salt and light. If we need restoration, may we look to those who have the word and Spirit to do the job.[30] Don't forget that the *psych* in psychology comes from the Greek word for *soul*. Counseling is discipleship.[31] Look to the Word and the Spirit, our only links to the light of the world, Jesus Christ.[32]

Notes:

Appendix 7

1. *The Diagnostic and Statistic Manual of Mental Disorders III R* (Washington, D.C.: American Psychiatric Association, 1987) and *DSM IV-TR* (2000).

2. "Sick or Just Quirky? Psychiatrists are Labeling More and More Human Behaviors Abnormal," *U. S. News and World Report*, vol 112, no 5 (Feb 10, 1992), 49-50.

3. *Lancet*, vol 338 (Dec 21/28, 1991), 1574-1576.

4. "The Medicalization of America," *Journal of Biblical Ethics in Medicine*, 5:4, 67-68.

5. *The Useful Lie* (Wheaton: Crossway, 1991).

6. Gerald R. Patterson, *Families: Applications of Social Learning to Family Life*, revised (Champaign: Research Press, 1975); *Living with Children*, revised (Champaign: Research Press, 1976).

7. Mary Stewart Van Leeuwen, *The Sorcerer's Apprentice: A Christian Looks at the Changing Face of Psychology* (Downers' Grove: Inter Varsity Press, 1982).

8. Raymond J. Corsini and Danny Wedding, eds., *Current Psychotherapies*, 5th ed. (Itasca: F. E. Peacock, 1995), perhaps the most widely used college text on the subject.

9. Corsini, ed., *Handbook of Innovative Psychotherapies* (New York: Wiley Interscience, 1981).

10. For example, the *Journal of Psychology and Judaism*; *Journal of Psychotherapy and the Family*; *Journal of Divorce: Clinical Studies and Research in Family Therapy, Family Mediation, Family Studies and Family Law*; *Child and Family Behavior Therapy*, to name just a few.

11. M. & D. Bobgan, *Psychoheresy: The Psychological Seduction of Christianity* (Santa Barbara: Eastgate 1987).

12. *The Myth of Psychotherapy* (Oxford: Oxford U, 1979); *The Myth of Mental Illness* (San Francisco: Harper and Row, 1984).

13. Seward Hiltner, *Pastoral Counseling* (Abingdon-Cokesbury, 1949).

14. Donald Capps, *Biblical Approaches to Pastoral Counseling* (Phila.: Westminster, 1981).

15. James P. Osterhaus, *Counseling Families: From Insight to Intervention* (Grand Rapids: Zondervan, 1989).

16. Edward T. Welch, *Counselor's Guide to the Brain and its Disorders* (Grand Rapids: Zondervan, 1991).

17. William L. Playfair, op. cit., chapter 7, "The Myth of Christian Origins."

18. Don Matzat, *Inner Healing: Deliverance or Deception*? (Eugene: Harvest, 1987).

19. Paul C. Vitz, *Psychology as Religion: The Cult of Self-Worship* (Grand Rapids: Eerdmans, 1977); William K. Kilpatrick, *Psychological Seduction: The Failure of Modern Psychology* (Nashville: Nelson, 1983); J. De Wyze, "An Encounter with Bill Coulson," *The Reader*, vol 16, No 33 (Aug 20, 1987).

20. John MacArthur Jr., *Our Sufficiency in Christ* (Grand Rapids: Zondervan, 1991).

21. M. and D. Bobgan, *Prophets of Psychoheresy II* (Santa Barbara: Eastgate, 1990).

22. *Focus on the Family*, Aug. 1993, 10-13.

23. J. Adler, P. Wingert, L. Wright, P. Houston, H. Manley, A. D. Cohen: "Hey I'm Terrific," *Newsweek*, vol CXIX, no 7, Feb 17, 1992, 46-51. (The issue is titled "The Curse of Self-Esteem".)

24. G. C. Scipione, "Self-Esteem is Sweeping over America," *Journal of Pastoral Practice*; vol X ; no 1, 1989, 26-37; J. Adams; *The Biblical View of Self- Esteem, Self-Love, Self-Image* (Eugene: Harvest, 1986).

25. Examples of works from this perspective that have useful material but call for discernment are *The Journal of Family and Culture*, published by the Free Congress Foundation, 717 Second St. NE, Washington, D.C. 20002; and George A. Rekers, *Counseling Families* (Waco: Word, 1988). Rekers has a naively uncritical respect for the social science literature, but does have biblical content that others do not.

26. Jay Adams, *Competent to Counsel* (Grand Rapids: Zondervan, 1970); *The Christian Counselor's Manual* (Grand Rapids: Zondervan, 1973); *A Theology of Christian Counseling: More than Redemption* (Grand Rapids: Zondervan, 1979); Wayne A. Mack, *Strengthening Your Marriage* (Phillipsburg: Presbyterian and Reformed, 1977); *A Homework Manual for Biblical Living,* vols 1, 2 (Phillipsburg: Presbyterian and Reformed, 1979, 1980); *Preparing for Marriage God's Way* (Tulsa: V. W. Hensley, 1986); *Your Family God's Way: Developing and Sustaining Relationships in the Home* (Phillipsburg: Presbyterian and Reformed, 1991); R. Ganz, *Psychobabble* (Wheaton: Crossway, 1993). Dr. Henry Brandt's works are also worth reading.

27. C.C.E.F., 1803 E. Willow Grove Ave. Glenside, PA 19038, 215-884-7676.

28. NANC, 3600 W. 96th St., Indianapolis, IN 46268, 317-337-9100.

29. IBCD, 5333 Lake Murray Blvd., La Mesa, CA 91942, 619-462-9775, e-mail: ibcdsdg@k-online.com; website: www.ibcd.org.

30. Rom 15:14; I Cor 2; Gal 6:1-2.

31. Matt 28:18-20.

32. Isa 8:18 - 9:7.

APPENDIX 8

The Family and the Civil Magistrate

The original edition of this book, titled The Biblical Battle for the Family (1993), was researched in the late 1980s and early 1990s. It stated that a consideration of the civil magistrate was beyond the scope of the book.[1] That is still true. However, the book has been used in courses at the Institute for Biblical Counseling and Discipleship and at Westminster Theological Seminary in California. In these courses, I deal with the critical issue of the state's mandated reporting of abuse cases. Recent California State law obliges clergy to report child abuse, rendering the topic extremely important. Although no questions about the church/state issue were raised by advisors or examiners when a revision of the book became a Ph.D. thesis at Whitefield Theological Seminary, serious questions arose from an editor revising the manuscript in 1997. These questions prompted me to clarify the interplay between the civil magistrate and the family.

Moreover, American politics from 1992 to 2000 cries out for comment. The religous right has had a dramatic reversal of fortunes.[2] The Clinton Administration, the debacle of democracy in decline, the legion of lazy legislators—all of these have lowered the Republic's reputation to new depths. The body politic suffered a stroke when, during the impeachment hearings, it would not render a verdict of guilty for criminal behavior. The weakened body politic nevertheless continues its self-destructive patterns by attacking the family.[3]

If these incentives were not enough, my short-term missions trips to Trinidad, Tobago, Suriname and Uganda made me determined to deal with the church/state issue. The countries I visited are all devoid of political structures influenced by the Reformation's political theology. You cannot imagine the impact of a hostile culture until you have studied and experienced one. I have found useful Mark Shaw's analysis of Africa, an extension of Neibuhr's work on the kingdom of God and America.[4] Dr. Timothy Monsma's course, "The Kingdom of God in Global Perspective" (Westminster Theological Seminary in California), wrestles with the issues of God's kingdom and the nations of the globe. The monthly magazine published by Voice of the Martyrs helps to expose and explain Buddhist, Hindu and Muslim versions of political persecution.[5]

The family and the church cannot escape the all-pervasive modern state and its deleterious effects. But in order to know how to understand and resist such influences, we need a biblical basis to evaluate the state,[6] as well as help in dealing systematically with biblical data on government.[7] A balanced, biblical evaluation of the state will help us not to overestimate nor underestimate its importance.[8] Before we can develop a biblical view of the state and its relationship to the family, we must be clear about three things: the Bible, history and authority.

A Biblical View of the Bible

The Bible is God's inspired Word and therefore, infallible and inerrant (2 Tim 3:15-17). Few hold to this historic and non-negotiable position; still fewer believe that it is sufficient for all of life. But God says that it is![9] God commands us not to add to nor subtract from His Word (Deut 4:21, 12:32; Prov 30:6, Rev 22:18). The Bible does not tell us *everything* we want to know or could know about a given subject, but it does tell us what God deems *necessary* to please Him. God tells us neither too much nor too little. This must be true for all of life, including the subject of the civil magistrate, or He has lied (which is impossible).[10]

A Biblical View of History

The Bible presents a clear concept of history: God is sovereign and, by His eternal counsel, plans whatever comes to pass.[11] Proverbs teaches that God's sovereignty includes minute details (Prov 16:1, 4, 9; 19:21; 20:24; 21:1, 30, 31; 29:26). Therefore, we must interpret history *theocentrically* rather than in any other way.[12]

God reveals His desires, decrees and will progressively through history. He reveals His gracious covenant to save His people through successive administrations, all accompanied by verbal information which is recorded for subsequent generations. Through covenants with Adam, Noah, Abraham, Moses and David, God reveals His ultimate covenant to save His people through the Messiah. It is imperative to note that these administrations are complementary and cumulative, not contradictory and compartmentalized. To imply otherwise is to accuse God of contradiction or of changing His mind. Christ inaugurates the new, final covenant as the crowning culmination, climax and consummation of the prior incomplete typological administrations. Christ's covenant administration not only completes the prior ones, but has cosmic consequences to which the others only pointed. All authority belongs to Him (Matt. 28:18), including everything in the heavens and the earth. Naturally, then, His authority is superior to demonic forces and civil magistrates (Ps 2; 1 Cor 15:20-28; Eph 1:20-23, Col 1:16, 2:8-15).

A Biblical View of Authority

The Bible defines the nature of authority. Ultimate authority rests in God alone (Ps 50, Rom 9), who is the Creator and Sustainer of all things. Therefore, creation has its structure and foundation in authority, not anarchy. God ordains human authorities as His servants. Parents, elders and magistrates are His servants to shepherd in the home, church and state. Therefore, creation rests and runs on God-ordained authority structures which did not evolve (Rom 13:1-2; 1 Pet 2). As created servants, God limits these human authorities. The parent, elder or magistrate is limited in the exercise of power (Deut 21:18-21; Eph 6:1-4; 1 Tim 5:17-22; Deut 16:18-20; Rom 13:1-8). All human authority is therefore delegated and limited, not original and absolute. Because God judges His delegated authorities, every parent, elder or magistrate answers to God not only as an individual, but also in his capacity as God's ordained servant. God hears and will adjudicate the cry of abused children, church members and citizens. Particularly pertinent is Psalm 82, in which God addresses unrighteous civil magistrates. He is not pleased at all! All magistrates should remember Herod's proud ways, which cost him his life (Acts 12:22).

A biblical view of authority will deal not only with the *nature* of authority, but also with the *number* of authorities. God's authority is not arbitrary, nor obtuse. Adding to or subtracting from the designated number of authorities can be very significant. For example, in the family, it is important to define the nature and number of roles, as well as their interrelationships. Practically speaking, feminism and the children's rights movement show us how confusing home and family life can be if we ignore God's designated authority.

In the Church, it is important to delineate the nature and number of offices and their interrelationships,[13] as well as the nature and number of the sacraments. Even a quick reading of Foxe's *Book of Martyrs* indicates that most of the people put to death in England during the Reformation died over transubstantiation. Today, most believers cannot explain the difference between the Roman Catholic view and the biblical view! Fewer still would be willing to die for their understanding of the truth in this matter.

In the State, the nature and number and interrelationships of the branches of government is no minor matter. The very nature of civil government itself is critical to freedom of individuals, families and the Church.[14] Puritan and Presbyterian political thought have strongly influenced the form of government in the USA.[15]

Someone needs to analyze systematically the biblical data on civil government, while remaining sensitive to all the changes in redemptive history through the various administrations of God's gracious covenant. Our attempt in Appendix 3, "The Family in Biblical History," is more extensive and comprehensive.

In the pre-Fall order, Adam is a prophet to declare God's *Word* and will to the world. He is a priest to *worship* God. He is a king to *work* for God's glory by multiplying, filling, subduing and ruling over the earth (Gen1:28). Functions of the civil magistrate are within the family in germinal form.

In the post-Fall world, Adam retains those three functions, but now needs God's mercy and blood atonement to hide his nakedness and negate the effects of God's curse on his rebellion (Gen 3). Ousted from the garden, only the promised serpent-shattering seed of the woman generates hope (Gen 3:15). Governmental functions remain in the family. God's kindness to Cain is to prevent his kinsman-redeemer from collecting the blood debt of Abel (Gen. 4:9-15). This merciful provision is mockingly perverted by Lamech (Gen 5:19-24).

Under the Noahic administration of the covenant, governmental functions and justice still reside in the family. God officially approves of the kinsman-redeemer's legitimate function within the family structure.[16] We note, however, the satanic undermining of this function in the idolatrous formation of Nimrod's kingdom of Babel (Gen 10:6-12; 11:1-9). Here is the first occurrence of humans forming civil government beyond the boundaries of the family. Not insignificantly, it is in the context of self-centered rebellion against God, built on man's self-esteem.

In the Abrahamic administration of the covenant, governmental functions and justice still remain in the family—at least among God's elect people. This occurs amidst the development of many more pagan kingdoms. The hereditary character of these kingdoms implies that civil governments develop out of family/clan structures. Abraham fights to protect Lot, but refuses any payment from a pagan government. There is at least one city-state whose king maintains the priestly or churchly function. Abraham is a prophet and priest, yet he pays the tithe to Melchizedek (Gen. 14).

Under the Mosaic administration of the covenant, we have significant developments. A mega-shift occurs that affects us today and will continue to do so until the new heavens and the new earth are fully realized. God changes the form and function of both the church and the state. While family overtones remain in Passover and the other major feasts, the center of worship shifts from the family to the tabernacle/temple under the strict supervision of ordained servants (Lev; Deut 16:1-17). This significant change is never reversed in the rest of the Old Testament economy. Nor does it change in the New Covenant, in spite of all its radical changes (e.g., no priests, only pastors and teachers; no physical central worship in the temple, only worship in spirit and truth; no sacrifices, only Christ. See the book of Hebrews).

God also sets up a civil government. He legislates a localized government under a tribal system. He establishes a new executive branch. The legislative branch consists of the Levites, who do not make laws, but teach and interpret God's revealed laws. The judicial branch consists of godly men appointed by the people to apply the law to real cases. Of course, other laws (e.g., those given about the cities of refuge) also help to regulate national life. The Levites and judges combine to administer justice (Deut 16). The lack of centralization or federalization is consistent (e.g., there is no standing army, but men from age twenty to fifty serve as needed).

God knows, however, that Israel's heart will lust with the

worldly desire to be like the pagan nations around them (Deut 17:14-20). They will demand a king and no amount of godly preaching and warnings will alleviate this perverse desire (1 Sam 8). God warns of the troubles a centralized government will bring: loss of wealth with oppressive taxation, forced subscription into standing armies, and other woes. In the midst of all this, God graciously limits the extent of Israel's slavery to government (Deut 17:14-20).

Contrary to John Frame's arguments (see note 7), this is the divine basis for civil government as a God-ordained entity *separate* from the family and church. (This is a shift from my facile reference to Gen 6:9 in the first edition.) God separates the functions of the *Word* (the prophetic office), *worship* (the priestly office), and *work* (the kingly office). Thus, the church and civil governments are *separate* and *each* is differentiated from the family.

Under the Davidic administration, the king's power and office come to an even greater focus. God promises to place a Davidic heir on the throne forever (2 Sam 7:8-17). The king is to protect family, church and nation. The civil government (Prov 16:10-15, etc.) is clearly by divine appointment (Ps 82). Samuel warns of the dangers of centralized, bureaucratic government. As usual, Israel has to learn the hard way. Truly they need a king greater than David, Solomon, Hezekiah or Josiah. Praise God, Jesus is David's greater Son.

During this later administration of the covenant, the prophetic office grows. The prophets preach to the family and church, but particularly to the king as the head of state. This is abundantly clear for Judah and Israel. Equally clear, and not to be missed, God sends prophets to preach to pagan kings and peoples: e.g., Isaiah, Jeremiah, Ezekiel, Daniel, Joel, Amos, Obadiah and Jonah. Psalm 2 is fulfilled preliminarily in the prophets and finally and fully in Christ.

A peripheral but significant issue arises in the Old Testament. Some believers hold significant posts in pagan governments: e.g., Joseph, Daniel, Hananiah, Mishael, Azariah, Esther. True, these are non-voluntary, but all are viewed with divine approbation. Jeremiah instructs all the exiles to seek the welfare of Babylon (Jer 29:7). To serve a pagan government is *not* the same thing as bowing to idols.

As in the Torah, the civil magistrate is differentiated from the Levitical priesthood as a separate unit of ordained authority. Although David is a prophet/priest, writing scripture and at times offering sacrifices, the kings of Israel normally are not. Therefore, they are forbidden to work in the temple and suffer severely if they ignore this sacred boundary (see the case of Uzziah, 2 Chron 26:16-21). Even more intriguing, God views pagan kings and civil governments as His servants. The pagan King Cyrus is called "[God's] shepherd" (Is. 44:28) and "anointed" (Is. 45:1), terms normally used only for the Davidic or Messianic king. When pagan shepherds overstep their God-given bounds, they suffer severely (cf. Nebuchadnezzar and Belshazzar, Dan 4 and 5).

In summary, the Old Testament portrays the civil magistrate as an ordained servant of God requiring obedient service (Jer. 29:7). Evil civil magistrates may be resisted passively *in order to obey God* (Daniel). Also, the civil magistrate can delegate the right of self-defense to God's people (Esther).

The New Testament picks up and extends this view. John the Baptizer, the last and greatest of the Old Testament prophets, preaches powerfully to individuals, church leaders and civil magistrates. In fact, his confrontation with Herod and Herodias costs him his life. Of course, as we see with Christ and Stephen, this is nothing new (Matt 24:37-39; Acts 7:51-53). Christ the Messiah, the final prophet (Heb1:1-2), who is the King of kings and Lord of lords, preaches to the Pharisees as apostate ecclesiastical leaders. Jesus also preaches to Pilate, a perverse political hack. Jesus teaches that we should render to the state its due, even though we are sons of the kingdom (Matt 17:24-27; 22:15-22). He refuses to take up the sword, or to utilize legitimate civil power to advance His kingdom.

The apostles' post-resurrection, post-ascension ministries and teaching are the most pertinent data for our present consideration, since we live in the same period of redemptive history. The apostles never take up arms against the government, even when it illegitimately uses force. The one exception is Peter, who is soundly rebuked by Jesus (John 18). The early church is willing to suffer even to death (Acts 4, 7, 12, 14), and teaches us that the church will suffer as the Savior did (1 Pet 2:11-17; Rom 13:1-7; 1 Cor 6:1-8; 1 Tim 2:1-8; Tit 3:1-8; Rev). As in the Old Testament, the civil magistrate is seen as God's servant (Rom 13:1-7), who answers to God for his conduct (Acts 12:20-23).

In summation, the biblical data contains several principles about the civil magistrate.

1. The civil magistrate is God's ordained servant.

O.T.: Deut 17:2-13; Ps 82; Prov 16:10-15; Is 44:28; 45:1

N.T.: Rom 13:1-7; 1 Tim 2:1-8; Tit 3:1-8; 1 Pet 2:11-17

2. The civil magistrate, as God's servant, answers to God for the exercise of his ministry.

O.T.: Gen 12:10-29; 20:1-8; Prov 16:10. Note the constant counsel given to the kings of Judah and Israel by God's prophets, the punishment of Judah by Babylon, then Babylon's own punishment (Hab). Note also Belshazzar (Dan 4).

N.T.: John the Baptizer preaches to Herod (Matt.14:1-12); Christ preaches to Pilate (John 18–19; Rom 13:1-7; 1 Tim 2:1-8).

3. The civil magistrate's standard for judgment is God's righteous standards in His word.

O.T.: For God's people, it is the law. The king is to keep a copy and read it (Deut 17:14-20). Among the pagans, the precision of the law is not in view, but the general outlines are. The pagans and Israel are condemned like Judah. Only Judah is cited for violations of the law per se because she is the only covenantal nation (Amos 1-2).

N.T.: Although it is a general reference to pagan society and not a specific reference to civil magistrates, Rom 1-2 echoes Amos. The hearty approval of evil, often heightened in the realm of civil courts, applies. The magistrate needs prayer not only generally, but specifically for salvation (1 Tim 2:1-8).

4. The civil magistrate bears the sword by God's appointment.

O.T.: Gen 9:5-6; Deut 13:12-18; 17:2-13; 19:1-13; 20:1-18; 25:1-3; Prov 16:14

N.T.: Rom 13:1-7

The family can use the rod, reproof and cutting off inheritance, but is limited in the use of force (Deut 21:18-21). The church can quarantine and excommunicate with the sword of the Spirit, but cannot use the sword of the state.

5. The civil magistrate's legitimate authority is limited.

O.T.: The civil magistrate's legitimate jurisdiction is limited by the law which reserves certain rights for the family, e.g. marriage (Deut 7:1-5); inheritance (Deut 21:15-17), etc., and for the church (e.g., worship, Lev). Also, the civil magistrate's use of force within its legitimate jurisdiction is limited. The law limits the use of force in civil punishment (Deut 25:1-3), and in the prosecution of war (Deut. 20). The king's exercise of authority is to be limited by the fear of God, the law in general and specific legislation in particular (Deut 17:14-20).

N.T.: Paul distinguishes between civil and ecclesiastical courts (1 Cor 6:1-8).

6. The civil magistrate's purpose is to provide providential peace, so believers can live quiet, godly lives.

O.T.: Num 27:15-23; Ps 82; Esther

N.T.: 1 Tim 2:1-8

7. The civil magistrate is a legitimate calling for a believer.

O.T.: Joseph, the Judges, Esther, Daniel

N.T.: Believers serve as soldiers and are not required or advised to resign. Paul utilizes his Roman citizenship. God decrees magistrates to be saved (2 Tim 2:1-8).

8. The structures of the state and civil government are not dictated directly in the Bible.

O.T.: God sets up a decentralized government in the law. However, He is willing to allow an earthly king (Deut 17:14-20). The exile brings about a different governmental status (back to bondage). Post-exile Israel is a theocracy, not a monarchy.

N.T.: The New Testament accepts the existing governments as a given.

9. The civil magistrate and the structure of the state are not, therefore, unimportant, nor free from biblical law.

All of life is important to God and, therefore, to the believer (1 Cor 10:31; Col 3:17; 1 Pet 4:11). Yet there are some things that are more significant and important than others (Matt 23:23-24). Priorities do exist. Paul alludes to this in his discussion of sexual and marriage issues with the Corinthians (1 Cor 6–7). Paul teaches us to be content in whatever state we are in when converted by Christ. We are not to think circumstances *must change* when called to Christ. *We* must not change our circumstances. In his argument, he refers to another example, slavery vs. freedom. Are you a slave? Be content. Are you free? Be content. Yet, he adds parenthetically to take your freedom, if you can get it. We are to be content even in suffering, but we do not have to volunteer. Why? Because freedom is better, but freedom vs. slavery is a secondary, less important issue for the gospel and the believer. The freedom is better for you personally, but also for gospel service.

The same holds for the state, politics and the civil magistrate. Can you be a contented Christian under a totalitarian state, a limited monarchy, a tribal system, a constitutional republic? Yes, the gospel and you are not bound. But of course, if you can have what you prefer and what is better biblically, take the freedom of a constitutional republic built on principles derived primarily from puritan political policies.

Obviously, the Church has the greatest significance, because it is the only eternal kingdom. The family comes next because of its building-block character. The state is the least important of the three.

10. The civil magistrate, as well as the family and Church, is an independent authority, but cannot function without the others.

O.T.: The law makes clear distinctions between the family, the Church and the state.

N.T.: This structure, built into creation and redeemed in the work of Christ, is foundational to the three spheres of authority and does not change. Modified differences occur because we are in the full, final administration of God's covenant.

The Church uses preaching, persuasion and church discipline to develop repentance, faith and faithfulness. The family uses the rod, reproof, education, inheritance and marriage to mold individuals. Each needs the other two to function efficiently in a biblical manner.

11. The civil magistrate must be obeyed by all citizens, including Christians, even though a Christian's primary and eternal citizenship is in Christ's heavenly kingdom.

O.T.: Defiance of parents (Ex 21:15; 17; Deut 5:16; Prov 19:26; 20:20), of church or civil authorities (Deut 17:11-13) is serious and life-threatening.

N.T.: While the Christian citizen has dual citizenship (Phil 1:27; 3:20-21), and the heavenly citizenship is the higher one (Matt 17:24-27; Phil 3:20-21), he still must obey earthly authorities, even evil ones (Eph 5:21-6:4; 1 Pet 2:11-3:7).

12. The civil magistrate must be disobeyed when he mandates sin.

Passive Disobedience and Martyrdom

O.T.: The examples of the Israeli midwives, Rahab, Hananiah, Mishael, Azariah and Daniel are high points in redemptive history.

N.T.: Peter and John, Stephen, and Paul are stellar examples (Acts).

Active Disobedience

Calvin and the major Protestant reformers addressed these issues. They avoided the two extremes: the sacramental submission of Catholicism and the anarchy of the radical reformation. The general consensus was that a righteous redeemer or lesser magistrate must lead the active resistance, not individual citizens.

A Biblical View of the Interrelationship between the three God-ordained Governmental Institutions

You need the correct number of institutions. The classic interpretation of the Protestant reformation is three and only three: the family, the church and the state. There are people who like to insist on fewer or more, but this confuses the issue. Other associations—voluntary ones—are really extensions of one of the three. Unions or educational ventures are really extensions of the family. Para-church organizations are extensions of the Church. When there are too few or too many institutions, authority is wrongly redistributed or watered down. This tempts one of the authorities to impinge on the authority of the other two. You need the right balance between the three or you will have tyranny of one sort or another.

Individual Tyranny

This is the belief that only the individual counts or is of paramount value. The family, church and society are tyrannized by individual men. This view tends to depict all authority as evil or severely tainted with evil, which leads to anarchy and societal breakdown. Many historical examples exist. The radical reformation tended to throw off all forms of authority and triggered anarchy. This position fails to have a biblical view of scripture, history, authority or the civil magistrate.

Family Tyranny

This is the idea that the family is paramount. The individual, the church and the state are tyrannized by the family, usually the father. Ancient Chinese society is a classic example. The family exists for the ancestors. A modern example is radical home-schoolers who start family churches. This position fails to grasp redemptive history and the significant changes from Moses onward noted earlier.

Church Tyranny

This conviction elevates the church over the individual, the family and the state. The papal state and Muslim countries under Islamic theocracies are the clearest examples. This position forgets that the church does not wield the economic power of the family nor the physical sword of the state. It confuses the nature of Christ's kingdom and superimposes the purpose of the second advent onto the first.[17]

State Tyranny

This stance elevates the state over the individual, the family and the church. This was the position of the pagan Greco-Roman states and some medieval states and is the position of the modern nation-state. This can take the form of Erastianism (see W. Cunningham, cited in note 17) or modern principled pluralism that isolates the church into the ghetto of private pietism. This way of thinking clearly misses the kingdom of heaven and its nature and deifies the temporal political realm.[18]

A Biblically Balanced Freedom

A balanced biblical view is imperative to avoid tyranny. The family, church and state have their own spheres of authority. Biblically, they are to be independent and not infringe or impinge on the others. Instead, they should support the others so each can do its job effectively and efficiently.

We live in a fallen world. God tells us to work with whatever government we have. If, however, you can do better or get the best, then do so. The representative republic form of government hammered out by the Scottish and English Puritans and attempted by the New England Puritans is the best form of government to date. A biblically sound, disestablished church which is Presbyterian in form (minimally on a local level) and a representative republican form of government with a balance of powers between the branches of government, where the people covenant to serve King Jesus, will best protect the family and enable a people to win the battle for the biblical family.

Only biblically structured families with regenerate members will enable a culture to have proper churches and a sound state. Only all three structures, functioning biblically, will cause a community to thrive and prosper. This is the biblical, trinitarian, balanced society which the world desperately needs.[19]

Notes:

Appendix 8

1. See chapter 3, note 33.

2. See G. Thomas's and Ed Dobson's warnings of worldliness in *Blinded by Might: Can the Religious Right Save America?* (Grand Rapids: Zondervan, 1999).

3. See J. Whitehead, *State vs. Parents: Threats to Raising Your Children* (Chicago: Moody, 1995); G. Grant, *The Family Under Siege* (Minneapolis: Bethany House, 1994).

4. Mark Shaw, *The Kingdom of God in Africa: A Short History of African Christianity* (Grand Rapids: Baker Books, 1996); H. R. Neibuhr, *The Kingdom of God in America* (New York: Harper and Row, 1937).

5. P.O. Box 443, Bartlesville, OK 74005, www.persecution.com.

6. J. Whitehead, *Christians Involved in the Political Process* (Chicago: Moody Press, 1994); C. Thomas and M. Olasky's editorials in *World*, e.g., M. Olasky, "Patrick Henry's Idea," *World,* vol 15, num 27, p. 34; "Surprised by Stories," *World*, vol 15, num 28, p. 34.

7. J. Frame, "Toward a Theology of the State," *Westminster Theological Journal*, vol 51, num 2, pp.199-226.

8. Jay Adams, *Maintaining the Delicate Balance in Christian Living* (Woodruff: Timeless Texts, 1998). See especially chapter 2, "Balance Your Two Worlds."

9. 2 Peter 1:3, *The Westminster Confession of Faith*, chapter 1, section 6.

10. J. Frame's "Hermeneutical Prolegomena" in "Toward a Theology of the State" is a useful starting point. (See note 7.)

11. Eph 1:11; Heb 6:17; Westminster Confession of Faith, chapters 3-5.

12. C. Gregg Singer, *A Theological Interpretation of American History*, 2nd Edition (Phillipsburg: Presbyterian & Reformed, 1981).

13. J.R. DeWitt, *Jus Divinum: The Westminster Assembly and the Divine Right of Church Government* (Kampen: J. H. Kok, 1969); W. Cunningham, *Discussions on Church Principles: Popish, Erastian, and Presbyterian* (Edmonton: Stillwaters/Revival Books, reprint).

14. Although you may not agree with everything these authors say, their works will stimulate your thinking: S. Rutherford, *Lex Rex* (Harrisonburg: Sprinkle Pub, reprint of 1644); T. McCrie, "Appendix: A Short View of the Plan of Religious Reformation and Union Adopted Originally by the Secession," *Unity of the Church* (Dallas: Presbyterian Heritage Pub, 1987, reprint); R.J. Rushdoony, *Law and Society* (Vallecito: Ross House Books, 1982), chapters 12, 19, 22 and *Christianity and the State* (Vallecito: Ross House Books, 1986).

15. Singer, op.cit.

16. Frame, op. cit.

17. See W. Cunningham, *Discussion of Church Principles* (Edmonton, Stillwater Revised Books); The Trinity Foundation Conference, *Christianity and Roman Catholicism* (Unicoi: The Trinity Foundation, 1998).

18. See R. J. Rushdoony, *Christianity and the State* (Vallecito: Ross House Books, 1986).

19. I have not argued extensively for John Murray's position or my modified Puritan politics. I have given some direction and suggested many books. You may also find the following helpful: On the issue of Old Testament law and its relationship to the New Testament believer, see Bahnsen, Van Gemeren and Kaiser in *Five Views on the Law and the Gospel* (Grand Rapids: Zondervan, 1993). For the best help, see *The Westminster Confession of Faith* and *The Larger and Shorter Catechisms* (Inverness: Free Church of Scotland, 1976). The most pertinent section is *WCF*, Chapter 19, "Of the Law of God" and *WLC*: Q&A #91-153. On the nature and danger of the modern totalitarian state, see Rushdoony, *Christianity and the State*. On God and politics today, see *God and Politics: Four Views on the Reformation of Civil Government*, G.S. Smith, ed. (Phillipsburg: Presbyterian and Reformed, 1989). (Bahnsen and Carson are helpful, Brown is inconsistent and Spykman is indefensible.)

APPENDIX 9

The Family: An Annotated Bibliography

Listed below are some of the best works on the family. Study and use them to strengthen your family and church. Also employ them in your cultural skirmishes as you battle for the freedom of the family.

To strengthen the quality of this bibliography, I solicited the opinions of some of the most godly leaders in the biblical counseling movement. Several responded with helpful suggestions which are noted. My team was:

Howard A. Eyrich: B.A., Bob Jones U; M.Th., Dallas Theological Seminary; D.Min., Western Baptist Seminary. Dean of Biblical Counseling at Trinity Theological Seminary in Newburgh, IN. Dean of Birmingham Theological Seminary and Associate Pastor of Briarwood Presbyterian Church (PCA) in Birmingham, AL. Fellow of the National Association of Nouthetic Counselors (NANC).

Wayne A. Mack: B.A., Wheaton College; B.Th., Reformed Episcopal Seminary; D.Min., Westminster Theological Seminary (Phila.). Ordained pastor, author. Former Director of Biblical Counseling Studies at The Master's College and Seminary, Santa Clarita, CA. Presently, Director of Strengthening Ministries, Center Valley, PA. Fellow and Board Member of NANC.

Robert B. Needham: B.A., Reed College; B.D., Westminster Theological Seminary (Phila.); M.A., Naval Postgraduate School, Monterey, CA. Commander, U.S. Navy (Ret.). Pastor of New Hope Orthodox Presbyterian Church, Hanford, CA. Level II member of NANC. Board Member of the Institute for Biblical Counseling and Discipleship, La Mesa, CA.

Andrew J. Peterson: B.A., Western Washington State University; M.A., U. of California at Berkeley; Ph.D., U. of

Pittsburgh. Formerly, clinical psychologist and licensed school psychologist. Served as counselor and Director of Educational Services at the Christian Counseling and Educational Foundation-West (now IBCD). Presently, Senior Vice President of the Virtual Campus, Reformed Theological Seminary, Charlotte, NC, and an elder in his church. Level II member of NANC.

George C. Scipione: B.A., M.A., Temple University; B.D., M.Th., Westminster Theological Seminary, (Phila.); Ph.D., Whitefield Theological Seminary, Lakeland, FL; D.Min. (Candidate) Westminster Theological Seminary, CA. Former Director of CCEF, Laverock, PA. Presently, Director of IBCD, La Mesa, CA; Adjunct Professor at Westminster Theological Seminary in California; and Associate Pastor of Bayview Orthodox Presbyterian Church, Chula Vista, CA. Fellow and Board Member of NANC.

Robert B. Somerville: M.Div., Trinity Evangelical Seminary; D.Min., Westminster Theological Seminary (Phila.). Speaker and author. Senior Pastor of the Evangelical Free Church of Visalia, CA. Fellow and Board Member of NANC.

Steven Viars: M.Div., Grace Theological Seminary; D.Min., Westminster Theological Seminary (Phila.). Senior Pastor of Faith Baptist Church, Lafayette, IN; instructor and counselor at Faith Baptist Counseling Ministries. Fellow and Board Member of NANC.

Roger Wagner: B.A., Westmont College; M.Div., Westminster Theological Seminary (Phila.); D.Min., Westminster Theological Seminary (CA). Senior Pastor of Bayview O.P.C.; faculty member at Bahnsen Theological Seminary, Valencia, CA; teacher at Covenant Christian School. IBCD Board Member.

In the outline that follows, the books are listed in order of importance under each category. Comments from members of the team noted above have been included.

I. Definition of the Family

A. General works on the Family

1. Jay E. Adams, *Christian Living in the Home* (Phillipsburg: Presbyterian and Reformed, 1972). Adams gives a clear, practical presentation of the family and its roles. Originally, these were talks given at family camps.

2. B. M. Palmer and J. W. Alexander, *The Family* (Harrisonburg: Sprinkle, 1981). This reprint of Palmer's *The Family in its Civil and Churchly Aspects* and of Alexander's *Thoughts on Family Worship* is the best theological treatment of the family. K. Ptacek gives an excellent evaluation of Palmer's work, "The Family in the Theology of B. M. Palmer," *Bulletin of Greenville Presbyterian Theological Seminary*, vol 6, no 3 (Aug-Oct 1993), 3.

3. Edith Schaeffer, *What Is a Family?* (Old Tappan: Revell, 1975). Schaeffer gives thoughtful consideration to the family and God's purposes for it.

4. Elizabeth Elliott, *The Shaping of a Christian Family* (Nashville: Oliver-Nelson, 1992). Elliott writes with a clean, clear style. This is a valuable book both for its pithy commentary on family life and as a model of how to save the personal history of a family for subsequent generations.

5. Gary Bauer, *Our Journey Home: What Parents Are Doing to Preserve Family Values* (Dallas: Word, 1992). Bauer gives the best conservative view of America in 1992. He shows how conservative thought differs from conventional liberal thought. However, he is typical of evangelical conservatives: virtually no scripture or biblical content and no acknowledgment of the necessity of spiritual regeneration or sanctification to accomplish a turnaround of an individual or of America. A warm style and personal reflections are the strengths of the book.

B. Workbooks on the Family

1. Wayne Mack, *Your Family God's Way* (Phillipsburg: Presbyterian and Reformed, 1991). Mack gives solid teaching on the family and relationships among its members as well as exercises that help with communication, problem solving and forgiveness.

2. Ken and Flo Smith, *Learning to Be a Family* (Norcross: Great Commission, 1990). This husband and wife team help you to study the family from a biblical perspective. Workbook format.

C. Periodicals for Families

1. *World*, and *God's World*, Box 2330, Asheville, NC 28802. General reading that keeps families informed from a biblical perspective. *World* is an adult magazine and *God's World* is for children.

2. *Christian Observer*, 9400 Fairview Ave., Manassas, VA, 22110. Billed as "the magazine for serious Christian families—since 1813," it has national and international focus.

3. *Focus on the Family*, P. O. Box 35500, Colorado Springs, CO 80935-3550. Contains some helpful hints, but must be constantly screened for its uncritical traditionalist dependency on erroneous social science "wisdom." (See Appendices 6, 7.)

4. *Journal for Biblical Manhood and Womanhood,* Council on Biblical Manhood and Womanhood, 2825 Lexington Rd., Box 926, Louisville, KY 40280. Pertinent articles and reviews on gender issues in the home and church.

5. *The Family in America,* The Howard Center for Family, Religion and Society, 934 N. Main St., Rockford, IL

61103-7061. This publication contains useful articles from a politically and sociologically conservative position. Its supplement, *New Research,* chronicles social science research that bears out the conservative viewpoint. While not Christian, it is thought-provoking and provides useful data.

II. The History of the Family

Andrew J. Peterson is responsible for directing me to Zimmerman. See chapter 9 for comments on these works.

1. Carle C. Zimmerman, *Family and Civilization* (New York: Harper and Brothers, 1947).

2. _____, *The Family of Tomorrow: The Cultural Crisis* (New York: Harper and Brothers, 1949).

3. _____, and C. F. Cervantes; *Marriage and the Family: A Text for Moderns* (Chicago: Regnery, 1956).

4. Emmanuel Todd, *The Explanation of Ideology: Family Structures and Social Systems* (Oxford: Blackwell, 1985).

5. _____, *The Causes of Progress: Culture, Authority and Change* (Oxford: Blackwell, 1987).

6. Allen Carden, *Puritan Christianity in America: Religion and Life in Seventeenth-Century Massachusetts* (Grand Rapids, Baker, 1990).

III. Marriage

A. General works

1. Jay E. Adams, *Christian Living in the Home.* See above.

2. R. C. Sproul, *The Intimate Marriage* (Wheaton: Tyndale, 1975). Sproul gives sound, simple biblical advice.

3. Wayne Mack, *Strengthening Your Marriage* (Phillipsburg: Presbyterian and Reformed, 1977). An excellent (the best) workbook on marriage, which combines solid teaching with helpful exercises and is so complete that some modification of assignments may be necessary.

4. Lou Priolo, *The Complete Husband* (Amityville: Calvary Press, 1999), or Stuart Scott, *The Exemplary Husband* (Bemidji: Focus, 2000).

5. Martha Peace, *The Excellent Wife*, rev. ed. (Bemidji: Focus, 1999).

6. Walter Wangerin, Jr., *As for Me and My House: Crafting Your Marriage to Last* (Nashville: Thomas Nelson, 1987). The paperback edition (which was published a year or so later) has a study-guide added to the back of the book for self- or small-group study. The great strength of this book is its personal and practical discussion of confession and forgiveness (which forms the heart of the book). Wangerin says that the biblical skill of forgiveness is the most important thing that spouses need to learn in order to build durable and lasting marriages. Though he does not come to the subject from the perspective of a Reformed worldview (he's a Lutheran), his approach to marriage is covenantal. He's more open at a few points to "professional" counseling than we would be, but it only comes in peripherally. The several chapters on "Marriage Work" (the last part of the book) are insightful and practical. The chapter which, in my judgment, has a very serious error is ch. 19, "Avoiding Adultery," in particular the section where he gives advice on what to do if adultery has taken place, but the betrayed spouse is not aware of it (pp. 199-204). He advocates not confessing to the spouse, but rather confessing to another, and being prepared to admit your

sin to your spouse should they become aware of it at some later point. His counsel on this point is very confused, and it is especially disappointing because of the real *hope* he builds in the effectiveness for healing of biblical confession and forgiveness in the earlier sections of the book. It's as if he got cold feet at this point and caved in. (Comments by Roger Wagner.)

B. Premarital Counseling and Preparation for Marriage

1. Wayne Mack, *Preparing for Marriage God's Way* (Tulsa: Virgil W. Hensley, 1986). The most biblical, practical tool available with teaching and exercises usable by individuals, couples and classes.

2. Howard Eyrich, *Three to Get Ready* (Grand Rapids: Baker, 1991) 2nd ed. An excellent tool, flawed only by its dependency upon the TJTA test.

3. Jim West, *Christian Courtship versus the Dating Game* (Palo Cedro: Christian Worldview Ministries, 1992). See comments in chapter 8, endnote 23.

4. Elizabeth Elliott, *Passion and Purity* (Grand Rapids: Revell, 1984). Solid advice on how to have a godly male-female relationship aimed at marriage.

C. Gender Roles

1. John Piper, Wayne Grudem, eds., *Recovering Biblical Manhood and Womanhood.* See appendix 2, note 52.

2. Andreas J. Köstenberger, Thomas R. Schreiner, and H. Scott Baldwin, eds. *Women in the Church: A Frank Analysis of I Timothy 2:9-15* (Grand Rapids: Baker, 1995).

3. Werner Neuer, *Man and Woman in Christian Perspective.* See appendix 2, note 52.

4. Stephen B. Clark, *Man and Woman in Christ* (out of print, available on-line through the Council for Biblical Manhood and Womanhood; http://www.cbmw.org).

5. James B. Hurley, *Man and Woman in Biblical Perspective: A Study of Role Relationships and Authority* (Grand Rapids: Zondervan, 1981).

6. Susan T. Foh, *Women and the Word of God: A Response to Biblical Feminism* (Phillipsburg: Presbyterian and Reformed, 1992).

7. Gary Smalley and Steve Scott, *If Only He Knew* (New York: Harpers, 1988). A good reminder of the differences a husband must note, even though poor theologically.

8. Elizabeth Elliott, *Let Me Be a Woman* (Wheaton: Tyndale, 1976).

9. ______, *The Mark of a Man* (Tarrytown: Revell, 1983). Helpful wisdom from one of the best Christian writers.

D. Sexuality in Marriage

1. Ed and Gaye Wheat, *Intended for Pleasure: Sex Technique and Sexual Fulfillment in Christian Marriage* (Old Tappan: Revell, 1981) rev. ed. The best work on the subject, even though it is weak theologically.

2. S. Craig Glickman, *Song for Lovers* (Downers Grove: InterVarsity, 1976)

3. Joseph C. Dillow, *Solomon on Sex* (Nashville: Nelson, 1982).

E. Help in Problem-Solving in Marriage

1. Jay E. Adams, *What Do You Do When Your*

Marriage Goes Sour? (Phillipsburg: Presbyterian and Reformed, 1977). A useful pamphlet that helps to create hope in the midst of despair.

2. _______, *Solving Marriage Problems* (Grand Rapids: Zondervan,1983). Adams systematically categorizes what can go wrong and what to do about it. Combined with his *Christian Counselor's Manual* (Grand Rapids: Zondervan, 1973) and *Christian Living in the Home* (see above I.A.1.), it can be a great help.

3. Wayne Mack, *A Homework Manual for Biblical Living: Vol 2, Family and Marital Problems* (Phillipsburg: Presbyterian and Reformed, 1980). Mack develops assignments that can be used to help yourself as well as others.

F. Divorce

1. Jay E. Adams, *Marriage, Divorce and Remarriage in the Bible* (Grand Rapids: Zondervan, 1980). The best exegetical and practical work to date on this subject written in Adams's usual lucid style.

2. John Murray, *Divorce* (Phillipsburg: Presbyterian and Reformed, 1961). Impeccable work comes from the pen of one of the premier exegetes of the 20th century.

G. Finances and Inheritance

1. Larry Burkett, *Answers to Your Family's Financial Questions* (Wheaton: Tyndale, 1987).

2. ______, *The Complete Financial Guide for Single Parents* (Wheaton: Victor, 1991).

3. Ron Blue, *The Debt Squeeze* (Focus on the Family, 1989).

4. _____, *Master Your Money* (Walk Through the Bible Ministry, n.d.). This video series and workbook are good).

5. George and Marjean Fooshee, *You Can Beat the Money Squeeze* (Old Tappan: Revell, 1980).

6. J. R. Rushdoony, "The Economics of the Family," *The Institutes of Biblical Law,* vol I (Phillipsburg: Presbyterian and Reformed, 1973), 174-182.

IV. Children

A. General

1. Tedd Tripp, *Shepherding a Child's Heart* (Wapwallopen: Shepherd Press, 1995). The best new book on this important subject.

2. Wayne Mack, *Your Family God's Way* (see above I.B.1.).

3. J. C. Ryle, *The Duty of Parents* (Choteau: Christian Heritage Pub., 1983). This reprint of the 1888 classic is still one of the best.

4. Carl K. Spackman, *Parents Passing on the Faith* (Wheaton: Victor, 1989). Good with only one flaw, a chapter that accepts the concept of self-esteem.

5. Gordon MacDonald, *The Effective Father* (Wheaton: Tyndale, 1981). Easy reading with great stories; the opening story is worth the price of the book in itself. The traditionalist approach is thin on biblical content.

B. Younger Children

1. Bruce Ray, *Withhold Not Correction* (Phillipsburg:

Presbyterian and Reformed, 1978). Ray gives excellent, balanced advice on the use of the rod and reproof. Particularly helpful is his use of Scripture and method of using it with children.

2. Lou Priolo, *The Heart of Anger* (Amityville: Calvary Press, 1997).

3. Richard L. Strauss, *Confident Children and How They Grow* (Wheaton: Tyndale, 1975).

4. J. Richard Fugate, *What the Bible Says About Child Training* (Tempe: Alpha Omega, 1980).

C. Older Youth

1. Paul D. Tripp, *Age of Opportunity* (Phillipsburg: Presbyterian and Reformed, 1997).

2. Wayne Mack, Set of audio tapes, "Understanding Teenagers", Strengthening Ministries, Center Valley, PA.

3. Ron L. Kotesky, *Understanding Adolescents* (Wheaton: Victor, 1986).

4. C. John Miller, *Come Back, Barbara* (Grand Rapids: Zondervan, 1989). Miller relates the thrilling saga of a prodigal daughter who comes back to the "father's house".

5. Donald Matzat, *Christ Esteem: Where the Search for Self-Esteem Ends* (Eugene: Harvest, 1990). Matzat helps people to focus on Christ, not self.

6. Jerry Johnston, *Why Suicide?* (Nashville: Nelson, 1987). An excellent biblical analysis of suicide and why teens take this route.

D. Education

1. Jay E. Adams, *Back to the Blackboard* (Phillipsburg: Presbyterian and Reformed, 1982). Adams lucidly lays out the biblical case for education in contrast to pagan models.

2. Jack Fenneman, *Nurturing Children in the Lord* (Phillipsburg: Presbyterian and Reformed, 1978).

3. Samuel Blumenfeld, *The NAE: The Trojan Horse in Public Education* (Boise: Paradigm, 1984).

4. ______, *How to Tutor* (Milford: Mott, 1973).

E. Single Parenting

1. Gary Richmond, *Successful Single Parenting* (Eugene: Harvest, 1989). Though this has few proof texts, it contains good practical advice.

V. Caring for Aging Relatives

1. Jay E. Adams, *Wrinkled, But Not Ruined* (Woodruff: Timeless Texts, 1999).

2. Howard A. Eyrich, *Did a Good God Make Old Age?* (Atlanta: P.C.A. Christian Education Pub., 1990).

The following three works are acceptable, but not very biblical in orientation:

3. John Gillies, *A Guide to Coping with Aging Parents* (Nashville: Thos. Nelson, 2nd ed., 1981).

4. Margaret J. Anderson, *Your Aging Parents* (St. Louis: Concordia House, 1979).

5. Doug Manning, *When Love Gets Tough* (San Francisco: Harper Collins, 1990).

VI. Ethical Issues and Family Decision Making

1. Jay E. Adams, *The Christian's Guide to Guidance* (Woodruff: Timeless Texts, 1999).

2. _____, *A Call for Discernment* (Woodruff: Timeless Texts, 1987).

3. _____, *Maintaining the Delicate Balance in Christian Living* (Woodruff: Timeless Texts, 1999).

4. John J. Davis, *Evangelical Ethics* (Phillipsburg: Presbyterian and Reformed, 1985).

5. Franklin E. Payne, *Biblical Medical Ethics* (Milford: Mott, 1985).

6. _____, *Making Biblical Decisions* (Escondido: Hosanna House, 1989).

7. _____, *Biblical Healing for Modern Medicine* (Augusta: Covenant Book, 1993).

8. John Frame, *Medical Ethics: Principles, Persons, and Problems* (Phillipsburg: Presbyterian and Reformed, 1988).

To order additional copies of

THE SWORD AND THE SHOVEL

contact the
Institute for Biblical Counseling & Discipleship

IBCD
5333 Lake Murray Blvd.
La Mesa, CA 91942

(619) 462-9775
E-MAIL: ibcdsdg@k-online.com
WEBSITE: www.ibcd.org